LITTLE
GIRL
LOST

LITTLE GIRL LOST

Drew Barrymore

with

Todd Gold

POCKET BOOKS

New York   London   Toronto   Sydney   Tokyo   Singapore

The author and publisher have made every effort to appropriately acknowledge all source material and to secure permission from copyright holders
when required. In the event of any question arising as to the source of any
material, we will be pleased to make the necessary acknowledgment in
future printings.

POCKET BOOKS, a division of Simon & Schuster Inc.
1230 Avenue of the Americas, New York, NY 10020

ISBN: 0-671-68922-3

First Pocket Books hardcover printing February 1990

10 9 8 7 6 5 4 3 2 1

POCKET and colophon are registered trademarks of
Simon & Schuster Inc.

Printed in the U.S.A.

To:
Mom, Jan, David, Beth, Betty,
Lori, Dallas and my father.

ACKNOWLEDGMENTS

Beth: Everlasting partnership and love.

J.J.: Thank you.

Ele: For giving me the most valuable lessons and friendship.

Betty: I'd be lost without you.

Lori: You're indescribably the best.

Dallas: You mean everything. I'm glad you kept me in line.

Jan: I love you more than words could ever describe.

David: I would have to write another book to express to you my love and thanks.

Mikey: You're really the best friend.

Anthony: Please believe me, you're wonderful.

Angie: Cup O'Noodles, kisses, hugs, and I love you forever.

Christine: To crazy nights and a beautiful friendship.

Cindy: To loud birthday cakes, and funky times.

Jimmy: To the most beautiful relationship and bananas. I love you always.

Steven: I love you for everything.

Todd: Thank you for giving me a great ground to stand on, and believing in me.

To Mom: Through good and bad, pain and relief, life and death, sun and rain there will always be us. I love you for everything . . . the mistakes we both made. We're coming out beautifully, I love you forever, and on-going everlasting support.

PROLOGUE

Over the past year and a half, numerous stories about my battle against drug and alcohol addiction have appeared in magazines, newspapers, and tabloids. None of them was flattering. And few of them were kind in the way that someone who needs help might appreciate.

More important, none of them offered a complete picture of how I lived the past fourteen years, and that by itself is an important part of understanding the problems I've had to face.

When I began working on this book in late winter 1988 I was but a few months out of rehab and still undergoing intense outpatient therapy. I was excited to be free in the world again and able to tell the happy story of my recovery.

I enjoyed thinking about how this book would end in a tidy scene of my being completely cured, waltzing away from my problems, and satisfied that I had proved all the doubters and cynics of gossip columns wrong about my chances for a happy, natural life. It was as if I'd gone through rehab for them, just to prove them wrong.

Unfortunately, while completing this book, I found myself writing one thing and living another. I suffered a relapse. Scared and embarrassed, I kept it to myself until it was impossible to hide, and by that time it was nearly too late.

The temptation in recovery is to believe that once rehab is finished, you will be completely healed. The reality, as I found, is quite the opposite. The truth is that you are never fully mended. You just learn how to deal with the problems that intensify your disease. That's what I discovered, and I believe the conflict between illusion and reality is accurately reflected in these pages.

It surprised me, I have to admit. I had fervently hoped for a nice, upbeat ending with no loose ends, like in the movies, an ending that would leave me feeling quite the heroine. I really believed it was what I deserved.

Instead, I found myself adding two chapters of a different tone from the rest of the book while in the final weeks of another stay in rehab. In place of the happy fantasy I intended as the ending, what I wrote is a truthful one, and a realistic one to anyone who is, or knows, a recovering addict-alcoholic. There is no happy ending because there is no end to the struggle for a clean and sober life.

The happiness comes from knowing that you're alive and have a fighting chance to enjoy it.

As of this writing, I'm in the final weeks of rehab—my last time in the hospital, I hope—and I'm looking ahead to the start of school, making movies, and just being honest with myself.

LITTLE
GIRL
LOST

ONE

HEADLINES

It was the best time of my life. I can't underestimate it. Making *E.T. The Extra-Terrestrial* was the most wonderful experience any actor could ever wish for. Just imagine a little wide-eyed giggly kid in pigtails making that movie and you get a sense of what it was like for me.

I was a six-year-old girl who always preferred make-believe and fantasy and playing dress-up to reality. Anything where I could lose myself in another character. And then I was introduced to this wonderful cute, wrinkled creature named E.T.

I fell in love.

To me, E.T. was extremely real. Yes, I knew he was something Steven Spielberg created, but I actually believed in him. I could touch him, hug him, kiss him. He put his arm around me. From the moment I saw him, E.T. instantly became my best friend. On lunch breaks, I used to take my food into the room where he was kept, sit down beside him, and carry on a conversation while I ate. I talked to him about my mother and where we lived. If it was cold outside, I wrapped a scarf around his neck. I was always excited to be with him.

Occasionally some of the older crew members sat down with us and tried speaking to E.T. When he didn't answer, they asked how come he talked to me and not to them. "He's very shy," I

1

explained in my most serious little-girl voice, "and I think he prefers talking to kids."

One day, when filming was near completion, I got very sad and depressed, which was the opposite of my usual lighthearted and laughing self on the set. Steven asked what was bothering me and I told him that I dreaded having to say good-bye to E.T. Who would ever want to lose a friend like him? But Steven understood. He told me that I could visit him whenever I wanted.

That was exactly what I wanted to hear. Letting out a cry of delight and grinning from ear to ear, I ran over to E.T., wrapped my arms around him, and planted a big kiss on his rubbery cheek.

Like I said, it was the best time in my life.

But the turnaround was dramatic. In the final days of December 1988, Drew was experiencing the worst time in her life. She had spent the past six months undergoing intensive rehabilitation treatment for a four-year addiction to alcohol and drugs, an addiction that had turned her into a bloated and bruised remnant of her public image. That whole enterprise had been hellish enough to make Drew think she'd been through everything life could possibly throw her way.

However, on the eve of her long-anticipated pre-Christmas discharge from the ASAP Family Treatment Center, the private drug and alcohol hospital where she had been residing off and on since early summer, Drew and her mother, Jaid Barrymore, were delivered a startling jolt of bad news. The gossipy tabloid National Enquirer was about to blow the lid off her tightly guarded secret. Whether or not she approved, Drew's struggle with booze and drugs was about to be made public.

There was serious concern among those close to her about the effect such a shocking revelation would have on Drew, who, at thirteen years old, was reentering the world as fragile as a baby doe learning to walk on wobbly legs.

My mental state at that point was delicate and raw. Excited to go home, I was struggling to digest everything I'd been dealing with in treatment. I'd been learning how to manage again in the outside world. I'd finally gotten reacquainted with myself after years of masquerading as someone else. It was a lot to contend with. The prospect of stepping beyond the safety of the hospital was frightening enough by itself. I didn't need to be worrying about gossip columns magnifying and distorting the difficulties I'd been trying to overcome.

Needless to say, I was furious. While everyone else, including my mother and my therapists, grew dizzy from concern, I erupted into a rage, a huge, horrible angry outrage that evidenced the dark and temperamental side I inherited from my Barrymore ancestors. It seemed to vent my frustration some. And then I cried. I cried so hard I found myself huddled in bed, trembling uncontrollably.

A low self-esteem had plagued me for years, almost as far back as I can recall, and repairing it had been a major part of my treatment at ASAP. Consequently, imagining the godawful headlines—"Drew Barrymore Cocaine Addict at Twelve Years Old" or "Barrymore Burns Out in Teens"—and the impression people would get of me was all my worst possible fears come true. I would've been the last person on Earth to deny my problems, but I wanted to have the option of confessing them.

In the position I found myself, I felt helpless, like a drowning swimmer gasping for air. I didn't know what to do and I fell into the worst depression.

In the years since making *E.T.* Drew had matured into a stunning teenage beauty who, by all accounts, had grown up much too fast for her own good. Six years and more than $700 million in box office receipts had passed since Drew, playing the effervescent Gertie, nearly stole scene after scene from the lovable alien in what became the most successful movie—and video— in history.

Yet the downcast teenager who sat on a hospital cot pondering an invasion of her privacy bore only scant resemblance to the winsome child who had charmed audiences with her wide eyes and ear-splitting scream. Drew's innocence had vanished along with her youth. In June she had been admitted to the ASAP hospital after an all-night drunken binge left her ill and babbling incoherently. Three months later she was readmitted to the hospital after a two-day cross-country jaunt fueled by cocaine, alcohol, and a credit card taken without permission from her mother.

On the threshold of her release from rehab, Drew was only beginning the lifelong process of recovery. She clearly recognized what she had previously chosen to ignore: that her consumption of drugs and alcohol was in inverse proportion to her ability to handle them. However, if she was to remain sober, like any addict she had to go beyond simply identifying the obvious symptoms of her sickness—hangovers, irritability, and constant fighting with her mother. Drew had to address and solve the underlying issues that caused her addiction, what the crux of treatment had been all about.

In retrospect, entering the hospital and confronting my problems was a matter of life and death. There's no underestimating that. For years I was so busy trying to mask the pain and fear that I always kept hidden—from myself as well as from everyone else—that I became a stranger to myself. And my own worst enemy. Stuck on a one-way avenue toward self-destruction, I have no doubt that I was writing my own obituary. I had to break out of that pattern of behavior.

I had to accept that I was an addict-alcoholic, and that proved the most difficult challenge I ever had to confront.

But the most frightening aspect of the whole process was facing myself. When I entered the hospital, I couldn't even sit in a room alone. The person I'd become was no one I wanted to hang around with. I had built a wall around me so thick and so high that even I couldn't penetrate it. Of course, I didn't really want to. On the outside I was this tough girl who thought she could handle anything.

Boy, was I deluding myself, though. In truth, I was anything but that well-adapted character. Actually, I was this vulnerable little child, bruised and tender on the inside, a kid who refused to acknowledge the tremendous pain that had built up and been ignored over time. In a bit of twisted logic, I dealt with that reality by not dealing with it. I numbed myself with alcohol and drugs.

As a girl, I once entertained thoughts of becoming a construction worker. I had this image of myself walking along the iron girders of a high-rise building, performing my tasks without regard for the dangers of being twenty floors above the ground. But acting was like that, too. Exciting. And I craved the work I got in the films *Firestarter, Cat's Eye, Irreconcilable Differences,* and *See You in the Morning.*

Acting is all I've ever thought of doing. It's something I've been inexplicably drawn to by enthusiasm and ambition. However, what I never admitted, not even to myself, is that my desperate need to perform was fed by a deep-seated insecurity and low self-esteem. I hungered for the love and affirmation I felt was absent from my life. It was my private wound, a wound that festered and grew over the years.

Yet stardom has always been a role which I've never really accepted. It's never seemed real, like anything I could identify, and yet fame is something that has to be dealt with. I've always grappled with the clash of image versus reality. The public saw me as Drew Barrymore, movie star, while I viewed myself quite differently—as a sad, lonely, and unattractive girl with not much to her advantage.

Fame changed everything so suddenly. Virtually overnight, everybody knew me, and yet nobody knew me. I mean the *real* me. From early on I was always this remote, dreamy little girl who loved escaping reality by acting in movies. I desired the attention and recognition as much as I liked becoming a different character. Without work, I believed, I was nothing. I was horribly insecure. It wasn't what anyone imagined me, Drew Barrymore, the celebrated actress and heir to the great Barrymore legacy, to be like.

I was supposed to be, as Steven Spielberg once told reporters, this perfect seven-year-old going on a mature twenty-nine, and that's the way I behaved. I always felt as if I had to live up to such incredibly high expectations. It was hard on me emotionally and, I believe, it made people think I was someone who I wasn't. I'd walk into a restaurant or some room where there were other kids and sense that everyone was looking at me, thinking, "I'm sure she's the biggest snob or brat on Earth."

But I wasn't. I was really this frail little thing who wanted to shout "Hey, I didn't want to be famous. I just want to be loved. I'm scared. I don't know how to deal with this."

Growing up, an only child raised by a single, working mother, I was riddled by insecurity, always fearing that people wouldn't like me. "How could they?" I thought. "My father hates me. My mother likes me only for the money I earn. And I know for damn sure that I'm nothing but a worthless piece of flesh."

As I got older, the problems magnified and it became harder and harder for me to deal with them. Especially between projects. Without the ego-boost of work, I got into trouble with liquor and drugs by trying to run from everything. Or to numb it. I was the party girl on the run. If I was high, I thought, everything was fine. The trouble was that I had to be high all the time.

By the time I got into rehab, my life was completely out of control. Everything was just so screwed up and so off kilter that I couldn't handle my life.

On the surface, people might blame Hollywood for my troubles. It would be easy to cast me as a fast-lane victim of the glitter and glamour. But that's not remotely close to the truth. If anything, work was my saving grace, the one tangible thing I could always rely on to boost my sagging self-esteem and confidence.

My problems had more to do with life in general. The family I was born into. The home in which I was raised. The times I live in. It's just so hard being a teenager today. And that's what pissed me off so much about the *National Enquirer* thing. It was just so shallow and distorted.

Nowhere is perception more clouded by illusion than in Hollywood, the place that made Drew the most loved child star since Shirley Temple. She became a fifth-generation actor and celebrity in a family whose name figured prominently in entertainment circles going as far back as England's George III. To the public, she was a charmed kewpie doll, a pint-size prodigy living out a fairy-tale existence. As she grew, Drew was photographed smiling, frolicking at play. As far as the public was concerned, she had money, fame, and attention. Problems? Not Drew. She was, after all, a Barrymore.

But that alone should have been clue enough to a more unsettling reality. For if acting was part of the Barrymore legacy, so, too, was the pall of tragedy. Drew's grandfather, John Barrymore, one of the finest Shakespearean and movie actors of the 1920s and 1930s, drank himself to death at age sixty. Aunt Diana Barrymore admitted her self-destructive hunger for booze and drugs in the 1957 best seller, *Too Much, Too Soon.* Likewise, Drew's own father, John Drew Barrymore, whom, by the time of her hospitalization, she hadn't seen in seven years, had a lengthy history of alcohol- and drug-related problems.

Given her tender age, there was little reason to suspect Drew would also succumb to the dark Barrymore destiny. As far as anyone imagined, she appeared to be a sweet, lovable scamp, radiating easy smiles and infectious giggles, and brimming with the endless possibilities of youth. The insidious demons that plagued her family seemed to have mercifully skipped a generation. Yet, unbeknown to anyone, Drew's precocious movie stardom was accompanied by a more shocking precocity offscreen—a premature appetite for drinking and drugs.

I started smoking cigarettes when I was nine and a half. I was smoking constantly, going out and doing everything I could do to be bad. It wasn't long before I began thinking, "Well, if I smoke ciagrettes, I can drink." It was an easy step, one that I didn't take alone. I started drinking with friends when I slept over at their houses. Just sneaking a drink here, a beer there. After a while, though, drinking became the only way I thought I could have fun. Only I didn't drink to have fun. I drank to get drunk.

I was also a club hopper at ten, as much as someone that age can be. I would sleep over at a friend's house and we would sneak out. One time a magazine ran a picture of me dancing and a headline that said, "Drew Barrymore Dancing at Two A.M. Shouldn't She Be in Bed?" Maybe other kids that age should've been in bed, but that wasn't for me. I didn't care what anyone thought. I was accepted in the club world, I felt I belonged and I wanted to be there.

After a while, though, I started thinking, "Well, this is getting boring now, so let's try something even better. If I can drink, I can smoke pot. There's nothing to it."

When I was ten and a half I was sitting in the backseat of a car driven by a friend's mother. She started smoking pot. I'd wanted to try marijuana for a long time, but I was afraid that if I asked, she'd say, "No way, Drew. You're too young." However, she offered me some and I said, "Sure, I'll try it." I was shocked. But she had a look that seemed to say "Isn't it cute, a little girl getting stoned."

Eventually, that got boring, too, and my addict mind told me, "Well, if smoking pot is cute, it'll also be cute to get into the heavier stuff, like cocaine." My usage was gradual. But what I did kept getting worse and worse, and I didn't care what anybody else thought about me.

The higher I got, the happier I imagined myself, the more miserable I actually was.

The pattern fit. Friends have always described me as obsessive and compulsive. And in the hospital I learned that an addict is nothing but compulsive, someone who compulsively pursues self-destructive behavior. My whole life became geared toward satisfying my addiction. In my case, it was a means to overcome great insecurities.

Someone once explained to me what the word *veneer* meant. Gloss. A shiny surface that's supposed to protect an inferior material underneath. That's me exactly. Whenever I'd look in the mirror, I'd think, "You're lost. Totally lost. How can anyone like you? You don't

even like yourself." Those moments when I realized how estranged
I'd become from myself, not to mention the rest of the world, sent
me spiraling into a depression. And my depressions knew no
depths. Imagine being trapped in a descending elevator that never
hit the ground floor. You get to a point where you'll do anything to
get out.

With her December release from ASAP imminent,
Drew could look back upon her six months in the
hospital and see how mistaken she was about her own
condition when first admitted in June. Back then, in
her own mind she was *the* worst-case scenario. No
one could possibly have sunk to such depths, she
thought.

Now Drew could see how wrong she was. However, it had taken quite a while in rehab before she
arrived at an important realization: She wasn't the
worst case. Not even close. In fact, Drew discovered,
her drinking and drug use were actually more common
among people her age—teenagers—than she'd ever
imagined.

In ASAP's multifamily sessions—frank discussion
groups that brought together parents and their children—the frightening fact of rampant substance abuse
was etched on the face of nearly every adult. Over
time, warnings from experts have gone virtually un-
heard, drowned amid the cacophony of the crime and
violence that permeates society, but drug use and
alcoholism among the young has been rising for years.

The problem, experts say, has surpassed epidemic
proportions. Surveys have shown that somewhere between thirty and forty percent of the adolescents na-
tionwide use drugs every weekend, and, according to
the National Council of Alcoholism, the percent of
students using drugs prior to the sixth grade has tripled
since 1975. When she thought about it, Drew con-

cluded that she was way out of line thinking she was worse than everyone else.

Her circumstance was dire. That was true. But her problems made her far more average than she ever dreamed.

Average. That was a hoot. The word ingrained itself in Drew's mind. Average was all she had ever wanted to be. It was also the last way she pictured herself. She based that on innocent observations. Her friends, she saw, all had mothers and fathers, siblings, and seemingly happy homes. Compared to them, Drew thought of her own life as empty, depressing, and bereft of the laughter and familial warmth she tried so desperately to absorb when visiting her playmates.

That's what gave acting its importance. The ensemble feeling that arose from being part of a production crew, the approval won from good work, it all fulfilled a desperate emotional need. Unfortunately, Drew learned these rewards were temporary. The end of a film always proved traumatic. She'd get close to people, then be yanked away and had to go back home, which sent her spiraling into a depression.

Early on, Drew learned not to count on her father, a volatile man of unpredictable personality who seemed determined to make her life miserable every time she saw him. And her mother, a part-time actress, worked so many jobs to make ends meet that Drew grew up feeling abandoned and starved for affection. There were times when Drew would have gladly and quickly traded all her acclaim from acting to be more like her pals at school.

When I looked out the window, I saw that everyone's situation was better than mine. I was sure of it. Their dads would drive off to work in their sports cars and their moms would stay home and bake cookies and pick up their kids at school in their station wagons. It was the total suburban-dream life-style, the kind of place where Steven Spielberg sets his films.

My life, it appeared, was directly opposite that. I'd ride along with my friends in their car pools, listening to their mothers talk about family business, and then they'd come to my house. I'd get dropped off and run inside to my baby-sitter. Our house seemed so empty and quiet and lonely. My mom was off working and my dad was out of his mind. One time a friend asked why my father didn't live at home with us. "Because," I replied, "when he's here, he beats the living daylights out of us."

I loved the book *A Wrinkle in Time,* and read it over and over. In one part there's a description of a neighborhood that I believed paralleled my life. The neighborhood is fashioned by a row of houses, all identical in shape and size, and all the children who live in them dress alike, do the same things and have the same experiences. And then there is this one oddball house that is completely different. The people who live there stand out like a sore thumb.

I felt as if I came from that different house. Anyway, that's how I saw my life. I always wanted to know why I couldn't be like one of the identical kids from one of the identical houses on the block, and I was always trying so hard to make my life like the book.

As Drew's discharge date from ASAP neared, one of the things she looked forward to most was being able to sleep late in the morning. That was enough of a Christmas present. Throughout her hospitalization, she was awakened each day at 7:30 A.M. by a staff member who knew enough of her bleary-eyed growls to be wary. Her two roommates were equally ornery at that early hour.

But that was life at the hospital—lots of rules and routine. Their cramped room, far from the ornate boudoir one might expect of a famous young actress, was stocked with the bare essentials of dorm life: beds, a dresser, and a bathroom. Pictures of good-looking guys—er, hunks—ripped from magazines adorned the otherwise plain stucco walls. In the midst of shared grumbles, Drew dressed quickly.

Like the others, it had taken Drew a while to get used to the rigidly circumscribed days and nights of rehab. After so many months, of course, it was all second nature. Following wake-up, she straightened her cot, tucking in the blankets and propping her favorite stuffed bear beside the pillow, an ironic reminder of girlhood. Drew took breakfast—usually a cup of black coffee—on the run, then headed for the hospital's classroom, where she attended school from nine till twelve. Lunch and dinner were both followed by a myriad of therapy sessions: individual, group, and family therapy, and multifamily meetings. The ensuing emotional confrontations, more like purges, were grueling, torturous ordeals. On an average day she went through an entire box of tissues.

When I first arrived at the hospital I was extremely standoffish, the most distant, obstinate person in the entire hospital. People asked me a million questions and I wouldn't answer them. I just sat in the various groups, twirling the ends of my hair around my fingers, letting whatever anyone said drift in one ear and out the other. Nor did I participate in any of the discussions. I wasn't going to admit that I had any problems. No way. That meant facing up to everything that I'd been running from.

Yet the pressure building inside me was enormous. The emotions I worked so hard to suppress were straining to get out, pushing against the seams of my consciousness. It was the program starting to work. Whether or not I wanted to admit it, which I didn't, the various therapies were affecting me. I didn't want to acknowledge that, though. All I wanted to do was drink my coffee, smoke my cigarettes, and get the hell out of there. Just do my time and be out with my friends. That was my frame of mind.

Then one afternoon in the cafeteria, during lunch, I overheard these two older girls talking about how messed up they were before they came to the hospital. I thought I was bad, but as I listened, I realized they were in it a lot deeper than me. They'd been doing lots of cocaine, speed, anything they could get their hands on. They experimented with different drugs, like acid and pills, and stole from their parents' medicine cabinet. One of them had even been arrested for stealing a car radio.

"What'd you do?" one of them asked me.

I told her about my two-day drug-induced romp from New York to Los Angeles.

"Yeah?" she raised her eyebrows. "Well, I've heard worse."

"You have?" I said, surprised.

"You bet. Everyone has. You just got here. But you'll see. You come in thinking you're the worst piece of shit here. But you learn different. We're all the same . . . screwed-up kids with screwed-up parents living in a screwed-up world."

I smiled.

"You scared?" she asked.

"Yeah," I nodded.

"I was, too, at first. You think a rehab hospital is like one of those gruesome prisons, like in the movie *Midnight Express*. But it's not. This is a bad place, but in a good way . . . if that makes any sense."

It made sense. By the end of December it made lots of sense. Drew didn't want to conceal anything from anyone. She knew well the dangers of that.

Drew had used her ample talent as an actress to conceal her addiction from her mother. She'd turned on Drew Barrymore, actress, smiling and sweet, laying on the saccharine coating heavy and thick, and for a long while that got her by. "Like most parents of kids with drug and alcohol problems, I had no idea what was going on," says Drew's mother, Jaid. "People want to know where I was when all this was going on. But the question, though obvious, is still somewhat of a shock, since our lives have always been so closely intertwined."

Perhaps too close. Jaid, as a single parent, had

always tried to be everything, and more, to Drew. Mother, father, best friend, confidante, and gofer. She'd turned herself into Supermom, always running, doing, and huffing and puffing from the weighty responsibilities she assumed to insure her daughter the finest life they could afford. From day one Jaid had vowed that Drew would never lack a thing if it was within her means to provide it. Clothes, the best schools, the choicest film roles. She did so many things to show Drew that she was loved. "If she grew up with tunnel vision," Jaid says, "then it's my fault."

However, in the end, nothing seemed to matter. Drugs and alcohol changed Drew, exercising infinitely more power and influence than her mother ever could. Jaid, like many other parents, missed the warning signals. The signs were almost lifted from a textbook: listlessness, poor schoolwork, dishonesty, a change in friends, personality swings. It even got to a point where Drew refused good-night kisses to avoid scrutiny of her breath. "In retrospect, you kick yourself for not noticing," Jaid says. "But you chalk it up to growing pains. You never think, 'My kid is doing drugs.' "

If it was any consolation, which it later was, Jaid wasn't alone in failing to recognize her child's addiction. It can be a difficult thing to see. Addicts, instead of admitting they've lost control, spin ever more complicated webs of lies and alibis to cover up their problems. And those people who are closest to them often find themselves unwitting abettors—or codependents—to the addiction. They're often so involved that they don't, or can't, recognize the problem until it's too late. The relationship is nearly as dangerous as the addiction itself.

Before rehab, the lines of our relationship were fuzzy. When I was little, my mother worked night and day so that she could afford to give me whatever I wanted. Left with a baby-sitter most of that time,

I felt abandoned. Later, as my career heated up, she quit her job and became my manager. That just confused everything even more. Not only did I harbor a longstanding anger toward her for abandoning me, but I also imagined that my primary worth to her was the money I earned. I was wrong, of course. It was a fabrication on my part. But I couldn't see—or was too selfish to see—that she loved me and had only my best interests at heart.

These issues weren't ever confronted, and over time our relationship disintegrated to where I didn't want anything to do with her. Not because I didn't love her. That wasn't it. It was more that my mom bore the brunt of the unhappiness I felt toward myself. The angrier I was at myself, the angrier, nastier, and meaner I was to her. She'd react in ways that only fed the inferno of my temper, and our problems escalated from there.

It's funny. I never would've treated a friend that way. But she was my mother. I knew that no matter what I did or said, she'd come back, hoping for a change of heart. It got to the point where I'd reduce her to tears. "I love you," she'd plead. "Why are you doing this to me? To us?"

I didn't know what to say.

Of course, when I needed a shoulder to cry on, I went to her, me playing the great manipulator. But the minute my tears went away, so did I. I vanished quicker than you can say Houdini. She'd want to get close and I'd ignore her. It was like, "See ya, I've got better things to do."

Life was a circle of vicious confrontations and evasions. I'd put on this nauseatingly sweet act whenever I was around my mom. It was all fake, though. I didn't want her to know how much pain and trouble I was in. If she found out about my using, she'd find a way to stop the only thing that I believed made life bearable. Besides, it was easier to blame her for all my problems. If she was mad at me, well, that proved what a jerk I was, which was reason enough to get loaded.

But that whole time I knew inside that I truly did love my mother. I wanted to change. I wanted to have a relationship. I just didn't know how. Thanks to me, she forgot as well. I'd gone too far over the edge. I didn't even know how to say I love you without acting. And that was scary.

In the hospital I learned to confront my fears. I had to recognize them, write them down, articulate them, explain them to others, and then figure out how to work through them. Nothing was sacred. The process makes you feel like a punching bag being pummeled by an unrelenting Mike Tyson. It's draining, exhausting, and painful. But it works.

In late October *E.T.* was finally released on home video amid much hype and ballyhoo. I wasn't aware of the event. However, one night I was eating dinner in the cafeteria, staring vacantly at the television tuned to the local news. Then the anchorman mentioned something about *E.T.,* which startled me out of my daydream, and a moment later I saw a photograph of me at age seven flashed on the screen.

"Oh, Gertrude, you space cadet!" someone chided me.

I'd heard teases like that for years and laughed along with the others. But the image that confronted me on the television screen was too startling not to have an effect. It was like seeing a ghost of yourself from an earlier life. I got a sudden rush of nerves and anxiety. I was intensely frightened and wondered if anyone could see me trembling.

See, in rehab, you get to a point where you feel very safe and protected, and I was at that point. I'd forgotten, as much as I could, that I was Drew Barrymore, the celebrity. I was relearning how to be an ordinary, average kid. But when my face came on the screen, all of a sudden it was as if I *was* open and vulnerable to the world.

For the next few days, though, I talked about that experience, my fright and sense of vulnerability, and discovered that being open and vulnerable to the world was an inescapable part of being alive. Somehow that chance encounter with the image of myself on TV became the turning point in my treatment. No longer was I going to run from my fears. Instead, I decided, I was going to confront them.

As the weeks turned into months, I began earnestly working the program, grappling with the big issues of my life: my relationship with my mother, with my father, and my sobriety. I began participating in my therapy, revealing my hurts and fears. Most important, I recognized that vulnerability wasn't a sign of weakness but a part of being human.

For the first time since who knew when, I found myself

enjoying my age rather than acting it. It was as if I'd made a new friend—me.

In the back of her mind, Drew wondered not *if* she would someday talk about all that she'd gone through, but *when*. She didn't tell anyone of her plan. It was her story, after all. She didn't need anyone's permission to speak. And she felt as if she'd know when the time was right to bring it up. Unfortunately, that seemed to be decided for her two weeks into December in a way she never expected.

One afternoon Jaid arrived at the hospital to take Drew to a dentist appointment. As she waited beside the outer reception desk for Drew, a father who had told ASAP officials he was interested in admitting his teenage daughter asked Jaid what she thought of the program. He had just finished touring the facility with a treatment coordinator, who had noted the unusual curiosity with which he studied each patient's face.

Jaid answered his questions until they seemed to cross an understood line of politeness. He was getting too specific, what one might term downright nosy. Then, without warning, Drew came bounding out, greeting Jaid with a hug, and the man with a skeptical nod. His eyes seemed to light up. He tried to strike up a conversation. "Aren't you Drew Barrymore?" he asked. "How is your treatment going?"

Alarm bells suddenly went off inside Jaid's head. Her piqued suspicion turned into paranoia. Grabbing her daughter's arm, she and Drew sprinted outside to their car, leaving the mysterious gentleman behind. Not for long, though. The tabloids were on the case. It confirmed their worst fears. Reporters continued calling for days. Their hearts sank. The elaborate precautions everyone had taken to keep Drew's treatment out of the gossip columns had suddenly been blown, and it didn't take a genius to know that this was going to be exploited for all it was worth.

Headlines in the January 3, 1989, edition of the *National Enquirer,* printed in glaring yellow letters, trumpeted the alarming news. "*E.T.* Star in Cocaine & Booze Clinic—at 13! The Shocking Untold Story." No attempt was made to hide the story from Drew, but there was concern over how she would react. However, she had already considered her reaction.

I can't even begin to describe how angry I was. Fortunately, though, after so many months of rebuilding myself, I was feeling better, less vulnerable, and more confident. I'd come to terms with a lot of stuff in the hospital and, I guess, that made me a stronger person. I felt like one, at least. I might've fallen apart when the story came out, a momentary loss of composure from the shock. But I was able to pick up the pieces and get it together.

There were lots of phone calls, hundreds of them, it seemed, where everyone talked about the story. It was dissected to death, until it was too boring to think about. My mom was terrific throughout. We cried on each other's shoulder. We talked. We held each other, which shows how far we'd come. But then it was up to me. I'd been through too much to let that trash beat me up.

I had to make a decision, a big decision. Was I going to let this horrible press about me go unanswered? Or was I going to take control of the situation and let people know what happened to me was wrong and that I was trying to do something about it? I wasn't ashamed or embarrassed, weak or injured. I was simply human, a human being whose dignity was being exploited in the worst possible manner.

Sometimes it's better not to respond to gossip. Most times, in fact, it's better not to respond. However, I decided that this wasn't one of those times. I think it took courage on my part. But I didn't want to be considered another Hollywood tragedy. That's the last thing I am. I'm a success. That's why I decided to tell my story. If I've learned anything, it's always better to tell the truth. And by doing so, maybe it will help other kids not to end up like me.

TWO

THE INHERITANCE

When I was very young, maybe four or five, I had a vivid dream that's stayed with me throughout the years. In it, I was surrounded by total darkness, not a speck of light anywhere. Surprisingly, I was very comfortable and conscious of being awake, but I wasn't aware of anything else. There was no sense of my body, no sense of my environment. The feeling was just very comfy and secure.

About halfway through the dream I began to feel a cool, breezy spray of air on my skin. It was the first time I realized that I had skin, that I might be associated with a physical shape. Moments later I heard beeps, tiny beeps that started out faint and distant and then became louder and louder. Finally, from out of the darkness, I began to glimpse a distant shimmer of light.

As the beeps got louder, the light grew nearer and became brighter and brighter. Suddenly the light eclipsed the darkness with a near-blinding brightness, and then I woke up.

The next morning at breakfast I sat with my mom and tried to analyze it. She guessed that maybe I was recalling the moment I was born, and that got me excited. I thought that was the neatest thing and concentrated hard on not ever forgetting any part of that dream.

I wanted so badly to remember something about being little, since I couldn't recall much of anything about my early childhood. My birth was a subject we never really talked about, I guess because I was always frightened of finding out that I wasn't really wanted.

The plain facts surrounding Drew's arrival give little indication of the drama that preceded it. She was born on February 22, 1975, at Brotman Memorial Hospital in Culver City, California. It was a few minutes before noon, and Jaid's delivery was uncomplicated, even though the diminutive woman felt "like the Hindenburg was coming into the harbor." But when the six-pound-five-ounce baby girl arrived, Jaid was overjoyed and promptly named her Drew. She had selected the name months earlier. Girl or boy, the baby was going to be called Drew Barrymore. Drew was an androgynous name, Jaid thought, a name that was good and strong, simple, respected without sounding trendy. And it was unmistakably part of the Barrymore lore.

I think my mom and dad were boyfriend and girlfriend for a couple of years, but they were apart by the time I was born. That's about all I know. Once, I remember, I wondered why they had even bothered to have me if they were already splitting up. But I never asked, and no one ever told me. I guess they wanted to leave it a mystery so I could make up my own story.

Drew's parents' initial meeting happened on a Hollywood movie set many years earlier. Ildyko Jaid Mako was a young, lithe woman of Hungarian descent, an only child who suffered what she terms an unhappy childhood, the result of her parents' divorce. From her girlhood in Pennsylvania, she was consumed by dreams of acting in Hollywood. With the dark, exotic beauty of a model—large, inviting eyes, exquisite cheekbones, and a thick mane of black hair—a charming intelligence, and witty repartee, the odds of making it seemed stacked in her favor. It was no wonder that her first encounter with John Drew Barrymore, Jr., was a memorable one.

At the start of the 1960s, Barrymore was the sort of virile man who cast an entrancing spell over women. He possessed dashing good looks, inherited from his father, the great actor John Barrymore, who was called "the greatest lover of the screen," and there was about him a Bohemian charisma, a sense of wild adventure and passion and living for the moment. Having acted in a slew of big screen films including *The Sundowners, While the City Sleeps,* and *Never Love a Stranger,* Barrymore was something of a movie star himself.

However, Barrymore, a true rapscallion, garnered the most fame from his offscreen adventures. A week after marrying his first wife, actress Cara Williams, he was tossed in jail following a domestic argument. Within several years he had been arrested on several counts of drunk driving, hit-and-run driving, and his unrestrained alcoholism cost him his good standing with Actors' Equity. By 1960, bearded and long-haired, he had fled to Rome, where between marrying and divorcing twenty-three-year-old starlet Gabriella Palazzoli, he seemed to rack up as many arrests as he did B-movie credits.

After a brief period of meditation in India, Barrymore returned to California, ever flamboyant and dangerous at a time when it was hip to be on the edge of what society deemed acceptable. He cast himself as an ascetic, and professed to lead a pious, vegetarian life in the desert while composing poetry and writing screenplays. But Barrymore remained as spontaneous, untamed, and explosive as ever. On March 21, 1972, *The New York Times* reported his arrest for possession of marijuana. It was Barrymore's fourth drug-related arrest since the mid-sixties.

Soon after that latest run-in with the law, Barrymore and Jaid were reacquainted at the Troubadour nightclub, a hip Los Angeles music venue where Jaid waitressed. When romance blossomed, they began living together on the outskirts of West Hollywood and soon married. It was easy to see how Jaid could be mesmerized by Barrymore. Yet their tenure together was a violent one. Like the women before her, Jaid thought she might rehabilitate Barrymore, temper the flame that drove him to drink and drugs. She tried persuading him to enter a treatment program. She tried to convince him to go to therapy. She even tried having his baby. But instead of rehabilitation, she turned into a doormat for his abuse. The more she tried to love him, the more he lashed out at her.

Ethel Barrymore, Drew's great-aunt, once asked, "We who play, who entertain for a few years, what can we leave that will last?" She needn't have worried. The Barrymore family, prominent in entertainment circles since the days of England's George III, has continued almost in spite of itself. Each generation has been blessed with its share of talent, beauty, fame, and intelligence, yet the hallmark of each generation has been a penchant for self-destruction.

In the mid-1800s actress Louisa Lane, who delivered her first lines onstage at age five, married the Irish comedic actor John Drew, a slight, outgoing spirit who fell dead prematurely at thirty-four after a period of excess barroom exploits. "Had he lived to be forty-five, he would have been a great actor," wrote his widow. Their daughter, Georgie, a strikingly beautiful blonde who made her stage debut at fifteen, was swept off her feet several years later by a flashy young British actor whose dapper taste in clothes and stiff, proper accent cultivated an air of charm and polish. His name was Maurice Barrymore.

Married New Year's Eve 1876, the Barrymores set up housekeeping in New York and established themselves as the most prominent family of the American stage, though Maurice's reputation as a bon vivant reveler, womanizer, and imbiber quickly usurped his chance for greatness. Wobbling home one Sunday morning after a night of carousal, Maurice found his wife heading out the door. "Where are you going, my dear?" he asked.

"I am going to Mass," she said, "and you can go to hell."

Their first child, Lionel, was born in 1878, and he was followed a year later by the birth of a daughter, whom they named Ethel, after a character in Maurice's favorite novel, Thackeray's *The Newcomes*. Their third child was born February 15, 1882, and christened John Sidney Barrymore. A bright child, he showed an artistic and athletic flair early on, though with parents who traveled constantly, he developed a wild streak that would lead him in and out of trouble for the rest of his life.

John's mother died when he was eleven, leaving him with precious few memories. He grew up unbridled and wanton, a lad who shared as much distinction in preparatory school for his fondness for brass knuckles, cigarettes, and whiskey as for his academic prowess. By fourteen, he was a chronic drinker; a year later he made his stage debut in a nonspeaking role supporting his father, and at fifteen he was seduced by his beautiful young stepmother, an event that Barrymore biographer John Kobler supposed "profoundly affected his sexual development, engendered conflicting emotions toward his father, and produced a trauma that contributed to his increasing alcoholism."

Although he readily preferred art to acting, Barrymore sustained himself by knocking about the theater on several continents, criss-crossing the Atlantic like a migratory gull, and acquiring the skills that would, by the mid-1920s, inspire critics in London and New York to describe him as the greatest Hamlet of his generation. In 1932, the same year John, Jr., was born, Barrymore, Sr., signed a multimillion-dollar contract spanning two years and ten motion pictures. The result was a string of unparalleled box office successes, including *Grand Hotel, State's Attorney, Dinner at Eight,* and *Counsellor at Law,* which enshrined Barrymore atop Hollywood.

However, the achievements Barrymore accrued were slowly and painstakingly destroyed by the private demons that had unrelentingly tormented his soul since boyhood. By 1942, a string of four divorces— "bus accidents," Barrymore called them—high living, and rampant alcoholism branded the great actor unhirable. Mortgaged to the hilt, his fifty-five-room mansion stripped of its antiques and paintings, Barrymore was a mere shadow of his former self, who possessed just sixty cents in his pocket when he was delivered to the hospital for the final time. He died on May 29, 1942, at age sixty.

His funeral, attended by more than two thousand people, included pallbearers W. C. Fields and Louis Mayer, and friends such as Clark Gable, Spencer Tracy, Greta Garbo, Errol Flynn, and George Cukor. The legacy of Barrymore's filmwork is unsurpassed, one of the finest bodies of work ever compiled by an actor. Yet it was not without compromise. Barrymore's legacy as a father might well be among the most negligent. His daughter, Diana, was also a victim of alcoholism, and shortly after the publication of her best-selling biography, *Too Much Too Soon,* she died at age thirty-eight. John, Jr., was ten years old when his father died, and the loss appeared to have left the wayward youngster with an irreparable pain that colored the rest of his life and those around him.

My mom hated going in to descriptions of my father, no matter how I pleaded. Of course, I didn't begin to ask her anything until I could talk, but even then I learned that he was a pretty sensitive subject. I'm sure it was very emotional for her to relive everything, or whatever parts she told me about, and so I learned about my father only gradually, in bits and pieces, over the years.

I can remember actually seeing my father only a handful of times, the last time when I was seven years old. By then, of course, I had a pretty good picture of who he was, and why it was dangerous to be around him, but there was still so much that I didn't know. Like I was curious about his and my mom's relationship. And why they had me if they were already broken up and all that stuff.

I was probably ten or eleven years old when I finally summoned the courage to ask my mother about that. It was afternoon, and we had fallen asleep on the couch together while watching TV. Both of us kind of woke up at the same time, feeling drowsy and close, and without giving it any thought, the words just kind of slipped off my tongue, softly and easily.

"Mommy," I asked, "what did Daddy do?"

She looked at me as if she didn't understand.

"I mean, what was one of the big things Daddy did to make you really not want to be with him anymore?"

My mom's eyes widened. She looked surprised. But probably not nearly as surprised as I was when it seemed that she was actually going to answer my question. She took a moment to collect her thoughts, a long moment in which she drew a deep breath. Then she started in a soft voice that I wouldn't have heard if I hadn't been lying right beside her.

"Sweetie, when I was pregnant with you," she purred, "I wanted you so badly. I couldn't imagine wanting anything more than you. I felt so lucky to be pregnant, and I wanted the world to roll out the red carpet for you. I'd dream of what a wonderful life you'd have and of how strong and beautiful you'd be. But it was a battle. Your father thought a baby would solve all of our problems."

"And?" I asked.

"Well," she said hesitantly, "it didn't. He was as bad and as obsessive and as violent as ever. So I left him. I had to. Not just to

25

protect myself, but to protect you too. And that just made him angrier and more resentful."

Then Mom started to cry, and I started crying along with her. She didn't want to continue the story, but I urged her on, begging and pleading that she had to. After a minute or two she dried her tears, and then told me that the rest might be too painful for me.

"No, it's okay, Mom," I said. "I have to hear it."

I guess she felt I was right, but as she began recounting that tale, I realized that she was right too. The rest of the story was painful. Although my dad thought a baby would mend the troubles in his relationship with my mother, it didn't. He was unable to handle the pressure of my mom's pregnancy and showed it when his anger reared its violent head. He raged at her all the time. Then one night, she said, he went berserk and beat her up. He hit her and kicked her in the stomach. I suppose he was trying to make me die inside her. Finally, though, someone heard her cries and came to her rescue and took her to the hospital.

"But we survived," she said. "Both of us survived."

The apartment Jaid brought Drew home to from the hospital was a comfortable one-bedroom duplex in West Hollywood, a middle-class neighborhood populated by an unusual mix of artists, Hasidic Jews, and senior citizens. The sun streamed in from large windows, making the plain furnishings appear brighter than they actually were. Jaid filled her baby daughter's tiny bedroom with a menagerie of stuffed animals, determined that she would have the best of everything she could afford, which wasn't much on her meager income.

Upon Drew's arrival, Jaid temporarily shelved her acting career. A baby, she knew, was not exactly what her agent termed a good career move, considering she was a newly separated, struggling actress who owned good stage credits but still lacked the lucrative work in television and film that would make life easier. Still, a baby was cause to celebrate. Jaid had wanted a child, and motherhood was something she felt deep within her soul. It gave her a biblical feeling, a sense of connection with past generations of her family, and that was good. Yet Jaid had no doubt that raising a child would prove a struggle, and that filled her with doubt and worry.

A look at Jaid, a slight woman of fragile, petite build, gave little to suggest the reservoir of inner strength she possessed. But she was a person who, having made a decision, could stand resolute and immutable. Drew became her sole focus, a solitary, overly protective interest that in retrospect seems to have been a reaction to the destructive, ill-fated union that had produced her. In Drew she would find the love that she couldn't find in her husband, and she would return the sentiment even more so.

It was tough. Jaid's priorities were suddenly changed from auditions and acting workshops to food, toys, diapers, and inoculations—and that cost money. A month after bringing Drew home, Jaid went back to work. She juggled acting jobs with a steady waitressing gig at the Troubadour, relying on a revolving group of baby-sitters to care for Drew while she was away. And when she was away her thoughts centered on her little girl. What new things was she doing? Did she laugh? Did she sit up? Did she roll over? These little things were big events.

Their duplex hardly seemed big enough for the two of them once Drew began to crawl. She was all over the apartment. In the closets, under the furniture, in the cabinets. And one day she was out on the balcony. It was a hot, sultry summer afternoon and Jaid had left the sliding glass door open, hoping to find a cool breeze in the heavy air. However, what she inadvertently created was a passageway to danger. When Jaid glanced up, a diaper-clad Drew was poking through the wrought-iron restraining bars on the balcony, a scant few inches away from a tragic fall.

That's all Jaid needed to see. With lightning speed she scooped up her baby and decided, then and there, to move to a safer apartment. The following week she signed the lease for a two-bedroom ground-floor apartment located directly across the street from the old place. It was more expensive. But nothing was too good for her daughter.

I was too young to realize it, but my mother worked extremely hard so that I could have nice things. It wasn't because she wanted to. She worked during the day and she worked at night, which meant that even though she didn't like it, I was left with a baby-sitter all the time. What effect that had on me at the time is hard to say. Later on I resented it. I felt abandoned. But as a little baby I don't know that it mattered. Maybe it did. I suppose it did. I've been told that I was a very good baby, real easy and good-spirited. Maybe I just wanted whoever was taking care of me to like me.

It was impossible not to like her. At eleven months Drew was a little bundle of tufted blond hair, dimples, and fat. She had a docile disposition and she seemed to laugh at everything. She was the picture of a perfect baby. Perhaps, as Jaid hoped, the world would roll out the red carpet for her. "Commercials," Jaid's friends would say. "You should get her into commercials." Jaid wasn't interested. For obvious reasons, she had a rather cynical take on the acting profession.

However, completely unknown to Jaid, a friend of hers snapped a photo of Drew and mailed it to a children's theatrical agent, who liked what she saw and responded right away with the date and time for a job interview. That was nice, a nice compliment. However, Jaid politely declined. She didn't want her daughter in the business, she explained. No matter. The agent, refusing to take no for an answer, telephoned the friend and begged her to persuade Jaid to change her mind, which she managed to do after a second lengthy phone conversation.

They showed up at the appointed place, a big, empty Hollywood soundstage, and entered the outer waiting room only to find it jam-packed with what seemed like every baby in Los Angeles. "Babies coming out of the walls, the roof, the windows and the Rolodex," Jaid recalls. "Half of them looked like Winston Churchill and the other half looked like the Gerber baby. I couldn't imagine how they were going to pick one kid out of that pack." The cramped room was a madhouse. Babies cried, nursed, crawled, kicked, and wet. The wait seemed interminable as each child was individually screened.

Finally, the casting director called Drew's name and Jaid carried her onto the set. The commercial was for Gainesburgers, and the audition process was a simple one. Drew, like the others, was set down on a large cloth spread out in the middle of this vast room. Then they let in a little white puppy. The child's reaction was studied. If they cried or tried yanking the dog's eyes out, they flunked. And if they just sat there, that, too, was grounds for dismissal. Drew did neither. She laughed when the puppy came running in. Then she stuck out her hand and the puppy licked her. She then started nuzzling the pooch. Suddenly, though for no apparent reason, the tiny dog bit her.

Jaid was stunned, stopped in her tracks. So was everyone else in the room who watched the incident. "You could have dropped a pin it was so silent," Jaid recalls. "The puppy scampered away and Drew just looked up at me. She was surprised too. Then she looked at everyone else in the room. There was something like twenty-five people there, and they were all shocked, probably thinking, 'Oh my God, lawsuit.' Then Drew suddenly threw her head back and started laughing, and everyone was charmed out of their mind. They all broke into applause, and Drew just looked around and beamed. She just drank it up. Oh, boy, was she a little ham."

Before they left, Drew was given the job.

I didn't work again until I was two and a half. I was in a made-for-TV movie, which, I think, is my earliest memory of working. I remember lying on a bed, pretending to be asleep. A man came over to me, picked me up, and then someone yelled, "Cut!"

Oh, yeah, I played a boy in that movie.

Acting wasn't in Jaid's plans for Drew. But her longtime friend, actor-director Stuart Margolin, who costarred with James Garner on the hit television series *The Rockford Files,* was making his film directorial debut with a TV movie called *Suddenly Love,* and he needed to cast the part of a little kid. The movie starred Cindy Williams of *Laverne and Shirley* as the mother of a young boy who begins a new life after her husband drops dead of a heart attack, and Margolin, says Jaid, "didn't want to deal with the unknown quantity of a child actor any more than he had to."

Because Margolin was a friend, Jaid agreed to let her daughter work on the movie. They cut her shoulder-length tresses short to resemble a boy's hair, and that was it. The two-and-a-half-year-old charmer was in heaven. Considering her age, she evidenced an extraordinary ability to concentrate while learning her part. When the camera rolled, she hit her marks perfectly. Her attention never waned. Her most difficult scene, the one where the mother learns her husband has died, called for Drew to run up and comfort her mother by pleading, "Don't cry, Mommy. Please, don't cry." It presented no problem. Drew delivered on the first take. "Even when she was supposed to be asleep, her eyes never fluttered," says Jaid.

Margolin was amazed. Drew's mother was

equally impressed. "She understood," Jaid says. "Somehow, at that age, she understood what it was all about." More than that, there was a purpose to Drew's acting. It's easy to underestimate the thinking of a two-year-old, if only for their inability to communicate. Yet by that age the ability to perceive and react to an array of complex emotions, like love and hate, fear and acceptance, is already well developed. So although she was unable to articulate it, there was, Drew understood, a purpose to her acting.

The earliest memory I have of my father isn't pleasant. I was three years old. It was afternoon, and I was wearing a pair of jeans and these cute Mickey Mouse suspenders, a favorite play outfit. My mom and I were standing in the kitchen, doing the laundry. Taking the clothes out of the dryer, folding them into the basket. Stuff like that. I was mostly dancing around the room while my mom did the work. Suddenly the door swung open and there was this man standing there. I yelled, "Daddy!" Even though I didn't know what he looked like, I just automatically knew it was him.

He paused in the doorway, like he was making a dramatic entrance, and I think he said something, but he was so drunk, it was unintelligible. It sounded more like a growl. We stood there, staring at him. I was so excited to see him. I was just coming to the age where I noticed that I didn't have a father like everyone else, and I wanted one. I didn't really know what my dad was like, but I learned real fast.

In a blur of anger he roared into the room and threw my mom down on the ground. Then he turned on me. I didn't know what was happening. I was still excited to see him, still hearing the echo of my gleeful yell, "Daddy!" when he picked me up and threw me into the wall. Luckily, half of my body landed on the big sack of laundry and I wasn't hurt. But my dad didn't even look back after me. He turned and grabbed a bottle of tequila, shattered a bunch of glasses all over the floor, and then stormed out of the house.

And that was it. That was the first time I remember seeing my dad.

The incident sparked a terrible memory. It occurred long ago, six months before Drew's birth, but still lodged in Jaid's mind like a grotesque image that refused to vanish, an unshakable nightmare. She had made up her mind. She was leaving John. She was going to walk out on him. If she wanted to survive, it was her only option. She'd had enough of the abuse, of his drinking and violence. She wanted to make something out of her life. Besides that, she was pregnant, and whether or not he wanted the child, she did. There was just one question: How would he take it out on her?

That was what frightened her most. He would, she knew, do something.

To her surprise, when Jaid announced that she was walking out, John didn't hit her. Not that the scene was quiet and peaceful. There was a pitched argument, all right. There was plenty of screaming, shaking of fists, and pounding on furniture that rocked their apartment like an earthquake. But what John did was worse than striking her. He issued a threat, Jaid recalls, a threat that caused her to tremble. Between drinks, in a smooth, controlled voice that struck like the terrifying calm before a storm, he simply stated, "If you leave me, if you hurt me by leaving, I'm going to hurt you back by making sure that your child's life is miserable."

Whether or not he consciously intended it, John Barrymore, not unlike his own father, cast a tragic shadow over his little girl. He was a puzzle Drew wasn't able to comprehend, an unfathomable mystery she learned to accept as part of her life. As hard as Jaid tried to keep him at bay, his presence hung over them like a ghostly stir.

I remember one time my grandparents—my mother's mother and father—were visiting, and we were coming back from a nice Chinese dinner. I think it was me who ran out of the car and went to get the hidden key. But when I looked, it was gone. Nobody except the four of us knew where that key was. It would've been impossible to just guess where it was. Someone had to have seen us hide it. Anyway, I just turned, motioned like the key wasn't there, and said, "Well, obviously Dad took it."

"He must've been watching us," someone said.

I guess my mom went and called him, because soon he drove up. It wasn't that we wanted to deal with him, to invite him over or anything. We just didn't want him to have the key. Not under any circumstances. Because then he could come in anytime he wanted, and that was too unsafe. We knew how violent he could be. So he drove up and let us inside, but he wouldn't hand over the key.

That's when my grandfather, who was around seventy, decided to get the key back. Rather than confront my dad, Grandpa asked if he wanted to get a drink. Well, that was great, and the two of them roared off in my dad's car. A couple of hours later my grandfather walked in, holding the key in his hand so that all of us could see it. I think everyone kind of applauded. But Grandpa didn't take alcohol real well, and he'd obviously had a drink or two. He looked so tired and disgusted. I remember him saying, "Jesus, what a jerk." Then he passed out in a chair.

After the TV movie *Suddenly Love,* Jaid was adamant about Drew not acting anymore. It was simply too hard. Not on Drew—on Jaid. If that was selfish, fine. Jaid barely had enough time to make her own appointments, never mind piling up a full schedule of auditions and shoots for her daughter. That would have only complicated what was already a complicated routine of juggling baby-sitters, doctor appointments, and play groups as well as Jaid's own career. "I was still a young woman with my own ambitions," she says.

Life was in a perpetual state of turmoil. During the day, auditions competed with Drew for attention. At night, the baby-sitter would suddenly cancel a half hour before Jaid was due on the set. Or Drew would be sick and the baby-sitter wouldn't take her. Jaid often found her own interests pitted against her daughter's. She wanted a career, yet she also wanted what was best for Drew, and it was difficult for her to swallow the aspirations she had harbored since girlhood.

"But everything in my life had to serve Drew," she explains. "Every breath had to be for her. I was determined that Drew wouldn't be raised the way I was. In retrospect, I can see the massive overcompensation. But that was my guilt for her not having a father as well as my unwillingness to bring a man into our lives. Drew was Queen of the Hop. She had to be the center, at least as far as I was concerned."

Consequently, when Drew, at four years old, surprised her mother by expressing a well-thought-out ambition with a clarity beyond her years, Jaid found herself taken aback. Not only did she reconsider her position on Drew's acting, but she had to reevaluate her own career as well. The decision turned out to be one that affected their lives for years to come.

A routine had already started. I would complain to my mom about her being gone so often, and she'd say things like, "Drew, just let me go. There are so many bills to pay." I didn't understand. All I knew was that she was leaving me. I felt like I was getting a cold shoulder.

One night she was running out to a play. The baby-sitter was there and I had on my nightgown. She was late and didn't want to be delayed by my whining. But I stopped her.

"Mom, I really want to act," I said. "I like it so much."

"I've got to get to the theater," she said. "Mommy's late already. She's got to go."

"But I really want to discuss this," I said. "I really want to act, and I've thought about it a lot."

My mom sat down and plopped me on her lap so that we were looking eye to eye. She decided to get serious with me.

"It's just so hard, Drew," she said. "Look what Mommy goes through. There's a lot of rejection. It's not always like what you've done."

I tried explaining to her that I still wanted to do it.

Out of exasperation she said, "Drew, you just don't understand. It's too hard."

And that was supposed to be that. My mom set me back down on the floor and started to put her coat on. I grabbed ahold of her hand, stopping her so that she'd pay attention to me.

"Mommy, I know it's too hard. That's why I want to do it."

If only for Drew's frankness and serious tone, it was a chilling moment that stopped her mother in her tracks. "I thought, anybody who expresses themselves in that articulate, elegant, and determined manner is obviously quite serious," says Jaid. "Drew just took my breath away when she said that. Mostly because it was so out of context for her age. It was like an older person speaking through her, and I just paid total attention. I said, 'Fine, Drew, if this is really what you want, we'll start something up and see how it goes.' "

THREE

WORKING GIRL

Why did I want to act? How did I know so early? The answer, I suppose, has always been pretty obvious—at least it has been to me. I loved being part of the group. Actually, I didn't just love it, I needed it. That's what drove me to club hopping later on. Being part of that really fun *in* group. As a little kid I was the girl who didn't think anyone loved her, which only inspired me to try to be accepted even more. When you make a movie, or work on any kind of production, I learned, you become part of a very close group. It's a lot like being in a family, a big extended family. And I loved that.

Jaid wanted to start slowly. Commercials first, then television and movies. Maybe her daughter wouldn't like acting, she thought. But Jaid couldn't have been more wrong. A prematurely self-possessed Drew snagged the first four commercials she auditioned for, and both the agent and Jaid thought the neophyte's feat nothing short of miraculous. "It was the most uncanny thing I ever saw," says Jaid. "My God, I wondered, what do we have here? I didn't go into the

37

interviews with her. I thought, what does she do in that room?"

It was something to see. The tiny blond cherub, who barely tipped the scale at thirty-five pounds and stood about that many inches tall, would wave good-bye to her nervous mother and confidently stride to her interview. There was not an ounce of shyness to Drew, who loved dressing in bright, frilly sundresses that made her look like the quintessential huggable little girl. When she faced the director, or whoever was conducting the audition, it was, Drew recalls, "as if a light switch turned on inside me."

Indeed. She came alive. She chattered, laughed, answered questions, and she was so intuitively bright and sensitive that it was hard not to like her immediately.

Jaid, who stood in awe of her daughter's successes, felt neither jealousy nor vicarious satisfaction from these successes. She still hungered for her own achievements. In fact, Jaid was about to pull the reins on Drew's burgeoning career to give herself more free time when the youngster went up for her first feature film, Ken Russell's *Altered States,* starring William Hurt and Blair Brown.

Drew was one of about three dozen girls, each one prettier and more charming than the next, who stood in a semicircle around Russell. The colorful director, an avuncular Santa Claus lookalike, began talking informally to the group and then, addressing no one in particular, asked a question. When nobody answered, Drew looked around, stepped forward, and offered a reply that made everyone laugh. Russell asked a second question and the same thing happened. Soon he and Drew were carrying on a private conversation while the other girls drifted off, and before she and her mother left, Drew got the part.

"I was shocked," says Jaid. "I'd gone out on eight

thousand interviews for films, and here Drew waltzes
in and gets one on her first try."

I was having a great old time. They'd say, "Actors to the set," and
everyone would kind of lollygag to their places. Except for me. I'd
run. I was always the first one there, ready to do it. That was a big
part of my wanting to act. I wasn't in that much of the movie, but
when it was time for me to work, I was so incredibly happy.

However, what I didn't know is that my work was hard on my
mother. She was schlepping me all over town, taking me to shoots
and auditions and fittings. Everything. It was a full-time job. We
were spending a lot of time together, which should've been nice,
but it was pretty much business, and not very rewarding for her.

I sensed, kind of, that she was not very happy. Thinking about
it, she didn't have much of a life. She was either with me or working,
trying to find time to go out on an audition of her own, maybe
wondering why she didn't have much of a social life, and always,
there was the pressure of bills that needed paying and all that kind
of stuff.

One day she was just so upset. She'd reached a breaking point,
and she sat on the couch and started to cry. Not from any one thing,
but from everything in general. I began stroking her hair, trying to
comfort her.

"I know why you're upset," I said.

"Why?" she asked, glancing up at me with a what-can-you-
possibly-know look. "What is it?"

"Life, Mommy," I said. "Life."

If she was prematurely insightful, Drew was also quite
similar to the other youngsters in her preschool. Like
them, she possessed an abundance of energy that
typically turned her into a song-and-dance monster.
The living room served as her stage. With the Go-Gos
or Blondie blasting in the background, she turned
cartwheels and somersaults and practiced the dance
steps she learned in ballet. When she tired of that,

Drew roller-skated, colored, or played dress-up in her mom's clothing.

She had fun. She reveled in her playtime, but there was, Drew noticed, something missing from her daily routines—her mother. Unlike the majority of her friends, it was the baby-sitter who often supervised Drew at play while her mother was off at work. The baby-sitter woke up with Drew in the morning, and at night, it was the baby-sitter who pulled back the Mickey Mouse comforter on the bed and reluctantly acquiesced when Drew fended off sleep by asking to play Let's Pretend.

"Okay," the baby-sitter would reply, "what do you want to pretend?"

"Ummmmm, let's pretend . . ." I'd say, pausing to think of something. "Let's pretend . . . that we're movie stars and we just got back from this big party . . ."

"You're already—well, almost—a movie star," she'd laugh, giving me a friendly tickle. "And we really have had a party all night."

"Okay, then let's pretend that we're . . . that we're sisters," I'd start again. "You're my big sister, and you've been watching me while our mother and father are out to dinner. And when they get home they'll come in, tuck us into bed, and kiss us good-night."

"Okay, we'll pretend that," she'd say. "But let's also pretend that you're going to sleep now."

I hated going to sleep. I was afraid that I was going to miss something important. Maybe my mom would come home early, wanting to visit with me. Or maybe my dad, my whacked-out father, would show up unannounced, looking for me. I didn't want them to say, "Oh, Drew's asleep. Better not wake her."

I was at that age where going to prekindergarten, playmates, and TV shows like *The Brady Bunch* made me aware of all that I didn't have. Maybe the baby-sitter sensed that I felt alone and uncared for. As a kid, you never really concentrate on what good stuff you have. It's always what you're lacking. And with me, that was a mother and a father. I knew that mine wasn't a normal family situation. It made me feel very alone.

The absolutely greatest day, as far as I was concerned, was always my birthday. Without question. My birthday was the biggest, best day of the year. I have this one photograph of my fifth birthday that I still love looking at. It shows me standing beside our apartment, wearing a pink party dress and surrounded by a bunch of friends who came over. For some reason I'm also crying. That's why I like it, I guess. I call it the "it's my party and I'll cry if I want to" picture.

Actually, the reason I loved my birthday, and counted down the days every month, was that all the people who came to my party were there just for me. Just for me. That one special day every year when I wasn't so alone. Which is undoubtedly why I never wanted my birthday party to end. Come to think of it, maybe that's why I'm crying in the picture. Maybe everyone was about to go home and I didn't want my birthday to end.

Drew's next project was *Bogie,* a made-for-TV biofilm about Humphrey Bogart. Though her part as Bogart's daughter, Leslie, was negligible, the movie affected the budding actress in a way that none of her previous work had. The director, an affable old-timer named Vincent Sherman, had worked with Drew's great-uncle, Lionel Barrymore, and known her grandfather, John, and he made a point of telling her stories of her legendary relatives. She had never heard these tales before. And for the first time, it dawned on the five-year-old that she was part of a family. Somewhere, she had a family, and she wanted to know more about them.

To this day I still haven't met my two sisters. One is named Jessica and the other is named Blythe. They're my half sisters. I also have a half brother—John Barrymore III. Even though he's twenty years older than me, I've always called him Johnny. When I was real little, like three, four, and five years old, Johnny was around quite a lot. Nearly every day I waited for him to show up. Besides my baby-sitter, he was the only person who played games with me, and I loved him so much, more so because it was such a treat when he stopped by.

Johnny was always hitting me up for bits of money. "Drew, you got any money for gas?" he'd ask, and me, little Miss Ready-to-Please, would run over to my bank and proudly give him the bundle of change that I'd collected especially for him. We had an avocado and an orange tree in the backyard, and I would put a whole bunch of fruit in baskets, load them onto a wagon, and take them around the neighborhood, selling the fruit for ten and twenty-five cents each. Then I'd give the money to Johnny, the love of my life.

What I didn't realize then, but later learned, was that Johnny was often drugged out, and if he didn't spend the money I made for him on gas, I suspect he spent it on drugs. I simply thought he was kind of strange and wild, like my dad. Here's a typical scene: Johnny would be sitting on the floor, playing Chutes and Ladders with me. That was fine. But when he'd lose, he'd go crazy. He'd just erupt into a huge temper tantrum, and I'd sit there wondering what I'd done to cause that. I mean, it was only a stupid game. What did I know about drugs?

Once my mom caught on to his behavior, though, when I was about six, she told him that it was probably best if he stopped coming around until he cleaned himself up. When I asked why Johnny stopped coming by, she tried to explain that he was sick. Or something like that. But I didn't really understand. All I knew was that someone else whom I was close to and loved abandoned me.

However, the one person I didn't give up on was my father. Despite his abusive outbursts, I talked about him all the time. My mom took the brunt of my complaints and anger. I'd always ask her if she couldn't try to make things work with Dad, and she always gave me the same answer: no. Because she left him, I always felt like she was the bad person. At that time I didn't know the situation, and my mother didn't want to depress me by telling me the truth. She accepted the blame while I piled up the resentment.

There were times when I talked of nothing else but my father. I begged to know more about him, to see him, to invite him over for dinner. I forgot about his violent temper. Why was he such a bad guy? I wanted to know. Couldn't I see for myself? When I was very young, my mother thought it was necessary to keep him away from me. But as I became more insistent, she didn't want her resentment of him to get in the way of any potential relationship— if there was going to be one.

Our conversations were always the same. I'd start by telling my mom how much I wanted to see my father.

"But I don't think you're going to be happy with the way he looks," she'd say.

"I don't care, Mommy."

"And I don't think you're going to like the way he treats people," she'd say. "Daddy is not always a nice man."

"Well, I have to learn that for myself."

I was very headstrong, and to my mother's credit, she was accepting of my desire.

So one day I went to my dad's apartment. When my mom dropped me off, I was practically bursting from the excitement and anticipation. I was all gussied up in a sundress, with ribbons dangling from my pigtails, which was a stark contrast to the way my dad looked when he opened the door. He was in tattered jeans and a T-shirt. His shocking white hair hung past his shoulders and he had a big, bushy mustache and goatee. A cigarette dangled from his mouth.

"Dad?" I said, handing him a flower I'd picked outside.

"Come on in, munchkin," he laughed.

What a dump that place was. He had a bed, a cardboard box, and a candle. That was it. He spent all his money on alcohol and drugs, I guess. For the next few hours, while he rambled on about everything from the Barrymore family to Buddha and meditation, I tried to make his place a little nicer. I made curtains out of paper towels and dusted and found a cup to hold the flowers I'd picked. Time must've passed quickly, because what I remember next is my mom honking from the car. Just before I left, my dad went over to this pile of boxes, rummaged through a bunch of junk, and pulled out a white stuffed bear.

"What do you want to name it?" he said.

"I don't know."

"How about Yogi Bear?" he said, handing it to me.

I practically melted right there. When he gave me Yogi, I thought it was like God's personal gift to me. As far as I remembered, that was the first nice thing my dad had ever done for me, and I skipped out of there feeling like the luckiest girl in the world.

Of course, it didn't last. Not too long after, perhaps a few months later, my mom was stuck for a baby-sitter and she decided to let my dad try it. He'd been pestering for a chance. But she didn't trust him alone with me. No way. So she arranged for her friend, Carol, to stay over too. We went and picked up my dad, who was acting really drunk, and before we even got home, a fight erupted and my mom booted him out of the car.

She was always tough with him. It was a side to her that I rarely saw. They'd be arguing and all of a sudden he'd say something like "I've got to go. I'm late for a doctor's appointment." She'd roll her eyes and say, "Yeah, Dr. Cuervo, right?" She called him on all his bullshit.

Anyway, he walked the rest of the way to our house, determined to be my baby-sitter. My mom left after Carol arrived, and she went into my mom's bedroom, where she made phone calls, leaving me and my dad alone. We turned on the TV and started talking, and, like always, he got kind of weird. He turned off the lights and lit a bunch of candles. At the time he was hanging around with David Carradine, who had worked on the series *Kung Fu,* and he was real into that karate stuff. For some reason he started showing me how to do the kicks. He'd whip around and, *bam,* snap a kick at me. Most of the time he'd just miss, but sometimes he'd hit me. In the arm, the stomach, the head. He didn't seem to care that it hurt. But I wouldn't cry. The more he continued, the more pissed off I got.

"Why do you always have to cause so much pain?" I asked him.

"What do you mean, little one?" he asked, while continuing to toss off kicks in my direction.

"Why do you always have to cause everyone so much pain?" I screamed. "You're always hurting everyone!"

He stopped and came toward me. There was a crazed sort of look in his eyes. He sat down on the sofa.

"Come over here," he motioned.

Kids don't know any better. So I sat down beside him.

"What do you know about pain?" he challenged.

I didn't know what to say. Then he took my hand and stuck it in the candle flame. It burned and I started to cry. My cries only seemed to make my dad angrier. He let go of my hand and thrust his own hand into the flame, running it back and forth in the fire.

"Don't ever be afraid of fire," he scolded me. "Never be frightened of fire."

He stood up, like he was lecturing me, but I was crying and not listening, holding my burned hand.

"It's all in your mind, Drew," he said.

I heard what he said, but it didn't matter. He was out of his mind. Finally, he drifted off to something else. I think he left the room, probably to go get a drink.

For a time Drew tried to understand her father. It was the only way she could attempt to reconcile her yearning for love and approval and his utter refusal to give it.

"How come Daddy's like he is?" I asked my mom.

Jaid didn't really have a good answer. She explained to Drew that her father had never been loved by his parents, especially by his own father, a man whose affection and approval he desperately craved. John, in fact, had once told his ex-wife that he had seen his own father for only one day, and that the senior Barrymore had been drunk the whole time.

"So your dad didn't ever learn how to love other people," Jaid offered to Drew.

She tried to understand. Nonetheless, the pain of abandonment was woven into the fabric of daily routines and accepted as part of the overall design of life. The lines uttered by Drew and Jaid were spoken so many times, they sounded like dialogue they were rehearsing for a play. "Mom," Drew would say, "do you have to go to work today?"

"Yes, honey, I have to go to work."

"But couldn't you stay home, just this once?"

"We've got bills, Drew. Mommy's got her career."

"Can't they wait?"

"Oh, come on, honey, gimme a break."

Gimme a break. "I heard that a lot," says Drew. At six years old, the only break she could afford to give her mother was silence. She wouldn't complain. She wouldn't tug on her mother's dress as she was getting ready to leave for work. She wouldn't argue. Drew would keep the frustrations to herself, just like her mother contained her frustrations, and she'd simply cope the best way she could.

Drew's recourse was to develop a magnetic, ingratiating charm and a fertile, unbridled imagination into which she could comfortably disappear from reality. The drawings she carried home from school and taped to the refrigerator were full of children playing amid flowers, rainbows, and hearts that floated in the blue sky like billowy clouds. At home she played all kinds of make-believe games with her baby-sitter, and when her mother returned home at night, Drew excitedly recounted her adventures with rock bands, dragons, and movie stars.

Drew especially treasured those cozy nights when her mother was home in time to read her a bedtime story. Over time, they pored through classics like *James and the Giant Peach, A Wrinkle in Time, Eloise,* and *Charlie and the Chocolate Factory.* One evening her mother brought home a new story, a script, and with Drew under the covers, she began reading a heartwarming fairy tale about love and life and concerning a sweet alien who's been left behind in a California suburb by his fellow extraterrestrials and the little boy who comes to his aid.

I loved it. It sounds stupid, like a cliché, but I cried and I laughed and at the end, I got a real warm spot in my heart. I mean, how could you not?

Two weeks before she listened to this fable, Drew was among the one hundred children who auditioned for Steven Spielberg's latest movie, *Poltergeist*. However, he asked Jaid if she could bring her daughter back to audition for another film he was directing himself. It was called *E.T.* In Drew, Spielberg spotted the pluck and cuteness he was looking for in the part of the little sister, Gertie. Drew's second interview, Jaid remembers, "seemed to last an unusually long time."

I was so nervous before I went in there. But instead of taking the nervous approach, I decided to pull it together and be the exact opposite. So I walked into Steven's office as this live-wire six-year-old, just laughing and saying hi to everyone. They all started to laugh with me and I relaxed.

"You like acting?" Steven asked.

"I love it," I said. "But you know, honestly, I'm a musician at heart."

He looked mildly curious and asked, "You are?"

"Oh, yeah," I answered. "I've got this punk rock band called the Purple People Eaters. I sing lead. We play the clubs on weekends, you know, Madam Wong's, the Troubadour, the Roxy. Stuff like that."

"And your mother doesn't mind?"

"Oh, no," I said. "She's a total rocker. She used to work at the Troubadour."

I was being a total geek about everything, answering his questions with any goofy answers I could think of, but, of course, then I thought I was being the epitome of cool and grace under pressure.

Apparently, Spielberg was entertained by the little wisecracker. When Jaid was finally summoned inside, she found the director, his producer, and the casting agent "laughing and having a great old time." A seemingly impressed Spielberg mentioned that Drew had spoken colorfully about her rock and roll band, which caused Jaid to raise an eyebrow. "Oh, did she?" sighed Jaid, wondering what other tall tales Drew had conjured up that she might have to explain.

"Do you think she has a good imagination?" he asked.

"I'm not really objective," Jaid replied. "But I think so. To give you an example, remember the punk rock band she spoke about?"

"Yes," he said.

"Well, that doesn't exist."

Spielberg laughed. Drew was open and creative. She was adorable. She had all-American stamped on her forehead. Spielberg felt he had found his Gertie. Still, the director, ever the perfectionist, asked Drew back for another test. He wanted to see if she could portray different emotions, like fear and awe.

I knew about emotions like fear and hurt, but I didn't have a clue what the word *awe* meant. I could barely read, being only in kindergarten. When I asked my mother, she told me to pretend I was looking at the most amazing thing I've ever seen in my life.

"Am I supposed to be scared?" I asked.

"No, not at all," said my mom.

"So it's like in *The Wizard of Oz* when the good fairy came in the big bubble?"

"Right."

"Or will it be like seeing the spaceship come in *Close Encounters?*"

"That's right too."

I had a good feeling about *E.T.* On the way to the studio I told my mother that I really wanted to do it. From the story alone, I knew it would be fun. But I also knew that I could learn a lot from Steven. Finally, we got there and I was asked to improvise with the two other kids, Henry Thomas and Robert MacNaughton. Apparently, that went all right because Steven then said there was just one more thing they wanted to see if I could do.

"What's that?" I asked.

"Scream."

So they led me into the sound room, sat me down in front of a microphone, and told me to scream.

"Just scream?" I asked.

"As loud as you can," the soundman said.

I was a little better than they expected. They told me that I almost broke the instruments.

E.T. was Steven Spielberg's intimate little movie. So personal was it that the Hollywood wunderkind guaranteed the cost overruns out of his own pocket. Spielberg had thought up the history-making story in 1980 while stuck in the Tunisian desert making *Raiders of the Lost Ark.* "I was kind of lonely at the time," he said. His girlfriend was in Los Angeles, and he thought to himself, "What I really need is a friend I can talk to—somebody who can give me all the answers." Days later Spielberg and *Raiders* star Harrison Ford persuaded Ford's screenwriter wife, Melissa Mathison, into writing the screenplay.

Filming began a year later under extreme secrecy, lest outsiders glimpse the squashy ten-million-year-old space mariner who was able to magically levitate colored balls, cure cut fingers, and make geraniums grow. From September to December Drew arrived on the set at Laird Studios at 8:30 A.M., where, by law, she, Henry, and Robert received three hours of tutoring every day. Shooting began after lunch and continued until six P.M., when Jaid drove Drew back home while listening to her animated talk about how wonderful Spielberg was.

Right off, I fell in love with Steven. In many ways he was—and always will be—the dad I never had. I wanted so badly to be accepted by him, and when I was, it meant a lot to me. I was thrilled when he invited me to his Malibu house. We'd run along the beach, collect seashells, and build sand castles. It was so much fun to hang out with him.

But working with Steven was even better. In most of the scenes he let me do whatever I wanted. All of us were free to offer input, but he especially seemed to like the silly things the kids came up with. Like in the scene where Henry, Robert, and I are hiding E.T. in the closet from our mother, Henry tells me that only kids can see E.T. There wasn't a line to go with that, and Steven told me to just make something up. So when we did the scene again, I just shrugged and said, "Gimme a break!"

He'd often take me aside and say something like "You're talking to me now. Do you really like this? Or do you have a different idea? Do you think it could be done a different way?" Eventually, I'd add something and Steven would smile and say, "Good, let's combine ideas." It made me feel so good. For once I didn't feel like some stupid little kid trying to make people love me. I felt important and useful.

One day I was really, really sick, but I didn't want to say anything because I was scared. Steven was under a lot of tension and the last thing I wanted was to let him down. After one scene he pulled me off to the side and reprimanded me. "How come you're not putting everything you've got into the work?" he said. I didn't say anything. I was too frightened to tell him. I loved him so much I didn't want to cause any problems.

He eventually found out that I was sick, and I ended up collapsing. I had a temperature of 104 degrees and had to go to the hospital, where they fed me ice chips to bring down the fever. And I remember Steven felt so bad for scolding me. He sent me home with a note from my director and told me to stay there till I got better.

Steven is also responsible for the best advice I've ever been given on acting—actually, on anything. One time he told me, "Drew, you can't act your character, you've got to *be* your character." I kind of nodded and said, "Oh, sure, Steven. See ya." However, when I got home, for some reason what he said popped back into my head and, I swear, it made the most perfect sense. What he said was so simple that it nearly skirted by me. But it's amazing how one brief sentence like that—don't act your character, be your character; don't act like you imagine yourself, be yourself—can be so profound and make such a big difference in your life.

After shooting Spielberg's *The Color Purple,* comedienne-actress Whoopi Goldberg lamented that the multitalented filmmaker provides actors with the most wonderfully creative, blissful experience they'll ever get and then leaves them to work with others and fend for themselves in less-perfect situations. In other words, a Spielberg picture ends and the actor runs headlong into reality. To Drew, that meant returning to her first grade classroom at the Fountain Day School, where she was a virtual stranger.

During the nearly four months *E.T.* filmed, Jaid had taken time off work to stay beside Drew, who was six when she made the film and seven when it was released. The money her daughter received, about $75,000, was enough to purchase some long-sought independence from the job runaround. When filming completed, Jaid quit waitressing, which allowed her more time to pursue an acting career as well as spend more time at home with Drew. Unfortunately, things didn't work out as neatly as planned.

Actually, even before *E.T.* wrapped, my mom worked at the Strasberg Institute in a play called *Playing for Time.* Daytimes she'd be on the set with me and then rush over to the theater at night. The play was about Jews imprisoned by the Nazis. It was very sad. On Friday and Saturday nights I played a small part, a little girl who was about to be sent off to death but who became the darling of a female German officer. That's where we met Lee and Anna Strasberg. Lee really liked my mom's work, and Anna became my godmother.

Right after, though, my mother was cast in a small part as a prostitute in the movie *Night Shift,* which starred Henry Winkler and Michael Keaton. For several months she was working long eighteen-hour days and I hardly ever got to see her. The days were unpredictable. There was no routine to her schedule and we didn't have any full-time help. So I was constantly being dumped with one sitter or another, and when that fell through, my mom carted me off to the set with her.

E.T. wasn't out yet, so I was still regarded as this bothersome little kid who no one wanted to have around. I'd wait for her in the ladies' dressing room and fool around with the makeup that nobody wanted me to touch or I'd wander around the set. I remember they'd always be worried that I would start screaming or hollering and ruin the scene. But I didn't. Still, I felt the pressure of everyone watching, of being an intruder, which wasn't comfortable.

Then, sometime during the filming, I got sick. Very sick with pneumonia. It was real hard for both of us. My mom was feeling guilty for not being with me and the people she worked with gave her a hard time too. She got upset, and that got me upset. I'd gotten used to her being there for me and suddenly, with me so sick, she wasn't there. Again, it was like I was abandoned. This time, though, she was feeling the same way because it was true. She would be gone before I got up and wouldn't come home till after I was asleep.

I was begging her to spend more time with me. And even after I got well, I continued begging her. Finally, we had this full-blown knock-down confrontation that ended with me yelling "Just quit this job and spend more time with me!"

What always appeared so fuzzy was suddenly crystal clear. "When she said that," recalls Jaid, "I thought to myself, 'What am I doing here? I don't really have a career that's so wonderful it's worth all this aggravation.' I knew my first responsibility was to Drew. Her father was not in the picture. There were no relatives to look after her. I was basically all she had, and that foundation was becoming very shaky at best. So at that point I decided to basically retire the career and pay attention to Drew. However, if I was going to do that, we had to first make a decision."

FOUR

THE
CELEBRITY

I remember the day when we talked and finally set things straight. My mom picked me up from the Fountain Day School, where I was in first grade, and on the drive home she mentioned that there was something very important she wanted to discuss with me. Naturally, I thought that maybe my teacher had told her something about me—though I couldn't think of what—but when I asked if I'd been bad, she told me not to worry.

"You're perfect, Budgie," she said, stroking my hair. "I love you so much."

It was nice spending so much time around my mother. She wasn't working like she used to. In fact, when *E.T.* began filming, she had quit working two or three jobs to give me the support I needed. Afterward, she went out on an occasional audition, but her schedule wasn't nearly as busy as it had been in years past. She was pretty much around the house every day, and that was nice. I liked her saying good-bye to me in the morning, and knowing that she would be at home when I got back in the afternoon was something to look forward to.

"What do you want to discuss?" I asked.

"I think we need to make a decision about the way we're living," my mom said.

"Isn't everything going fine?"

"I think so, and that's what we need to talk about," she said. "We both like the amount of time I've been able to spend at home lately, right?"

I nodded.

"Well, Drew, here's the thing. We can go back to living our normal lives, with me working and you going to school and auditioning when I have time to drive you. Or we can turn it all over to you and let you pursue your career."

"I want to keep acting, Mommy," I said.

"Think about this carefully," she cautioned. "I love you very much, and I want to know what you want, because you're a part of me and your happiness and my happiness depend on each other."

"I just want to keep acting," I said. "I love it. I love doing it."

I understood what my mom was saying perfectly, and my mind was made up before she even finished. At times when I imagined myself a grown-up, I thought perhaps that one day I might like to work as a television news anchorwoman. Either that or as a construction worker on a big high-rise building. One or the other. But rationally, I knew that acting was in my blood, that I felt best about myself when I was working in front of the camera. The attention I received was great, but I also loved becoming a different person with a different name, bringing this person on a piece of paper to life.

"Then that's what we'll do, Budgie," my mom said.

That decision made, life for the mother and daughter assumed, for the first time since the initial months following Drew's birth, the flavor of a routine. For both Jaid and Drew, it was a welcome respite from the constant shuffle of schedules they'd tolerated for so many years. Their quality of life didn't suddenly get remarkably better—it merely stabilized. Jaid drove car pools to and from school, and afterward she took

Drew to her weekly dance lesson. She was home to make dinner and to put Drew to bed.

In addition to her motherly chores, Jaid assumed the task of managing her daughter's career. She'd earned her battle stripes as both actress and wife and thought herself as well-versed and sharp-eyed as anyone when it came to show business. She previewed scripts, rehearsed with Drew, discussed characterizations, and mapped out long-range career directions. It was a decision that would color and confuse their future relationship. But it seemed a natural move. Who better to look after Drew's interests than her mother?

But my mom didn't have anything to do with my next role. I got that by myself. My class was putting on a production of *Sleeping Beauty* and I was one of several girls who tried out for the part of the princess. I was probably more nervous about getting that than any of the other work I'd done, but there was a reason for that. His name was Alex.

Alex was the cutest boy in the class. There wasn't a single girl who would dispute that. He had brown hair, chestnut eyes, and dimples. He was playing Prince Charming.

Needless to say, when the teacher told me that I was chosen to be the princess, I flipped. Why make such a big deal about a dinky school play? Because at the end the prince kisses the princess, and I, like everyone else, wanted to smooch with Alex. We rehearsed for a week before getting to the end of the play, when it was time to practice the kiss.

"Okay, now, Alex," I remember the teacher saying, "you kiss Drew."

Both of us pretended it was no big deal, but I was melting inside. With the entire class watching, many of whom were hooting and making fun of us, Alex bent over and gave me a quick little peck on the lips. It was so fast, but it was so wonderful. My first kiss with a boy. Ahhhh.

School let out in June, a few weeks before *E.T.*'s premiere, which allowed Drew and her mother to fly to New York for several sneak screenings of the film. Despite great anticipation, no one knew what to expect from "Steven's little movie." That summer's blockbuster, the critics assumed, was going to be Spielberg's other movie, *Poltergeist.* "However, each audience that saw the movie loved it," remembers Jaid, "and more and more it became apparent that it was going to be big." Indeed, by the time of its gala, star-studded premiere at the Cinerama Dome in Los Angeles, critics and moviegoers alike knew *E.T.* was something special.

There was absolutely no way to prepare for what happened to me—to all of us—from the morning after *E.T.* came out and on. For me it was like walking into a thunderstorm without warning or protection. I was staying at the Universal Sheraton Hotel with the two other kids from the film, Henry and Robert. All of us were best friends. We'd stay up all night telling ghost stories and playing Dungeons and Dragons. The night before we were having a messy food fight, and I remember screaming, "Look! Look! Look at what's on TV!"

It was the local news, and a reporter was standing out in front of the Cinerama Dome, talking about this "film event" and the incredibly long line of people waiting to see it, the longest line ever, he said, for the opening night of a movie. "We're in that," I said incredulously.

When we walked downstairs the next morning, the place went wild. Absolutely wild. The movie had been out one day and people all around were whispering, "Check them out. It's the kids from *E.T.* I'm telling you, that's the little girl from the movie." Everyplace we went, we were followed. People asked for autographs. They stared. They knew my name. They wanted to talk to me. They wanted to touch me. They asked me to tell them what E.T. was *really* like. I thought it was insane. I didn't know how to deal with it, and that frightened me.

Later that night I lay in my bed and tried to make sense out of everything that had happened. It was dark and I was alone, feeling probably more alone than ever. My mother was asleep in an adjoining room. As I lay there, listening to the silence and feeling overwhelmed by all the commotion, I came to the obvious conclusion that very suddenly my life was going to change.

Maybe it seems odd that a seven-year-old can know that her life is changing. But there comes a moment, I suppose, when all of a sudden you become aware of something like that. It's so abrupt, it's unavoidable. I didn't try to figure out if it was good or bad. It just was. It was a fact of life. Literally overnight, I wasn't just this pain-in-the-ass little seven-year-old girl anymore. I was someone who people knew by name. It made me feel that I must be different. And quite honestly, from that day forward, my life was never the same.

In its first two months of release, *E.T.* grossed an amazing $200 million, spinning off E.T. dolls, games, posters, and bedsheets. Audiences were smitten. The only parallel to the lovable alien's phenomenal rise to fame was the equally rapid ascension of its costars. Both Henry Thomas and Robert MacNaughton came from stable two-parent families, who acted as buffers to the onslaught. Drew, however, was out there alone.

"It was trial by fire," says Jaid. "We were complete neophytes, totally unknowledgeable about handling what came at us."

Reporters literally stood in line outside their West Hollywood bungalow once it was learned that Drew was part of *the* Hollywood Barrymore family. Hers was a story too good to believe. *People* magazine branded her "the hot tot." Indeed, she provided a great angle within an already terrific story. "Everyone asked what I thought of my grandfather as well as Lionel and Ethel," shrugs Drew. "What could I say? I'd never met them. I just smiled and said they were great and that I hoped one day I would be considered as accomplished as them."

That one day came sooner than Drew ever thought. Comparisons were rife. Photographers posed her alongside shots of her grandfather, John Barrymore, "the great profile." She talked about doing Shakespeare. She shrugged off questions about her father, saying only that she "saw him on occasion" and nothing more. Only in retrospect did Drew realize what pressure she took on simply from being a Barrymore.

People would sit me down and tell me an endless stream of stories about my grandfather. Or they'd compliment his talent, and I'd sit there thanking them. At first I didn't really understand what it was all about. I just knew that I was a young Barrymore, an actor, and that according to what everyone told me, I was supposed to be great.

And then I got to understand what my family was all about— the good and the bad. I was invited to attend a ceremony honoring the Barrymores at the Shubert Theater in New York. There was even a commemorative stamp issued by the post office. I went with my mom and sat beside Johnny, whom I hadn't seen in quite some time. We were seated in the center a few rows behind the front. I wore a little white dress that had been made up especially for me at Bonnie's Wee Shop, white tights and shoes, and a long frilly bow in my hair.

It was awe inspiring to be among so many great actors. Actually, it was embarrassing too. I didn't recognize anyone, but they all knew me from *E.T.* and they'd introduce themselves so sweetly. Lillian Gish was so nice. She talked to me about acting. "If this is your heart's desire," she told me, "and what you really want to do, I hope you do it always. It will be good to you."

Needless to say, I was honored by the attention. Dumbfounded is more accurate. For me it was an event of self-discovery. No one had ever told me about my family. I was a Barrymore—so what? One time I'd tried asking my dad, but he never gave a straight answer. Finally, I got so frustrated, I stopped asking. But at this event, suddenly, I heard people reminisce endlessly. There were plenty of individuals there who knew all about my grandfather's drinking and wild ways, and I listened to several of those tales, disgusted because they reminded me of my own father. But there were so many more stories about the Barrymore talent, and that was wonderful. In the midst of just such a speech, director George Cukor, who was then in the final months of his life, mentioned that there was another generation of Barrymore seated in the audience, and he asked me to stand up. I did, but I was so short, no one could find me. So Johnny lifted me up on the chair and everyone applauded.

I felt strangely connected to all of that heritage—strangely because it was only through the complete accident of birth and nothing I did. Yet I felt it, and, I suppose, subconsciously began to assume the role of the latest Barrymore actor, which was a lot to live up to.

After the ceremony we stopped at Sardi's, where I was interviewed for about an hour. They asked the same questions that have followed me through life: What do you think of your grandfather? What was it like to make *E.T.?* Then we finally went back to my hotel—my mother, her friend, and Johnny. Keyed up from all the festivities, I asked everyone if they'd play acting with me. My mom yelled "rolling," Johnny hollered "speed," and my mom's friend called "action." Then I pretended to act. I just danced around a bit, acting kind of silly.

But the fun was interrupted by Johnny. Every time he hollered "speed," he griped about how much he wished he had some speed— the drug. I didn't know what he was talking about.

"What's speed?" I asked my mom.

"It's something that's bad for you," she said.

Johnny continued asking for it though, until he finally got too weird to be around, and my mom told him to leave. Like I said, that night I encountered both the good and the bad in my family.

Life became a whirlwind of activity. There were endless parties, interviews, and personal appearances.

Routine flew out the window; only the confusion was fun. Drew adored the limelight, and rather than shun it for a normal life, which she had really never had, the precocious child embraced the commotion with wide-open arms, gravitating to the attention like a moth drawn to a bright light. She was refreshingly unspoiled, wide-eyed, and innocent. She said please and thank-you. Yet Drew was no ordinary kid. She showed an uncommon maturity, handling herself like a show-biz veteran. As Spielberg quipped, she "was seven going on twenty-nine." "People expected me to be like that, so I was," she says. When Drew appeared on *Saturday Night Live*, the youngest guest host ever, the cynical, wisecracking cast fell in love.

Eddie Murphy always called me Precious. However, he didn't exactly say it that way. He'd exaggerate it, draw it out, saying, "Praaaaaay-cious!" I'd break up in giggles.

The show took a week and a half to do. We rehearsed day after day. Finally, though, Saturday rolled around, and I was so nervous I didn't think I could do it. First we did a prerecorded show, which they called "Saturday Night Dead." Then, after a break, a different audience was brought in for the later, live version. When they knocked on my door and said, "Five minutes till air," I got so nervous. But Eddie and Joe Piscopo came in right after and told me that everything was going to be fine, and that made me feel really good.

I was too scared to do the opening monologue. So instead they passed out note cards to the audience and asked them to write down whatever questions they wanted to ask me. Then, when the show started, Tim Kazurinski accompanied me out onstage, read me the questions, and I answered them.

The funniest part of the show was the takeoff we did on *E.T.* Steven was sitting in the front row, and he'd brought Robin Williams with him, which frightened me so much. But I saw both of them laughing and that made me feel more relaxed.

When the show ended, the entire cast started hugging me and

holding me up. I never wanted to leave. It was the best feeling. Afterward I asked my mom if there was any way I could become a cast member. I'd had so much fun.

Fun. By summer's end there was still no end to the dizzying tumult, which the good-humored little girl viewed as an abundance of fun. While her friends at home prepared for the start of second grade, shopping for new school clothes, buying pencils and paper, and arranging new dividers in their notebooks, Drew was off on a month-long promotional trip to Europe, stopping in France, England, Norway, Germany, and Japan as *E.T.*'s goodwill ambassador to the world.

She was a remarkable sight, stepping off the plane at Tokyo's Narita Airport, for example, droopy-eyed and jet-lagged after a tedious fifteen-hour overseas flight, clutching a teddy bear and smiling without complaint for the army of photographers who camped out to meet the plane. She traded quips with Johnny Carson on *The Tonight Show*. It was stupefying how much Drew had grown up in such a short time.

Finally, though, Drew and Jaid were on their way home. One day they were at John F. Kennedy International Airport in New York, waiting for a flight to Los Angeles, when Jaid noticed that Drew didn't quite seem herself. She looked uncharacteristically glum, preoccupied.

"Do you feel okay, Budgie?" asked Jaid.

Drew nodded.

"Then is anything wrong? Anything bothering you?"

Drew shook her head.

"I'm tired," she said softly.

She was also not telling the truth. Not one to complain, Drew was concerned about returning home. She didn't want to say anything though. On the set, she knew, no one wanted to hear complaints, and she followed that rule off the set as well. But she was worried. Home was suddenly such a strange place, as strange and as frightening as had been that sudden onset of fame after *E.T.*'s premiere. Life had changed, and going back was full of uncertainty.

Two days later Drew returned to her first grade classroom at Fountain Day School.

God, it was so different. Everyone looked at me as if I were the Creature from the Black Lagoon. Or some kind of mutant celebrity. I wasn't the same little kid anymore, that much was obvious, and it was a very scary feeling.

Five months earlier my biggest claim to fame was that I kissed Alex the cutie in the school play. That made me a bigshot for about a week. But from the moment I checked back into school, I was set off from everyone else, as if I was some kind of alien. Kids called me E.T. "Hey, E.T.," they'd call. "How come you look so funny?" Or "E.T., why don't you phone home?"

It was everywhere. Teachers came up to me and told me how much they enjoyed the movie. Their children enjoyed the movie. Everyone wanted to know what E.T. was really like. And if I didn't want to talk about it, I was branded a snob. It was as if someone had secretly stuck a sign on my back that said "Outcast."

Before, the fact that I'd been in a few movies and commercials was no big deal. A few of the other kids at school had too. But fame really set me apart. And honestly, that was the last thing in the world I wanted, especially at school. I needed to be accepted.

It had always been that way. I wanted to be just like them. I wanted to have a mother, a father, and brothers and sisters. I didn't, and that made me feel different. Then I became famous and felt even more out of it. I couldn't stand up on a desk and scream, "There's nothing special about me." But I wanted to. That's the way I felt.

If anything, I felt a lot less special and more insecure than most of the kids I knew. It was a far cry from the way people perceived me.

Maybe Spielberg the surrogate father sensed that Drew's reentry to everyday life might be a trifle bumpy. He never said so. But one day he did present his favorite little actress with a fluffy little kitten. Drew named him Gertie. A boy with a girl's name. Drew thought it was pretty funny. "Like the cat was a misfit," she laughs, which, when she analyzed it, wasn't that far off from her own self-image.

Many nights Drew curled up on her bed with Gertie, her compassionate confidant, and expressed those feelings she kept hidden to everyone but herself. "I told him how alone I was feeling," Drew says. "One night I told him everything about my dad and, I swear, I thought I saw a tear in his eye."

Indeed, John Barrymore was an ominous presence Drew wasn't able to reconcile. Nor could her mother, for that matter. Separated since before Drew's birth, Jaid was in the midst of attempting to acquire John's signature on the official divorce papers. It was a fierce, messy battle. Each try would result in a pitched, screaming battle that would end with John ripping up the papers and storming out.

One night I went with my mom to a friend's house, where we waited for my dad to show up. It was neutral ground. I was always so full of mixed emotions every time I came into contact with him. On the one hand, I knew what an unreliable, violent, drunken man he was. I couldn't even recount a pleasant experience with him. Whenever I thought about him, I heard his gravelly voice telling me, "You weren't meant to be. I didn't want to have you."

On the other hand, I was his daughter. I shared his blood, his last name. And I wanted so much to be loved by him. I needed it. When I didn't get that love, I figured that it was my fault. I know that's crazy. But at the time no one told me any different. So whenever I was going to see him, I always hoped that something would change.

Despite what my mom and he were going through, I thought,

as usual, that evening might prove different. Who knew? Maybe, I thought, the reason he always tore up the divorce papers was that he wanted to patch everything up and be a family. Ha! Talk about wishful thinking.

When my dad finally walked through the door, he was weaving and unstable, all wobbly-kneed and obviously loaded. He was being a complete jerk.

"So how's the so-called movie star?" he laughed. "Haven't caught your flick yet."

"Thanks a lot," I said. "I can always count on you."

For some reason, for the first time in my life I was able to put some distance between us and look at him objectively. What I saw disgusted me. I said to myself, "Drew, why don't you just stop lying to yourself and understand that this man is not the father you dream about."

He sat down right next to me and asked for something to drink.

"Hey, Drew, you want to get me an autograph too," he said. "How 'bout putting it on a check?"

"Dream on," I said.

He was so out of it. I felt like hitting him. Or scratching his face. Anything to hurt him. Instead, I carefully lifted his cigarettes out of his pocket and started drawing over them. I wrote things like "You're an asshole." "I hope you die from cigarettes." "You're going to die really soon." All sorts of horrible stuff. Then he reached for them.

"Where're my smokes?" he asked, patting his jacket pockets and looking around.

"Here they are," I said, holding them up.

"Give 'em."

I threw them in his face and he looked surprised.

"Here's to all the horrible things you've ever said to me!" I yelled. "To all the times you've ever cut me down! Made me feel like a useless piece of garbage!"

He was trying to ignore me, but I knew he couldn't completely block it all out.

"Your goddamn drinking and drug use makes me sick and I want you out of my life!"

Then I stood up, kicked a chair at him, and walked out of the room. I hated him. I was so disgusted and angry. I'd never felt like that before. But it all of a sudden came out. And that was the last time I ever saw him.

> Refuge came soon after in the form of a movie. No longer a supporting player, Drew was being given star billing on theater marquees. The picture was *Irreconcilable Differences,* a mediocre drama costarring Ryan O'Neal and Shelley Long that concerned a young girl who sues her callous, career-oriented parents for divorce due to emotional neglect. The movie had its moments, and it proved a wonderful showcase for Drew's ripening talent. Yet the irony of the role was too much to ignore. Without intention it was life imitating art—almost.

When my mom read that script to me, I identified with that little girl. Our situations weren't that different—emotionally, anyway. For a while I wondered if I shouldn't try divorcing my parents. At least my father. My mother was not having much luck with divorcing him. I thought that if I did, it would make it easier for her. Maybe the pain both of us were feeling would subside.

But that was a short-lived idea. I didn't want to divorce my mother. Later on, maybe I would've entertained the notion more seriously, but not then. However, I liked the girl's attitude and went into making the movie closely identifying with her. It wasn't hard for me to get upset with my movie parents, especially Ryan's character, considering the scene I'd recently had with my real father.

Unfortunately, my excitement was dampened by the unpleasantness of making that movie. Compared to *E.T.,* which was sheer heaven, *Irreconcilable Differences* was utter hell. It was racked by nonstop fighting. The director and the producer always wanted different things. When they did finally agree on something, which was rare, the actors wouldn't be satisfied. The littlest shots literally took up to thirty or forty takes. It was unbearable.

Ryan kept my sanity. There was one particular shot—not even a scene, just a tiny shot—that involved me, and it took us somewhere in the neighborhood of forty takes before everyone involved was satisfied. By that point I was so emotionally drained that I broke down and cried. I hadn't ever felt stress like that, and no one even looked at me sympathetically. I fled to my dressing room. A few moments later Ryan came over. He was very fatherly. He draped his arm around me, then gave me a hug and shrugged, "Shit happens, you know."

"I know," I nodded.

"We're professionals, and sometimes we're forced to work with amateurs."

He made me smile.

"Tomorrow's going to be better," he said, grinning with me.

"Really?"

"You never know."

FIVE

GROWING PAINS

Despite Ryan O'Neal's paternal optimism, Drew nearly quit the acting business after *Irreconcilable Differences* finally wrapped. Tension from the arduous three-month-long production sapped the eight-year-old's enthusiasm and left her disillusioned. Acting, Drew believed, was supposed to be fun. It was her only means of escaping real problems, and she depended on it. But if acting was going to prove unpleasant, then, she told her mother, she didn't want to do it.

That was fine. There was no pressure on Drew to continue. As far as Jaid was concerned, whatever Drew wanted regarding her career was the right decision for her.

In the meantime, there were other changes. After paying fees to Drew's agents and business manager, and depositing a large portion of the remainder of Drew's earnings into a trust fund, there was still enough money left over for Jaid to purchase a lovely two-bedroom ranch-style home in Sherman Oaks, a comfortable upper-class neighborhood in the San Fer-

nando Valley. Compared to the West Hollywood bungalow they left behind, the move marked a significant
leap up the economic ladder.

Not that the Barrymores were rich. Not even
close. But they were comfortable, and for the first time
they were no longer encumbered by the constant
worry of making ends meet each month.

Drew started the second grade at Westland
School, a small, progressive private school. It was a
big transition from Fountain Day, which went only to
first grade. But Drew had gone there since preschool
and known everyone. At Westland, where the term
was already in progress, not only was she the new girl
in school, but her celebrity led to unmerciful scrutiny
by the other kids.

There was a big difference in the way I felt at the two schools. When
I returned to Fountain Day after making *E.T.,* I was treated differently. A little bit had to be expected. The kids made fun of me, they
asked questions and perhaps were a bit intimidated. I think a lot of
it was born out of jealousy. However, they'd known me before I was
famous, so it wasn't *that* big a deal.

But changing schools, the first of several times that I went
through that, was something else. There's a huge difference between
people you know making fun of you, which is uncomfortable, and
a whole bunch of people you've never even seen before just staring
at you, waiting for you to make a mistake. The one is understandable, the other is downright mean. Kids can be the meanest too.

School wasn't a total waste though. Eventually I made a few
friends who invited me to play at their homes, which opened my
eyes to the way other people lived. At this one girl's home, I
remember, I was introduced to her mom and her mom's boyfriend.
They weren't married, but they lived together.

"What about your dad?" I asked her, so naive at that time.

"My mom and dad are divorced," she answered. "Robert lives
with us. He's kind of like a dad without being a dad—if that makes
sense."

It did. I began thinking about my mother. My mom didn't have a social life. I was all she focused on. Me and my career. She didn't have a boyfriend. She didn't even date. The way I saw it, she wasn't trying to remarry. All that bothered me. I really wanted a father, a man around the house, like all my friends had, and I didn't see her trying to do anything about it. If she wanted to help me . . .

"You should go out more," I said to her one night at dinner.

"But I'm happy the way things are now," she said.

"Well, why don't you get a boyfriend, at least? I mean, my friend's mom has a boyfriend, and he lives with them."

"I think I just need to be on my own," replied Jaid. "For now that's what I think is best—taking care of me and you."

I let the subject drop. What more could I say?

But I still didn't understand why my mom was so opposed to having a man around the house. Especially if, as she always said, she really cared about my happiness. Time and time again I told her that I wanted to be a regular family, with a mother and a father. At that time what I wanted most in the world was to be loved by my father. Realizing that was impossible, I wanted my mother to find a replacement. But, I thought, she didn't seem to care.

All Drew saw was a mother who read over scripts, huddled with agents, and worried about good career moves. Although Drew had put acting on the back burner, Jaid knew it was only a temporary situation. In the meantime, scripts continued to flow in without interruption. After all, Drew was a brand-name actress in big demand. Despite Drew's hiatus, Jaid didn't interrupt her routine of screening prospective projects and ferreting out the best possible roles. She didn't want Drew to have an ordinary career. No, she wanted a film career. The distinction between film and, say, television made a big difference in terms of longevity, the way people in Hollywood thought of you and, not to be underrated, money. When Jaid found something interesting, which wasn't often, she read it to Drew.

It had been a while since my mom found anything that seemed right for me. Then one afternoon she told me there was a script she wanted to read to me. I was kind of half interested, like, "Okay, I'll listen." But lo and behold, I liked the story and wanted to act again. Just like that, as if my mom flipped a switch and my old enthusiasm for getting in front of a camera and creating a character returned.

There was only one problem. After preparing for the audition—I can't recall the movie—I didn't get the part. But that was okay. Rejection wasn't ever a big deal with me. For some reason, I always knew it was part of the business and not anything personal. Years earlier, I'd tried out for *Annie* and didn't get that either. It was my first major turndown. But then, right after, I got *E.T.,* and that convinced me that certain things were either meant or not meant to be. It was beyond control.

Not long after, another script that I liked a lot came in. It was *Firestarter.* At that time, my friends and I were into horror stories, and *Firestarter,* written by Stephen King, was a great one. It was about this little girl who was able to set things around her on fire at will—and sometimes even when she didn't want to. I liked it immediately. Maybe—ha! ha!—because there were times when I thought that special power might come in handy.

Anyway, this time I got the part, which wasn't just a regular part, but the starring role in a cast that included big-timers like George C. Scott and Martin Sheen. The movie was produced by Dino De Laurentiis, who was an absolute doll, so sweet and so very Italian. Because it was Dino's film, we had to travel to his studio in North Carolina, and that was exciting.

It was my first extended trip away from home. The picture was scheduled to shoot for three and a half months. That meant I had to fit my whole life, literally everything in my room—clothes for every kind of weather, hair dryers, stuffed animals, books—into several suitcases. Before we left, my mom checked to see if I'd packed properly.

"Do you have everything, Drew?" she asked, holding a checklist.

"I must have," I laughed, gesturing around the barren room, "there's nothing left anywhere."

Eight hours later we were in a new place.

Drew and Jaid situated themselves in a charming old two-bedroom home located in suburban Echo Park, North Carolina, where they seemed to step into the slow rhythms of a different culture. From the outset, though, the shooting schedule proved grueling, particularly on Drew, who was in nearly every scene of the movie. Work began when the sun went down and continued late into the night. Drew slept until early afternoon, then attended three hours of school before arriving at the set.

Fortunately, though, the stress of working long hours under adverse, sometimes frightening and dangerous conditions, was ameliorated by the friendliness of the cast.

At first my biggest fear was working with George C. Scott. He's a big man, who looks kind of rough and gruff. When I first met him, I didn't know what to think. He seemed like he could be mean. But I saw he had a dog, a big, cute dog whose name, I think, was Max, and he was always out playing with Max. It was really sweet the way he treated him. When I saw that, all my concern about being intimidated disappeared.

George turned out to be a wonderful, friendly man, the kind of man who you want to hug a lot. Working with him, you always knew where you stood. He's honest and direct. He'd give me different directions, but always in a kind, helpful way. It was never like he was talking down to me, which made me feel good, like I had the respect of someone who was at the top of his craft. Early on, he told me, "Drew, just forget about the camera and do your job." And I think that, along with Steven's advice, are the two best things I've ever been told.

Of course, the special effects I had to work with made it easy to forget the camera. Practically every day, I'd exclaim, "Oh, my God, I've just seen my life flash in front of me." It really was that scary! For instance, the first time they filmed the fire chips flying around me there was no Plexiglas protecting me. Later on, when they saw the red-hot glowing embers engulf me, they set me behind some protective glass. That was a relief. But I can't believe how brave I was—or how stupid. I'd just stand there, hoping I didn't get hurt.

In another scene I was told to stand in a certain spot while they dropped burning pieces of metal from a helicopter. I felt one touch my shoulder. It burned for a second, then blew off. But I got all queasy and thought I was going to faint. That wasn't even the worst though.

At one point, my double and I were instructed to stand and watch the special-effects people set this stuntman on fire. (A double is someone hired simply to stand in for an actor during long, tedious moments when equipment is adjusted, but in this instance, my double, an eight-year-old girl named Jennifer Ward, also became my friend.) This was supposed to ease my fear. The stuntman, they told us, would burn, nothing more than a match flame. But this guy just exploded—I mean burst—into huge, leaping flames, and we freaked. My double and I screamed and held on to each other, trying not to cry. It seemed like a disaster, like the guy was being fried right in front of us, and everyone was clapping. We didn't realize the stuntman was protected. But then the fire was extinguished and he popped out smiling. "Is it hot out, or is it me?" he asked.

Things were also kept light and humorous by Stephen King. We hit it off great. He's like a kid himself. You can see it in his eyes. When he gets an idea, his eyes light up, like this devilish boy full of mischief. Later, before *Firestarter* premiered, I spent two weeks up at his house in Bangor, Maine. It was a great time. Stephen makes the best french toast, and, as you'd expect, he tells the best ghost stories.

Every night his kids and I would sit in his office, a converted attic, and listen to him make up these incredibly scary tales. And Stephen doesn't just say a monster jumped out. He describes a monster in the goriest details, with eyeballs dripping blood, bashed-in noses, hatchets for fingernails, and always, a fondness for defenseless little girls dressed in their nightgowns. When we were good and frightened, he'd send us off to bed, where I knew for a fact we'd be easy prey for one of those beasts.

On the set, Stephen and I would talk for hours about music, TV shows, movies, and even things as ordinary as who makes the best hamburgers. Interested in everything, he was a good example of why I loved making movies. People such as him appreciated me. It meant so much to me when someone like Stephen, whom I saw as a fatherly sort, complimented or hugged me. At those times I felt fulfilled and loved.

One day Stephen asked me if I wanted to be in his next movie, and I said, "Sure," thinking that I'd hear about that in a few years. But the next day Stephen handed me a portion of a script to read. It was *Cat's Eye,* based on two stories from his book *Night Shift.* He'd written it overnight.

"It's great," I told him a few days later after reading it. "But can't I have a couple days off now?"

I was always pleading for a day off. The work was a strain. Most of the film was shot at night. I'd go to sleep very late, then wake up late in the day and go off to three hours of school in the afternoon. It was a tough schedule. I was so tired that much of that time is a complete blur. All that stands out in my memory is the horrible creamy chicken soup and salad I ate for lunch every day, and how I'd try to sneak hot salsa into my friend's bowl of soup.

Given the difficult hours, the strain of the special effects, and the grind of working in virtually every one of the movie's scenes, Drew's memories of *Firestarter* might have been less favorable if not for the companionship of her stand-in, Jennifer Ward. Jennifer was an outgoing, smart girl of similar age who became Drew's constant companion. The house Drew and Jaid rented was a few doors up the street from the Wards' home.

Jenny and I became best friends right away. She was one of those girls I wanted to be. That might sound strange, since I seemed to be a girl with everything. But Jenny was from a family, and that was something I didn't have. She had a younger brother, John, who was lots of fun, and her mom and dad were always there. Although my mother and I rented our own house, I seemed to spend all my free time at the Wards'. For me, just sitting at the dinner table, where the Wards said grace before eating, was a radical departure from the world I lived in back home.

But it was more than that. I went to church—something I'd never done—with them. I sat in the car when Mrs. Ward did errands, and I got in trouble with Jenny and John. I was part of a family, and it gave me a secure and comfortable feeling.

The only disturbing part of living in that town was that the homes were haunted. Jenny once mentioned that to me.

"People have died in these old homes," she said one night when she was sleeping over at my house.

"Yeah, right," I scoffed.

"They have," she insisted, "only they don't leave."

"Shut up," I said.

"Erika's house is where they mainly live," she told me.

Erika was another girl our age, a friend of Jenny's, who lived on the same street.

I didn't believe any of what she was telling me. Considering the gruesome stories Stephen always told us late at night, I figured Jenny had been hanging around him too long.

"Just go to sleep," I said.

Both of us fell asleep—until the shades on both the windows in my bedroom suddenly rolled up by themselves with a loud, startling noise. Needless to say, we bolted upright in bed, eyes wide, looking around the room.

"What just happened?" I asked, spooked.

Then the bedroom door slammed.

"Turn on the light," urged Jenny.

I sprang out of bed and flipped the switch. Nothing happened. It was still pitch black. There were streetlights on outside. I saw that through the open window. But the electricity inside the house didn't work. That did it.

"Let's split," I said.

We flung open the bedroom door and ran to the front door. I tried it. It was locked. I unlocked the latch. It still wouldn't open. I pulled as hard as I could.

"This is too weird," said Jenny.

I didn't need to be told that. Calm as always, I started to scream my head off. We ran back into my bedroom, hopped out the window, and spent the rest of the night at Jenny's. Several days later Erika invited us to sleep over at her house. We didn't think anything of it until right after we got into bed. That's when Erika flipped the light back on.

"You guys, don't worry if you hear footsteps," she said. "Okay?"

It wasn't okay. In the middle of the night Jenny and I heard footsteps. Or thought we did. Only we didn't wait around to make sure. We sprang out of bed and ran to her house. Why her house? That was my idea. "Your dad's there," I remember saying. "He'll protect us." I really believed that too.

After living in North Carolina for more than three months, I'd convinced myself that I was part of the Ward family, which gave me tremendous security and comfort. I liked having a dad, a brother, as well as a big family. It was what I'd always imagined a family to be like, which made saying good-bye one of the most difficult and emotional things I'd ever done in my life. I broke down and cried and pleaded with my mom to stay.

"No, Drew," she said. "You know you can't."

I did know, too, and that upset me even more.

If there's a part of making movies that I've always passionately hated, it's having to say good-bye. I'd spend months growing close to people, which is what I loved most about the work, and then I'd be torn from them without any consideration for how much I needed their companionship. The frustration sent me into a depression as deep as the high I got when a project began. I never knew how to react, except to cry.

However, before the *Firestarter* crew packed up and departed, there was one final blowout. The wrap party. Like a caravan of Gypsies preparing to pull up stakes, the cast and crew gathered at DeLaurentiis's beach house for one last farewell.

The place was already packed when my mom and I showed up. It was fun, sad, all those different emotions. We went our separate ways. At some point I was talking with these two guys who worked on the crew. They were close friends, the way everyone on a movie becomes close, and they were gobbling up hors d'oeuvres and drinking champagne.

"Hey, I bet I can down two of those glasses," I boasted.

"Sure you can, Drewster," they said, laughing at me.

Of course, I'd never even sipped anything remotely alcoholic before, but I'd been to enough parties, including this very one, to have noticed that most everyone drank, and that as they sipped their drinks, they appeared to be having a swell time.

"No, I bet I can," I persisted.

The two guys exchanged a look that asked, "Well, should we?" Then one of them shrugged, filled his glass, and handed it to me.

"Down it, champ," he said.

I took the crystal glass and studied it for a moment. There wasn't that much in it, I thought. It was bubbling. It looked pretty, refreshing.

"Here goes," I said, and gulped it down in two big swallows.

I set the glass down and smiled.

"One more to go," he said, slapping me on the back and refilling my glass.

"No problem." I smiled.

But in that short amount of time, the champagne hit me. I felt a trifle dizzy, definitely light-headed, and even a little sick to my stomach. I hadn't eaten much of anything all night. Even so, I took the second glass of champagne, downed that one as quickly as the first, and set the glass down.

"There," I said, and a few seconds later I asked, "What does passing out mean?"

"Falling asleep," one of them said.

And that's the last thing I remember. I passed out. The two guys must've set me down on a couch in one of the bedrooms. The next thing I can remember is Dino's fiancée, Martha, a beautiful woman with the longest blond hair, standing over me, fanning me, and asking if I was okay. My mom was there too.

"What happened?" she asked.

"I think I had a little champagne," I said, a bit groggy.

"Well, stay away from that," she said.

"Okay, Mom."

Do I have to? Oh, please, do I have to? Drew asked her mother that question over and over, as if the repetition would cause her mother to change her answer. Drew had to go to school. There was no room for debate of any kind, her mother told me. She had been enrolled in the Country School, a private, competitive grade school in the Valley, since second grade. Her work schedule had prevented her from starting then. But Drew returned to Los Angeles only a few weeks after third grade had begun.

Drew's reluctance was understandable. Once again she was the new kid, entering a strange school without knowing a soul and everyone knowing her. She dreaded the stares and whispers she knew would greet her arrival.

However, in addition to that, which was natural, Drew had been exposed to so much more than most nine-year-olds that sitting in a classroom from nine to three every day was stifling. Given extraordinary independence on the movie set, she was suddenly expected to buckle down, and that seemed unrealistic, at least to her.

After coming back home, my interests changed quickly. I had been used to playing dolls with Jenny, but after a while I got accustomed to the L.A. nightlife. Party invitations were plentiful, there were publicity events and various openings, and my mom and I got in the habit of going out a couple times a month. In a way, it was all quite innocent. I was always by far the youngest person wherever I went, and I'd kind of float around, talking to people or keeping to myself.

Yet the partytime environment was intoxicating. I loved it for the same reason I hated school. I belonged. If for no other reason than I was Drew Barrymore, the celebrity, I was part of it. Someone. Being in the thick of all those people was like a big security blanket.

I didn't necessarily understand what the fuss was all about. I remember going to a party at Ma Maison, which was then the drop-dead trendy restaurant, and everyone there was talking about how wonderful it was to be there. I wandered around, my head about waist level to everyone else, and listened to them talk endlessly about the marvelous food. I didn't get it. On a plate would be one bite of steak, a pea, a carrot, and half a melon ball. People drooled, "This food is to die for," yet I was pleading with my mom to stop at Burger King on the way home.

Somewhere around this time I also learned about sex. Sex. It was a word I heard a lot. "Darling, you look so sexy." Or "There's too much sex in this movie." Or "There's not enough sex in this movie." Or "They're upstairs, having sex." I picked that up at a party once and wondered what that meant. Why were they— whoever they were—upstairs having sex when everyone was downstairs at the party having fun? It was a mystery to me.

But one night I was watching a movie on cable. I don't remember what it was. Some horror picture like *Friday the 13th.* And in it there was a sex scene. I watched the guy and girl kiss, get into bed, hug each other, and roll around. It looked great, like they were having a lot of fun. Several days later I got out my Ken and Barbie dolls, but instead of whatever game I usually played with them, like house or disco, I removed their clothes and pretended they were having sex.

It was all embarrassingly naive. Just how naive I discovered one night at a party when I was standing around with my mom and some people. It was still early and everyone was trading ideas of what to do afterward.

"Why don't we have sex?" I chimed in.

Everyone's jaw dropped. I could almost hear the thud as they hit the floor. I didn't understand.

"Isn't it like a joyride?" I asked, using the language I'd heard in the movie, which I thought referred to something like going on a Ferris wheel.

My mom's eyes nearly bugged out.

"Oh, my God!" she exclaimed, taking me aside and saying, "Drew, I think we need to have a talk."

Compared to the experience I was collecting, third grade was a lesson in futility. Scholastically, I suffered, and that became a situation I came to accept as normal. I wasn't stuck-up. Nor did I consider myself too good for school. That wasn't it at all, since I didn't feel that way. If such a thought had ever hit me, I could've said, "Why practice handwriting when I have Stephen King writing a script for me? Why study arithmetic when I have a business manager who handles everything? Why do this? Why do that?" But that wasn't me.

No, compared to what I knew existed out in the world, school was just plain boring. In class I was restless, and the teachers came down hard on me. I worked at about a C level, under what I was capable of, but I got into trouble fairly often and found myself in a rut where I didn't want to try to do any better. It was the opposite way I felt about myself when I worked on a movie. There I desperately wanted to excel, even if it meant expending every last ounce of energy.

The start of summer found Drew and Jaid returning to the languid southern charm of Wilmington, North Carolina, to film *Cat's Eye*. For Drew, it was as much a relief to be away from the rigid demands of school as it was comforting to return to the familiar warmth of Dino DeLaurentiis, Stephen King, and the rest of the crew who'd worked on *Firestarter*. Best of all, though, was meeting up with her close friend, Jennifer Ward, who was again hired as Drew's stand-in.

Seeing Jenny made me so incredibly happy. I thought my life was complete. At first it was obvious how much I'd changed. I spoke differently, using a lot of slang I'd picked up in Los Angeles, and I talked about things that just weren't part of her world, like the Carson show, various clubs I'd been to, and entertainers I'd met. It wasn't intentional. I wasn't trying to make myself seem better than I was. That was my life.

But within a week all those cultural differences melted away and Jenny and I were the same as we always were. It was as if nothing had changed during the six months I'd been away. And in many ways nothing had. My mom and I rented a home one door down from the Wards, and like before, I was at their house all the time. Or Jenny and I were on the set, six days a week, always looking for free time to spend with each other.

We liked hanging out with James Woods, who was very funny, and I worked a lot with Candy Clark. One scene we did together, where I found my pet parakeet, Polly, dead and blame my mother, required lots of crying. Candy was curious how I always managed to summon the tears so convincingly on cue. I'd never told anyone my method before. Whenever I had to cry, I got very intense, and if there were a break in the scene, I'd keep to myself or hide out in a dark corner so the mood wouldn't be broken. It seemed mysterious to others, I suppose.

But there wasn't any secret. When I needed to cry, I explained to Candy, I thought about Gertie, the kitten Steven Spielberg had given me, who had run away.

"He was about the only one in the world I could tell my problems to," I said. "And then he split. One day he just never came back. He was probably sick."

"Yeah," she said, "cats are like that."

"But it's always made me sad to think about losing him."

Sunday was our day off, which meant all week we looked forward to Saturday night. I'd usually show up at the Wards late in the afternoon, my pajamas and clothes in a little suitcase. Jenny's mom would make iced tea, and we'd play outside till dinner, petting her cats, making masks from the hanging moss, or riding bikes. At night we'd have a pajama party, trying on clothes and dancing to all of Jenny's 45 rpm records. I loved dancing to Madonna's hit, "Borderline." We also liked acting out our favorite scenes from *Mommie Dearest,* which would end with us laughing on the floor and me screaming, "No more wire hangers!" Our giggling probably kept the neighbors up all night.

The movie wrapped at the end of the summer, and just like before, just like always, I didn't want to leave. However, this time, being a year older and more aware than before, I knew there was no other choice. I cried. I cried so hard. I loved Jenny and her family. I loved the life I had there, but I knew it wasn't mine.

On the way to the airport I saw my relationship with the Wards as no different from the parts I played in the movies. They were a fantasy brought to life. A dream. My dream. Only I knew that the next day I'd wake up and it would all be over.

SIX

LITTLE MISS BAD

Saying good-bye was never easy, but it was nothing compared to returning home. When Drew arrived back in Los Angeles, her loneliness had changed into anger. She was upset that she'd worked the entire summer even though it had been her own choice. Before *Cat's Eye,* Jaid had tried persuading her to take some time off. But Drew had replied, "I don't want to just sit around L.A. for three months." Not when she could reap all the emotional benefits from being part of a production.

However, that only made returning home more of a letdown. In Los Angeles it was just Drew and Jaid. Compared to the set, compared to the Wards' bustling home, their two-bedroom house was empty and subdued.

Right away Drew called her two best friends, Gigi and Chelsea, to tell them she was back. All three shared the same complaint—school. None of them were particularly good or attentive students. Like Drew, they were advanced for their age, and from single-parent homes that lacked stability. Even so,

Drew was the most vociferous of the trio when it came to griping about school.

She had her reasons. School didn't provide the same positive emotional nourishment that moviemaking did. In front of the camera Drew was confident, upbeat, and accepted. She performed her job with the aplomb of a veteran. She reveled in the closeness of a cast, the bonds of shared effort, the compliments, the hugging, the constant affirmation. She was a whole person. At school Drew was an outsider, distanced from classmates by her fame, insecure, and full of self-doubt. She had difficulty buckling down and concentrating. Her teachers pegged her as a problem. Students singled her out.

The disparity between life-styles aroused a frustration that eventually turned into rebellion.

I started fourth grade slightly behind in the work, even though I'd been tutored regularly on the set. But instead of encouraging me to do better or giving me extra help, the teachers put me down. They criticized me for placing my career ahead of education. At times they treated me with a pettiness that I imagine was due to jealousy. They showed little sensitivity toward me.

There was trouble every day, but on one day in particular, when I didn't do an in-class assignment properly, the teacher called me on it. He didn't just tell me I did it incorrectly. He didn't even criticize me. No. Instead, in front of the entire class, he told me that I was stupid. Stupid! Also that I wasn't ever going to amount to anything.

"I think you're headed toward failure, young lady," he said in front of everybody. "And I don't think there's anything I can do to help."

I wanted to crawl inside myself and die. But there was no escape. I vowed not to show any emotion though. I sat there, stone-faced, crying on the inside and completely humiliated. Why that teacher seemed bent on destroying me is beyond my comprehension.

If that wasn't enough to ruin whatever self-image I had, there was this nasty group of guys who were constantly on my case. They delighted in belittling me. Their torment was endless. Jealousy is the only reason I can figure they acted like that. Almost daily they hit me with books, called me names like fat ass, pig, fatso, and said my nose looked like Porky Pig's.

The worse they treated me, the more I wanted to fit in and the harder I tried. I had suffered enough rejection, I didn't want any more. One time I thought that if I wore surfer shorts, if I dressed more like them, I'd fit in. I got this kind that had a spaceman design on them, not exactly what I wanted, but I was just happy to get anything. When I walked into class, they burst out laughing and called me a "cosmic cow."

I was crushed, absolutely mortified. But I wasn't a person who would fight back. I didn't have it in me to lash out. I didn't have the self-confidence that required. From day one, my dad had made me feel like such an unworthy person that I accepted all these deprecating remarks as if they were gospel. Instead of telling them to take a leap, or something to that effect, I just took their cutting remarks until, eventually, I let them completely undermine everything I knew to be true.

Out of self-preservation, I began looking for some other kind of situation that would provide me with the type of positive emotional support I got on a movie set. See, I knew there were times when I felt good about myself. It was always when I was working. Work was my salvation. But what was it about work that made me feel that way?

The obvious answer, at least to me, was that I became another person. I didn't act my character; I became my character. Which was lots better than being fat, ugly, and stupid Drew Barrymore. But it was more than that. I seemed to be more readily accepted by older people. I always got along with everyone on the crew. I knew how to talk to older people. My place with them was so much better defined than it was with kids my own age.

Only one situation came close to substituting for work—the clubs and parties my mom and I attended on weekends. They were as near to make-believe as a nine-year-old could find. I'd spend hours getting ready, putting on the right dress, doing my hair, trying to sneak on as much makeup as I could get away with. It was like getting in costume. Then, when we'd arrive, they knew me. It was always, "Hey, Drew, how's it going?" And there was nothing as invigorating as walking in and being engulfed by the thud of blasting music and the swirl of flashing lights. It was Disneyland for adults, only I got to be part of it.

We went out pretty regularly, sometimes once a week, other times up to five times. But nothing was ever enough for me. Being the youngest person at every party spoiled me. People treated me like a little toy, always telling me how cute I was, patting me on the head, or giving me a playful squeeze. However, since I was dependent on my mom, I couldn't always go when I wanted, which was all the time. That led to numerous arguments. I'd want to go out and party; my mom would want to stay home. I'd storm out anyway.

It was a tug-of-war that marked the start of what became my constant struggle for more freedom. We started getting into fights pretty often. I couldn't understand why I could go out only when she wanted. It didn't seem fair.

It made me hate authority. I thought the key to happiness was being older. Adulthood. Yeah, that was it. Twenty-one became my magic number. Adults, I figured, didn't have to answer to anyone, they didn't have to follow rules. My role models were those people I saw at clubs, dressed up, laughing, carrying a drink, staying out till two or three in the morning. They seemed to have all the fun, and I didn't have any. Or at least not enough.

That's the way I saw it, anyway. One day I'd be struggling with a vocabulary word or a math problem, and later that night I'd be at some club or party, twirling around on the dance floor beside someone like Jack Nicholson or Cher. Compared to school . . . well, there was no comparison.

Though I was not yet ten years old, events in my life seemed to accelerate, starting with the night Gigi came over. She and I were best friends, and her mom and my mom were best friends. We were always together. When they came over, our mothers went into the kitchen to dish and Gigi ran into my room.

"I've got something to show you," she said excitedly one afternoon.

"No, I've got something to show you," I said. "Let me show you first."

"No, let me show you first," she argued.

We went back and forth like this for half an hour, till we were driving each other crazy. Finally, we agreed to show each other at the same time. Both of us closed our eyes, took out our little packages, and yelled, "Surprise!"

Boy, was it. Gigi was holding a toothbrush case crammed full of cigarettes, and I was holding a pack of Marlboros. We started laughing at the coincidence. Then Gigi pulled out a book of matches and said, "Let's go in the bathroom." We shut the door and within an hour, we had smoked every single one of them, which was probably the equivalent of an entire pack.

We were going out that night to our favorite haunt, a super-exclusive nightclub in Silverlake that's run by a woman who is one of my mother's dearest friends. She first held me when I was about two weeks old. Something like that. Her club is always packed with famous people, like Sean Penn, Jack Nicholson, Madonna, and Warren Beatty. That group. There is a big dance floor and a place to eat. To me, the club was like a second home.

Anyway, we were still holed up in the bathroom when my mom called to us that it was time to leave. Naturally, Gigi and I panicked, thinking that our mothers would smell the cigarettes and nail us for smoking. That would surely put an abrupt end to the evening. My mom, for one, hated cigarettes, and if anyone could smell them, she could. So we spent an inordinate amount of time washing our hands and face and brushing our teeth. Then we smelled each other's breath. The breath check. It was my first and certainly not the last.

We were so nervous climbing into the car with our moms, but they never smelled anything, and when we arrived at the club, Gigi and I knew we'd gotten away with it. Walking inside, I realized for the first time that I'd gotten away with lying to my mom. She didn't suspect a thing. That was an eye-opener . . . as well as an invitation to try the same thing again some other time.

"Be good girls," she called as Gigi and I loped off toward the dance floor. "I love you."

"Love you too, Mom."

Love. One day the teacher asked Drew's class to write an essay describing the emotion. There were twitters and giggles. Everyone thought it was easy, a cinch assignment, until they put pencil to paper and began ruminating on the question.

What is love?

Drew looked up to ponder her answer. She knew what love wasn't, that much was certain. But what *was* love?

Thinking, she turned her head to the side and saw the answer sitting two rows away. Love was four and a half feet tall, with a thatch of longish brown hair, a pug nose, and, that particular day, he was wearing blue corduroys.

His name was Brecken, and we'd been friends for about a year, since third grade. I thought he was pretty cute, my type. Nothing really happened between us for a long time. We definitely liked each other, but I think we were embarrassed to admit it was anything more than just friendship. It was Gigi who began noticing that I liked Brecken.

"How much do you like him?" she asked.

"We're just friends," I said.

"Would you like to kiss him?" she asked.

"Oh, yeah, right," I scoffed, refusing to admit that kissing Brecken didn't seem like a bad idea at all.

At the same time, Brecken started hanging around me more than usual. We became better friends. Then one night he telephoned and said that he had a problem he wanted to discuss with me. There was this girl, Tracy, he explained, who really liked him a lot. I mean, *a lot.* She wouldn't leave him alone and kept pestering him to go steady. At that age, everyone was really into going steady. Except Brecken didn't like Tracy that much and he was too scared to tell her that. Also, he didn't know how to get rid of her.

"What should I do?" he asked.

I offered a few suggestions, but he didn't go for them.

"Maybe you could pretend to be my girlfriend?" he said. "You know? And then she'd leave me alone."

"You mean, like go steady?" I hedged.

There was silence. The biggest question a guy could ask a girl then was "Do you want to go with me?" I'd never been asked, but I'd begun hoping Brecken might. The situation was perfect. Only he was too embarrassed to come right out and say the words. So I made a suggestion.

"What if we ask each other?" I said. "We'll trade words."

"Okay," he agreed.

"But you go first," I added.

So Brecken said, "Do," and I said, "you," and so on until he finished with the word "me," after which I quickly said, "Yes."

Less than a week later Brecken and I, a steady couple, were at Gigi's house. The three of us were sitting on the floor in her bedroom. She wanted to know if we'd kissed yet. We shook our heads. When she asked why not, both of us shrugged.

"Well, why don't you," she said.

Tentatively, we turned toward each other, puckered tightly, and bumped lips. Or so it seemed. It was so quick.

"How was it?" asked Gigi, who, when I think back on it, was incredibly nosy. "I think you need to practice."

That sounded good to us, I suppose, because Brecken and I sat there, smiling, ready and waiting for Gigi's expert instructions. I have no idea where she picked up her expertise. Nevertheless, Gigi had a plan. She hastily stenciled a set of signs that said, ROUND ONE, ROUND TWO, and so on, all the way up to ROUND SIX. Then she held up the first card and said, "Okay, Drew and Brecken kiss, round one."

We kissed. A little longer this time, but still quick.

"Okay, now talk about it," said Gigi, "and then we'll try the next round."

By round six Brecken and I were smooching like mad, passionate lovers. Thanks to Gigi's coaching, we spent nearly an hour instructing each other exactly how we preferred to be kissed. We trained each other, and it was great.

From then on, we kissed all the time. In class, Brecken and I would always pretend to drop pencils or books. Then both of us would bend down to pick it up and we'd sneak in some heavy kisses. One time my mother was driving a carload of my friends to dinner at the Hard Rock Cafe. The car was packed. I was sitting on Brecken's lap. Someone tossed a jacket over us and we made out the whole way there without my mom knowing.

To this day—I swear—I can't kiss a guy without, at some point, thinking of Brecken. Really. He was the best kisser. Why? Because I trained him.

More important, though, was the feeling I got from kissing Brecken. It was like a big "wow!" that made me feel great. Becoming intimate with a boy seemed to satisfy my craving for affection. I was always searching for father figures in older men, particularly the ones I worked with. But kissing boys gave me a way to get closer than I'd ever dreamed. It made me feel so good. I became guy crazy, an addiction in which I used boys to find love, affirmation, and self-worth. I was like that song, "searching for love in all the wrong places."

The cigarette was a symbol, a sign of age, maturity, and coolness. It was prevalent in magazine ads, on television, among performers. Never mind the health warnings. More than anything, Drew wanted acceptance. She ached to be older and hip. A cigarette got her closer to that goal. If there was a smoke dangling from her pursed lips or poised between her index and middle fingers, she felt more like the others.

There was another symbol too. A drink. If she was going to complete the picture, she needed a cig *and* a cold bottle of beer. A brew. A brewski. A tall, cool one. She knew the jargon. In her mind, the two were indispensable to having come of age. And since she already smoked, Drew reasoned, she might as well drink too. Everyone cool smoked and drank. She saw them herself. It didn't matter if they were twenty-one, if they were legal. She knew lots of underage people who drank. They were at all the parties. They even had their own parties. It was all a part of being "in," of being accepted.

I knew I was going to take a drink that night. It was Rob Lowe's birthday party. I think he turned twenty. We walked up to the club—me, Gigi, and my mom—which was packed, and the doorman waved us all through. That was always one of my favorite parts of going to clubs. The fact that everyone knew me. Even if they didn't know my face, they'd say, "Aren't you the little girl from *E.T.*?" It was instant acceptance. I was part of the hip crowd.

All the Brat Packers were there. Rob, his younger brother, Chad, and stepbrother, Micah, Emilio Estevez and Demi Moore, Melissa Gilbert, and so on. The music was blasting. Almost everyone had some kind of drink, even though no one was of age, and the dance floor was humming.

As was our routine, my mom went off in one direction to visit with people she knew and Gigi and I went off on our own. First we cruised the place. I knew most everyone there from other parties or premieres. I introduced Gigi to Rob and gave him a little birthday kiss. We danced to a few songs, but then I had an idea.

"Let's snag a beer," I said.

"Cool," smiled Gigi.

There was a slew of cold, open bottles set up on the bar. We walked up, quickly snatched one, and ran off to the bathroom, where we got into a stall and split the bottle while puffing on a couple of cigarettes. We were a trifle light-headed after downing the beer and walked out feeling more grown-up than before. We were like everyone else: swigging brews and smoking—even though we had to sneak them.

Later, I got braver. I sidled up to one of the Brat Packers, a real Mr. Nice Guy, who was holding a bottle of beer by his side.

"Can I have a sip of your beer?" I asked.

"Yeah, sure," he said, handing me the bottle.

I'm sure he thought it was cute to give a little kid a sip of beer.

But I quickly downed the remainder of his bottle.

"Hey, I said a sip," he said, taking the empty from me.

"Sorry," I shrugged coyly.

"That's okay."

"You know, you just gave me my first beer," I said.

"Really?" he said. "Cool."

Feeling a slight buzz, I began to flirt, innocently, with Emilio Estevez, whom I had a crush on. It was like batting eyes at your big brother. Then a slow song came on and I made some comment about everyone slow-dancing, about how much fun it looked to be cuddled up against someone, and Emilio smiled.

"Do you want to?" he asked.

"I don't know how," I said. "I've never done it before."

"Cool," he smiled. "I'll take you on your first slow dance."

He hoisted me up off my feet and carried me out to the dance floor. I wish I had a picture of that sight, which had to be amusing. I was about half Emilio's size, not to mention half his age. He was being especially nice to me. I looked around at all the girls, noticing how they leaned in tight on their boyfriends, and nuzzled in close to Emilio, wrapping my little legs around his waist. It was the perfect antidote to being called fat and ugly at school. My heart was thumping. I was definitely in the throes of a heavy-duty crush.

When the song finished, Emilio set me down, patted me on the rump, and went off to talk to someone else. I ran over to Gigi.

"I'm in love," I sighed.

He made me feel so special, though sometime after that, emboldened by the alcohol and my attraction to virtually any guy who winked at me, I started making out with Micah, Rob's step-brother, who was about twelve. It was that kind of party. We were imitating the older people. But the big scene came at the end of the party. As I was leaving, Micah called me. I didn't respond and kept walking with my mom. But he came up, grabbed my arm, pulled me back, took me in his arms, and we started to kiss. Really kiss, like passionate thirty-year-olds.

Everyone was shocked. I mean, dumbstruck. Then I turned away and sighed, "Good-bye."

"Good-bye." He bowed, blowing me a kiss.

In the car my mom rolled her eyes in disbelief.

"Drew, what's going on?" she asked.

"Nothing," I said in the sweet voice I always used when I wanted to appeal to my mother.

"Good," she said. "I hope not."

Drew was supposed to follow household rules. Jaid set definite parameters. Or tried to. Drew had the requisite chores of keeping her room straight and helping with the laundry. She had to attend school every day and then do homework, if any, before playing with friends. Bedtime was at nine on weekdays, midnight on weekends.

But none of that ever got through to me. A party or some publicity event for a film would come up during the week and we'd be out a little past my bedtime. And on weekends we'd usually stay out long past midnight. So I never took any of the rules seriously. They were always altered a bit or being broken.

For example, my mom once found cigarette butts in a tree in our backyard that Gigi and I had left, and she erupted. Gigi's mom was shocked. My mom was royally pissed. But that was it. She just got angry. Then, a few weeks later, she caught us again, with a third friend, and got even madder. This time she gave me a huge lecture about smoking.

"Why do you do it?" she asked.

" 'Cause I like it," I said.

"Why?"

" 'Cause I do."

There was no getting through to me because of what cigarettes meant to me. I wasn't going to give up any part, no matter how small, of being accepted by people I liked. Even when my mom caught me and two friends smoking a third time, and grounded me, it didn't deter me. Know why? Because a party, or some other event, came up that we went to and suddenly I wasn't grounded anymore. It was becoming clear, I believed, that rules didn't apply to me.

Several months later Drew's girlfriend was promising her that teen hunk Matt Dillon was guaranteed to show up that evening at the Limelight, the fashionable New York disco. That was exciting. It was the night of her tenth birthday. Drew wanted to go out to dinner and celebrate her birthday, but her girlfriend, Stacy, a beautiful teenage model, persuaded her that Matt Dillon at the Limelight was better than any dinner they could buy. Drew agreed.

Drew and Jaid had made regular sojourns to Manhattan for years, ever since the publicity grind of *E.T.* They had a favorite suite at the Mayflower Hotel overlooking Central Park and a varied network of friends who made their trips feel like a homecoming. Drew loved the excitement of New York, the hustle and bustle, and especially the late-night clubs such as Limelight. With Stacy as her guide, she was discovering the labyrinth of nocturnal playgrounds and developing the fast-track sensibility of a professional nightclubber twice her age. She knew the clubs from promotional events, and many of the people partying there were of the same group as in Los Angeles.

A cab let Drew and Stacy out in front of the Limelight, where they knowingly pushed past the throng of would-be partiers waiting in line for entry and headed straight for the doorman. The doorman recognized her. She could see it in his eyes: Ah, Drew Barrymore. She was famous. The most prized type of guest. He kissed her on the cheek and motioned her inside. Drew had played out that exact scene dozens of times before and loved each one.

Inside, where it was dark and the air was energized by pulsing music, Stacy led Drew upstairs to the private gallery.

"So where's Matt?" I asked Stacy as we were walking up.

"Matt?" she said with a puzzled expression.

"Yeah, Matt," I said. "Matt Dillon."

Just then we entered the private room and all these people yelled, "Surprise!"

I was shocked. My mother and her friend had organized a surprise party and they'd pulled it off perfectly. I was unsuspecting and totally surprised. So what'd I do first? I looked around the room for Matt. I saw my mother. Some friends. Even Billy Idol. But when I learned that Matt Dillon was just the bait and not actually there, I got angry . . . for half a second. Maybe I was spoiled, but I had such a mad crush on him, and Stacy had built him up all day, so it was somewhat disappointing.

But there were lots of fun people there, like Moon and Dweezil Zappa, and Stephen Pearcy, the lead singer of the rock group RATT. There were balloons and streamers hung from every conceivable spot, a huge cake, and everyone sang this raucous, scream-till-you're-hoarse rendition of Happy Birthday that ended with all of us in hysterics. And we danced for hours and hours, till I was exhausted. To anyone but me, it was a dream party.

What bummed me out was the fact that I couldn't sneak a drink. Off and on that entire evening I complained to Stacy that there was no place where I could escape and secretly down a beer. I'd see one of the older people holding a drink and think, "Hey, this is my party. I should be able to drink too."

I couldn't, though. My mom and her friends were all over the place, and complicating matters even more, I was the center of attention, which made sneaking anything difficult. But that's all I thought about, drinking and a smoke—instead of what a nice surprise the party was. The lines of right and wrong were hazier than ever.

Of course, now I understand what was going on. I was succumbing to the tease of alcohol, developing a mindset that had me believing I couldn't have fun—or as much fun—without sipping a drink or two.

SEVEN

MORE, MORE, MORE!

Everything seemed to conspire to shake Drew's foundation, which was tenuous at best. For years she had worked consistently. Then, suddenly, the work slowed to a trickle. The lack of work, combined with an already shaky self-image, sent her self-esteem plummeting. Drew wasn't the cute darling anymore and yet she wasn't the desirable teenager for the desirable teenager market. One thing set off another, like a domino effect, and the net result was that Drew didn't feel good about herself.

Of this period Jaid says: By this time, regardless of Drew's lack of work, we had entered into a world that hadn't existed for us before. Business-related events like the Golden Globes or the People's Choice Awards, kept us out late at night more than ever. No one seemed to mind when Drew was out late for business. Yet when it came to private things, like going to a club, keeping Drew out at night was not okay. I was expected to explicitly draw the line between business and social. Gradually, though, the business activities Drew's work made us a part of extended into a social thing. We ran into a lot of the same people at both.

When we went out it was always the two of us together. It wasn't ever Drew going off to a party while I stayed home and knitted. Nor was it me going off and leaving her at home with a baby-sitter. This was still a period when I considered us an inseparable team. She and I together. I just felt that if we were together, somehow it was all right to be out late. Or to go to a club. There's no way I can justify that feeling. But I don't feel the need to.

It also wasn't as though we were skipping around town. We basically went to one club, which was owned by one of my dearest friends. I thought it was fairly low key. But in retrospect I can see that going there was bad, no matter what the atmosphere. However, I don't think if we'd come in—and I don't mean this to sound snide—two or three hours earlier, our lives would have turned out much different. Going out was, I think, one contributing factor to what happened to Drew. But I thought—wrongly, it turns out—that if I were there with her, I could have some measure of control.

We handled that time the best we could. Had I known more, I would have done things differently, but I didn't know. As adults went, I thought I was one of the stricter among Drew's friends' parents. One time I caught Drew smoking cigarettes with a friend who was two years older, and I blew my lid. I got very angry. The girls were apologetic and promised never to do it again. And that was one of the few times I ever really saw Drew doing something wrong.

As a brilliant actress, Drew has an amazing capacity to hide things. That combined with the fact that girls her age were involved in sleeping over at someone's house every weekend kept me pretty much in the dark as to what she was doing. One time I took her to a girlfriend's house to sleep over. They went into a back bedroom and smoked a cigarette. When she came out to kiss me good-night, I smelled the smoke and said to her, "You've been smoking. Get your things. We're going home." Just like that. And she never slept there again.

When I did catch her, when there was a glimmer of awareness, I tried to do what I could. Most of the time she slept at a place where I knew the parents. And not being an overly suspicious person, I always wanted to give Drew the benefit of the doubt. I wanted to trust her. I felt it was important for her as a person to feel that her mother trusted her. Which was obviously a big mistake. Hindsight is brilliant, but it doesn't help. In retrospect, I should have paid much more attention to my instincts and trusted Drew a lot less.

But it wasn't just Drew whom she should have been more wary of. There was no reason to distrust Alex Kelly. Jaid had met him years before through friends. Alex, a successful, extremely handsome model in his mid-twenties, was a regular visitor to the Barrymore household. "A good friend" is how Jaid described him. Drew thought him "mondo cool." They shared the same taste in nightclubs, where Alex would good-naturedly oblige Drew with a spin on the dance floor. But they saw him most frequently on their living room couch, where he often rested his feet on the coffee table and held a beer in his lap. Drew loved coming home and seeing his cherry-red Corvette parked in their driveway.

I was always begging him for rides. One night I convinced him to take Chelsea and me to Magic Mountain, an amusement park known for its spine-chilling roller coasters. He said okay, as long as we got permission from my mom. She said fine. Why not? My mother trusted him. So we went to Magic Mountain, had a great time, and then started back a little before midnight. When we were almost home Chelsea and I convinced Alex to stop at a liquor store for some beer.

"A beer?" he said, looking at us like we were crazy.

"Yeah, it'll be fun," I said. "A little beer."

"I don't know," he puzzled.

"Oh, come on," I argued. "We've drunk beer lots of times."

It was the truth. A few weeks earlier Chelsea and I had gone with my mom to a party at my agent's house in Beverly Hills and gotten smashed. We hadn't planned to get drunk. It had happened. We had dared each other to steal a little sip off a half-empty glass someone had set down. That led to hiding behind the bar and pouring glasses of vodka. Though we didn't realize it, we were hooked into the cycle. We thought it was fun to drink and, before we knew it, drinking became the only way we could have fun.

By the end of the night we'd each downed about six or seven glasses and were drunker than ever before. Amazingly, nobody noticed. Not even my mom. We just laid low, kept chewing sticks of gum after each drink, and everything was cool. When the party broke up, my mom drove home with us passed out in the backseat. She didn't suspect a thing.

After giving Alex a carefully edited version of this tale, he debated the dilemma for a moment, and then said, "Okay." We smiled, pleased. The fun was just starting. He pulled into a liquor store and came out a few minutes later with a six-pack of Corona and some cups.

"Pour it in the glasses," he instructed. "It'll look kind of weird to have two little girls in my car chugging from bottles."

For the next hour and a half we drove around, drinking and laughing and listening to the stereo. We had two beers apiece, then returned home. We were absolutely having a blast when we walked in the front door laughing and singing. My mom kissed me hello and gave me a funny look.

"Is that beer I smell?" she said.

I turned on the actress in me.

"Yeah, Mom," I smiled. "Alex gave us a sip of beer."

"Really?" she said, glancing over to him.

"Yeah," he nodded, lying through the teeth, "they were begging me."

"Yeah, just one little sip, Mom. We wouldr't leave him alone. He kind of had to."

She reluctantly said, "Okay," and let it drop.

Amy's mom fell into the same category as Alex. She was an indisputably trustworthy friend of Jaid's. Her credentials were even better than Alex's though. She was a parent as well as an adult.

Amy was another of Drew's close school friends, what Jaid might have called a "proven commodity." Amy and Drew were constantly sleeping over at each other's homes. They had fun together. Over time, Jaid also became friendly with Amy's mother, a divorcée and musician, and the foursome often went out together on weekends to the small, ultrafashionable club preferred by Jaid and Drew.

The excitement of a typical night at the club began when we started getting dressed. We dressed to kill—miniskirts, black lace, high heels, heavy makeup, perfume. The works. It was as if we were getting into costume. My mom seemed to always approve. She'd come in my room to check on our progress and say, "Oh, you girls look adorable." That was hardly the right word though. Because by the time we piled into my mom's car, we looked eighteen instead of eleven, like we'd stepped out of an MTV video.

Then again, we were going to an exclusive, ultratrendy nightclub, where dress standards were set by the likes of Madonna and Cher and the onlookers were comprised of Jack Nicholson, Angelica Houston, and Warren Beatty. So if anything, people thought we looked cute and stylish rather than what we actually were: little kids playing dress-up.

We'd arrive at the club and my mom would go off and do her

thing, leaving me and either Chelsea or Amy, my usual companions, to ourselves. If I was going to get away with hanging out at the club, I knew I had to be cool and keep my behavior toned down—relatively speaking. It wasn't like I'd hide. I didn't have to. Everyone at the club knew me. I knew them. It was kosher.

I'd sashay in with my mom and friend like I was at a relative's house—which it sort of was—and there was an enormous party in progress. Like everyone else who showed up, I'd first check out who was there, then glance over at the dance floor and inhale the rhythm of the evening. The layout of the club was such that Chelsea and I set up camp in an upstairs loft that was off limits to clubgoers. It was our private balcony, a perch from where we overlooked the entire club—particularly the bar.

Early on I told the club's owner, "If someone comes in who shouldn't see me, I'll stay upstairs. Just tell me."

A former actress and one of my mom's dearest friends, she was cool.

"Okay," she said, "but only you and your friends are allowed to go up there."

That was perfect. With my mom doing her thing, we'd go up to the loft and immediately take out our cigarettes and start smoking, not unlike the people down below. And we'd start out watching the bar for drinks people set down that were still half full. When we spied one or two, we'd make a beeline down the stairs, swipe the glasses, and quickly bring them back up. If anyone had seen us, we would've been nailed. It would've been serious. But the club's owner never had a clue what we did. She would've killed me for drinking. She's always been unmerciful whenever she's seen me smoke.

It's hard to judge how much we drank on an average night, but it was a lot. A few times we passed out up there, slept for several hours, and woke up with monumental headaches—a combination of the alcohol and lying with our ears right beside the speakers. But we were always game for more.

We loved dancing too. We'd try especially hard to look very sexy on the dance floor, mimicking perfectly whatever moves we saw the older women make. And believe it or not, despite our age, guys came on to us all the time. It was understandable; we looked so much older than we actually were. We loved that part. If a guy was cute, we were all over his case, flirting, trying to amuse him, waiting for him to ask one of us to dance. And when the question came, our answer was always the same.

"Sure, if you'll get us a drink."

That was our line.

Anyway, one particular night we left the club—me, Chelsea, my mom, Amy, and her mom—around two A.M. Chelsea and I arranged to sleep over at Amy's house, so we said good-bye to my mother out in front of the club and got into Amy's mom's car. Amy cranked the radio and all of us started singing. A few moments later I began smelling the familiar scent of marijuana. Chelsea and I looked at each other, then leaned forward and saw Amy's mom was holding a tiny gold pipe. She glanced at us over her shoulder and smiled.

"Anybody interested?" she asked after exhaling a wisp of smoke.

Okay, that was weird. Our friend's mother was offering us pot. A parent is supposed to be like a cop. But we quickly—immediately—got over the awkwardness and thought Amy's mom was being exceptionally cool.

Neither I nor Chelsea were strangers to pot. We hadn't smoked any, but we knew all about it. We'd watched people smoke it. We'd talked about smoking it. We'd plotted how to steal joints and how to persuade someone to let us try a puff. In school we'd been lectured about the evils of pot. We'd heard stories of friends getting busted by their parents, by the police. We'd even heard stories of parents being busted by their kids for dipping into their children's stash. We would've had to have grown up in a vacuum to be uninformed about dope.

"Yeah," I said. "I'll try some."

So Amy's mom handed the gold pipe and a Bic lighter to me. I put the pipe to my lips and inhaled.

"No, honey," she chuckled. "Hold the lighter to the pot when you inhale."

I tried it, got a huge hit of smoke, and coughed like a backfiring engine.

"In little puffs, Drew," she said, "and hold the smoke in a long time."

A few attempts later I got the routine down and passed the pipe over to Chelsea. For the duration of the twenty-minute drive back to Amy's house, the four of us continued to smoke, going through a couple of bowlfuls by the time we entered the house. Unfortunately, other than the excitement of finally trying pot, I didn't feel anything—or so I thought—and kept complaining that I wasn't stoned. However, I couldn't keep myself from laughing.

"I don't feel anything," I said inside. "What's being stoned?"

"Look in the mirror," said Amy. "You're stoned, Drew."

Our little dope party continued in the living room. Around three A.M. Chelsea started telling me that I'd smoked enough. She didn't want me doing any more, even though I kept asking for the pipe. So I snuck off to the bathroom and smoked even more. When I got out they told me that my mom had called. As long as she was up and out, she had said, she was going to stop by for a minute to drop something off.

"Shit," I said.

"Shit is right," said Amy's mom, who was as freaked as everyone else.

Frantically, the four of us took turns straightening up the house, opening windows and spraying air freshener, brushing our teeth, and chewing gum.

My mom stayed for a short time and somehow didn't catch on. Of course, we should've gotten Academy Award nominations for the performance we were putting on. On her way out, my mom asked for a hug and a kiss, but I fended her off with some lame excuse and instead pretended to blow her friendly kisses. Anything to get her back out the door.

"Call me in the morning, Budgie?" she asked before leaving.

"Sure, Mom," I said. "I love you."

Ten minutes later, Chelsea, Amy, and I began walking down the street to get some doughnuts and Slurpees at 7 Eleven, which was several blocks away. It was almost five A.M. We got down to the end of the front walk when Amy's mom called after us.

"Girls! Where are you off to?"

"Seven Eleven," said Amy.

"Oh. Would you bring me back some juice?"

And so began the practice of getting stoned. It was a welcome addition to Drew's already considerable repertoire of cigarettes and alcohol. It also became her preferred antidote to the psychological distress of school. Pot was more easily had than alcohol too. All Drew had to do was pop over to Amy's and smoke out with Amy's mother. The odd assortment of musicians and stragglers who collected there were always ready for an impromptu party.

Amy's mom would've hit the roof if we'd asked for a drink. She was into natural things—foods, holistic medicine, crystals, all that—and alcohol was forbidden. However, pot was fine.

"It's an herb, Herb," she liked to joke.

Their house was like a magnet that drew me there as often as possible. For a while it was a helluva lot of fun. We'd find any excuse to light up.

"Hey, I just got my braces off," I'd say. "Let's party."

There was always someone willing to toast any occasion with a hit off a bong, a tall, slender water pipe, or a joint. The excuses I made up for partying were always ridiculous, like getting a new dress or flunking a paper, ditching a class and getting away with it, or, worst of all, not having anything else to do. "Hey, I don't have anything to do," I'd say. "Let's get wasted."

In school, where we learned about marijuana in health class, pot was always said to be nonaddictive, unlike alcohol, cigarettes, cocaine, and harder drugs, which nobody ever expected to encounter anyway. Never mind that that waiver almost—almost—made pot seem okay to try. You knew you weren't going to shrivel up and die in an alley from it. However, what no one ever explained is that the way marijuana enables you to forget your problems *is* one hundred percent addictive. The drug itself may not be addictive, but if you've got things bothering you, as I did, you're going to get hooked on whatever helps you to shove them aside. And I was someone who had problems.

> She was a different person at school. In class Drew was a morose shadow of the lively sprite who bebopped around nightclubs with the confident bounce of an adult. Her appearance was disheveled, her head hung low, and her grades bore no relationship to test scores that indicated she possessed exceptional abilities as well as a photographic memory.
>
> Drew complained constantly about the group of boys who insisted on making her school life miserable, and three quarters of the way through the fifth grade, the Country School's principal asked Jaid to come in. Something, he said, had to be done about Drew's relationship with the boys, and he felt it was time for the parents to get involved.
>
> He called Jaid and asked her to meet with the mothers of the boys and resolve the problem.

But only one of the other mothers showed up and my mom came home frustrated. The rest obviously didn't think there was a problem, which shows how out of tune parents can be on issues involving their children. My mom badly wanted to do something to help, but there didn't seem to be any solutions.

No matter how much I complained, though, there weren't many alternatives. I had to go to school. It was a no-win situation. I was trapped between the guys who picked on me, the teacher who humiliated me, and my mother, who didn't understand why I wasn't bringing home better grades. I suffered through, getting C's and D's and feeling like the lowliest, homeliest, and dumbest creature at the place.

All that was compounded by drug use. In the hospital, drug use is called "self-medication." Instead of dealing with whatever pain or troubles you have, you medicate them. The problems are still there, you just don't feel them until the drug or alcohol wears off. Then you medicate again. That's the cycle I was entering. When I felt pain, I medicated it.

Alcohol. Marijuana. She knew they made her feel good when she was down. Though Drew's use was still infrequent, it was still enough to alter her personality and change the relationship she had with her mother. It revamped the way she thought about everything.

When I began smoking cigarettes and drinking, I taught myself how to lie to my mother and, soon enough, became an expert at it. When I started smoking pot, I became even more secretive and went to any length to hide my use. It was as if I'd enlisted in an underground army. I carried breath freshener and gum. I became evasive about my possessions and whereabouts. I made sure that whatever I told my mom about my activities, I was sketchy enough to present everything in the best possible light.

But my evasiveness exaggerated the wall that was growing between my mother and me. At the time, I thought my mom was constantly putting me down, pushing me away from her. I couldn't see that she was reacting to the way I treated her—a real codependent relationship. We fed off each other, egging each other into more extreme behavior and reactions.

Eventually, I had less and less to do with her. I began seeing her as an intruder, a hindrance to the nonstop fun I desired. That's when the fighting between us started to flare on a regular basis. Our relationship turned into a constant struggle for independence and freedom. She'd try to set limits and rules and I'd ignore them. She'd remind me that I was only eleven, and I'd say, "So what." She'd say one thing and I'd do the opposite.

It was easy to look at her as the enemy, the source of all my difficulties. In reality, she was looking out for my best interest, but I saw my mom only as preventing me from drinking and smoking dope and hanging out with my friends. She represented reality and

I was groping for fantasy. With every reprimand, resentment built inside of me like a furnace reaching its boiling point.

> Near the end of the school year Drew was cast in a three-hour television movie called *Babes in Toyland,* which filmed in Munich, West Germany. Shooting was scheduled over a four-month period. They'd be gone the entire summer, and that appealed to Drew and Jaid. Both looked forward to the change of scenery as a welcome relief from the stress of school in Los Angeles and their constant jousting. The project was Drew's first major work in nearly a year and her long-suffering ego badly needed the appreciative strokes acting was guaranteed to bring.

What a relief! We landed in Munich, checked in with the production, and suddenly I was no longer an outsider. I was greeted with hugs and kisses by my co-workers, and accepted right off the bat as a peer. Still, there were changes from the way things were when I was younger. For one, I demanded more independence from my mother. I didn't want to eat every meal with her or accompany her on my days off. Consequently, within days of arriving, we locked horns.

Several days before shooting began, Rod Stewart, one of my favorite rockers, rolled into town for a concert. He invited me to ride to the stadium on his tour bus and hang out backstage. I was in heaven. Afterward we rode back to the hotel on the bus, and Rod and his girlfriend, Kelly Emberg, a gorgeous fashion model, said good-night and went to their room. But I remained with the band, drinking all night long in one of their suites. We got crazy drunk, the whole lot of us, and someone took a video of everyone stumbling around the room, falling off the beds, downing the tiny bottles of liquor from the minibar.

Around four A.M. we filed outside, carrying all sorts of instruments, from trumpets to drums, and started playing them as loud as we could. There were about eight of us, and we were obnoxiously, recklessly drunk. The hotel manager ran out and threatened to kick us all out that very instant unless we quieted down and went to our rooms. Miraculously, though, no one else ever found out about that disturbance, my mom especially.

The next afternoon Rod invited me to go to Vienna with him for the weekend. I didn't have to work until Monday, so I had the time. To me, Rod and his band were like the circus, and I was ready to run away with them. Just like that. Two minutes, I thought, that's all I needed to get packed and situated on the tour bus. My mom seriously debated letting me go for the weekend, but then finally said no, which caused me to erupt in a volcanic temper tantrum that lasted for several days.

That tour bus represented the fun I had when drunk, which had fast become the only way I knew how to have fun, and I saw it rolling away, leaving me behind in a cloud of dust.

It shows you the pull alcohol and drugs have on the mind. There I was, on a movie set, the one place where I felt confident and appreciated, really good about myself, and I was panicking over the loss of my suppliers.

Much to my surprise, though, the ensuing months turned out to be the best I'd had in years. I still snuck cigarettes—I was a regular smoker by then—and there was an occasional secret drink, but I didn't find myself dwelling on the various insecurities and problems I suffered from when I was back home. My place on the set was well defined and I was treated the same as everyone else.

Best of all, I had a boyfriend, Michael, a fifteen-year-old guy who was also working on the picture. Michael was the first boy with whom I ever seriously made out. When word got around the set that we were a hot and heavy item, Mom felt it necessary to give me what amounted to my sex talk.

"Drew," she said, "do you need any help understanding boys?"

I shook my head, no.

"Well, if you do," she said, "come to me first. Okay?"

"Yeah, sure."

More important, at least to me, is that Michael was the first boy who ever told me that I was beautiful in a way that I believed it. He told me one night when we were out on a date, walking through town, browsing in stores and looking at our reflections in windows, and he said it so casually and matter-of-factly that it rang true. He gently kissed my cheek, looked at me with loving eyes, and said, "Drew, you *really* are beautiful." I felt good about myself . . . for a day or two.

At the movie's wrap party, Drew kept her good-byes short and sweet, promising to stay in touch with everyone she'd become close to over the past four months. But she never did. No one ever did. That was the toughest part. As always, she grew attached to people who filled a significant void in her life and then, at the end of a project, they were torn away.

Drew arrived home more certain of one thing: her fondness for getting drunk and stoned. Later, she recorded those sentiments in a journal she tried keeping for a brief time. She wrote:

I truly believe it was over that period that I decided being loaded was a new way of life for me. My depressions were more frequent and deeper than ever before and getting loaded was the only way I could rise above those depths. Six months after getting back, I had an awful fight with my mother and slammed the door to my bedroom so hard the house shook. I sat down and stared for the longest time at a bottle of extra-strength aspirin I'd grabbed from the bathroom. I was meditating on the possibility of death. Suicide. I entertained the thought. To just close my eyes and be done with the suffering struck me—death seemed so peaceful. All those pills. I wondered how fast I could get them down.

I didn't do it. I don't know why, since I clearly saw myself swallowing handfuls of pills and then lying down on my bed and going to sleep forever. But I remember thinking, "Well, if I'm not going to die and get rid of the bad feelings, then I will drink them away."

The near-fatal moment recorded in her diary was all but forgotten in the morning when Jaid pulled a sleeping Drew from bed and forced her to go to school. She was then in sixth grade at Cal Prep, another small, exclusive, and expensive private school. Jaid hoped the environment at the new school would be kinder to Drew and the teachers more understanding of her erratic schedule. As for Drew, though she hated the prospect of being the new kid in class for the fourth time in six years, she felt anything was better than a repeat of the agony she incurred the past two years at the Country School.

However, her adjustment to Cal Prep turned out to be a pleasant surprise. It wasn't that Drew suddenly found her new classes stimulating or her teachers inspiring. No, her improved outlook had nothing to do with a better academic climate. Rather, for the first time, Drew was attending a school where there were other children, eleventh and twelfth graders, and, unlike kids her own age, she related to their maturity. They accepted her, too. Within a matter of weeks she fell right in step.

The older kids laughed at my jokes, listened to my stories and, basically, accepted me for who I was. There was none of the pettiness or jealousy I expected from kids my own age. It was a big leap in confidence for me, one that I wouldn't give up for anything, and that eventually proved detrimental and destructive. See, the crowd I hung out with—all seniors—was a collection of good kids turned bad. They smoked cigarettes and pot, ditched school, and generally had a poor attitude about anything that prevented them from having fun—which usually meant getting high.

Also, having friends with cars made me mobile and changed my life. Suddenly I had the freedom I'd craved, and I exercised it without discrimination. Together we ditched school pretty often, usually to go out and smoke a cigarette or eat lunch out. Anyplace where we could hang out and bitch about what we thought were our rotten lives. On weekends we'd cruise around town until midnight, then get high and see the *Rocky Horror Picture Show*. That was a regular routine. Or we'd find out whose parents were gone for the evening and hit their liquor cabinet. Anything to catch a buzz. That was our entertainment.

I was so much younger than everyone else, but it never mattered. I made up for it in experience. I'd been to clubs and they hadn't. I could teach them how to blow smoke rings. I knew how to drink. Little, stupid things like that. I was adopted almost like a mascot, an advanced teenybopper like Tatum O'Neal's tough-talking, cigarette-smoking character in the movie *Paper Moon*. See, I wasn't a dopey eleven-year-old who tagged along. I fit in with them because I knew how to smoke, drink, cuss, and flip off authority with a disrespectful joke.

In retrospect, I understand how their acceptance of me served to reinforce my growing addiction. I belonged to the gang because I used cigarettes, dope, and booze. They were my insignias of association. But if I didn't do any of that, I worried, maybe then they would've seen me as the dopey eleven-year-old girl I was: one with not much of a figure, a wealth of insecurities, and little self-esteem. Not the fun-loving, party girl I made myself out to be. It was an act, a coverup, and all part of desperately wanting to be liked and respected by friends. I'd been an outsider for so long that I wasn't going to do anything that might jeopardize my position as part of the gang.

Not anything. If that meant shutting her mother out of her life, then fine, that's what she'd do.

As weekend partying overflowed into weeknights, Drew found herself becoming increasingly alienated from her mother. It was inevitable. There was so much to her life that she had to keep hidden from Jaid. There was so much she had to keep hidden, period. But pot and booze and cigarettes turned her into a whole different Drew from the one her mother knew. In the house they were like two strangers meeting for the first time and discovering they had nothing in common except for an old friend. In their case that old friend was the old Drew.

Forget it. Never mind. Lay off. That's how I talked to my mother. God, was I getting to be a bitch.

But that was me, and yet that wasn't me—if that makes sense.

The whole process of shutting down my emotions, of excluding my mother from my life, was a slow, painful one. It picked up steam as the school year progressed and my attitude toward partying changed to one of more, more, more! I was constantly jockeying for more freedom. We clashed almost daily. I wanted to get out and get stoned. When I wasn't able to it was automatically her fault. She became the villain, the cause of all my unhappiness.

In my mind I concocted an elaborate sense of injustice for which I blamed her. Looking back, I can see how unhappy and miserable I was with myself. But somehow I managed to blame all that on her. I saw her as my manager and no longer my mother. I convinced myself that she was trying to exploit me, living off the money I earned and going to clubs on the carpet of my fame. None of the good things she'd ever done for me, none of the love and affection she showered me with, mattered anymore.

I wouldn't have dared treat any one of my friends that badly. No way did I want to lose them. But my mother, she was different. I knew that she was always going to be there for me, no matter what I did, and she'd always come crawling back for more.

"Why are you doing this?" my mom snapped one day after picking me up from school. "I love you so much. But you're no longer letting me be part of your life."

"Oh, bug off," I said.

Whenever I sensed that my mom was hurt, I just got angrier. Alarm bells went off in my head. She hurt me, I figured, and I was going to hurt her back.

"I don't know why I even bother," she said. "You know, I'm really trying here. But for the past year you've done nothing but make our lives miserable when you could be making it so much better."

"Who cares," I argued. "Our life has always been rotten."

The truth was that my life, not my mom's, was miserable and rotten. I just didn't want to see that. I didn't want to acknowledge it. My mom was trying to help me, trying to get me through what she could see was a difficult period. She didn't have a clue as to how difficult, but I didn't offer any clues. I turned her away at every opportunity.

EIGHT

SEE YOU IN THE MORNING

To Drew, the Italian movie producer and his actress wife, a sex symbol throughout the 1960s, owned the quintessential happy marriage. They were longtime family friends who struck her as "the perfect couple, as if they'd stepped out of *House and Garden* magazine." With their two boys, one a few years older than Drew, and his younger brother, they resided on a picturesque ranch in Thousand Oaks, California, about a half hour drive from the Barrymores. For several summers Drew was a regular visitor, spending numerous days and nights at the luxurious ranch, playing with the boys in their summer camp setting.

It was an idyllic life. Breakfast, lunch, and dinner, formally served at appointed hours, were attended by both parents and the children. The table overflowed with food and conversation, family stories and constant joking, which reminded Drew of the warmth she'd experienced at the Wards' in North Carolina and the "normal" family that she'd always dreamed of having. Between meals there were plenty of distractions, like swimming, tennis, and driving go-carts around the driveway. When they tired, the house-keeper made lemonade or iced tea.

But even this house of plenty, protected by concerned, loving parents, wealth, vast stretches of property, and imposing electronic gates, couldn't escape the scourge of drugs and alcohol. By the time Drew was eleven, she and the oldest boy had graduated from what they considered to be boring childish games to more mature activities, like raiding his parents' liquor supply and drinking themselves into a stupor that had them sleeping away the better part of the next day. By twelve, they added pot smoking and were getting stoned as often as possible.

In the same way that we used to spend the day swimming or running around, we drank and got stoned at night. His room was far away from his parents', which made it easier to sneak. Plus, it was right next to an entertainment room, where there was a huge bar. Whenever we'd sneak a bottle of wine or champagne or liquor, we'd have to finish the entire bottle to cover our tracks. We went to great lengths to keep everything secret, not just from his parents, but from the maid as well.

Only one night, as we were downing vodkas one after the other, that became impossible. Sitting on his bed, I told him that I was going to be sick. He was concerned and asked what he should do. But it was too late. I ran into the bathroom and threw up. The next morning his dad came into the room and asked if I was feeling okay. The maid had told him I'd made a mess in the bathroom.

"I'm feeling better," I said groggily. "I had a horrible stomach-ache all night."

"Really? Are you feeling all right now?"

"Much better, thanks," I said.

"My son took care of you," he smiled.

"I know. Isn't that sweet?"

"Yes."

His son and I exchanged guilty looks. I hated lying to his parents because I loved them so much.

The drinking and drugs weren't *really* fun. Not in the way Drew had once used the word to describe what it was like making *E.T.* In fact, Drew couldn't help but notice the down side of her use. There was the nausea she suffered at night, the excruciating headaches she woke up with in the morning, the increasingly complicated lies she'd tell to cover her tracks, her poor schoolwork, and her mounting sense of alienation.

She had ceased to drink or smoke pot to have fun. "I did it to get drunk or wasted," she admits. It was her method of blotting out everything she didn't want to think about. Rather than deal with her troubles, she pushed them to the back of her brain and let them collect. But one summer night when she was visiting the ranch, the pressure became too much to ignore. It was an early warning that she was, in the parlance of experts, a "bad addict."

I had an anxiety attack. A full-blown anxiety attack that struck me like an eruption, a huge, uncontrollable emotional explosion inside my head. It totally scared the shit out of me.

That night, as always, the oldest son and I were holed up in his bedroom. His was an ordinary room: a bed, a stereo and television, posters on the wall. Nothing that special. We'd been watching TV, probably David Letterman, waiting for the house to quiet down. Finally, with everyone asleep, he brought out an enormous bag of pot and his bong.

"Oh, my God," I said. "Look at that bag."

"It's so strong," he said proudly. "And mostly all buds."

"Cool," I commented with a stoner's admiration.

For the next several hours, well into the early hours of the morning, we smoked one bongload after another, inhaling the pipeful of thick, acrid smoke and holding it in our lungs for as long as possible, trying to get the maximum effect from the high-potency marijuana. We started out laughing, changing records on the stereo, cracking stupid jokes, and exchanging those lightning-quick flashes of brilliance you get when you're stoned but can't remember three minutes later. Then I began feeling a bit tense.

"How strong is this pot?" I asked.

"I don't know," he said. "I just bought it. But the guy said it's really stoner pot."

"I feel kind of trippy," I said, "kind of weird."

"Maybe it's laced with LSD," he cracked.

"That's not funny."

We'd been fairly animated up till then, but both of us were pretty high and we gradually laid back on the floor, drifting inward into our individual thoughts. My eyes were closed. I ran my fingers through my hair and felt the music vibrate through me. I could almost see the wheels in my mind spinning too fast, like playing a 33⅓ record at 45. Nothing was clear, nothing was focused. Then, suddenly, the thoughts came fast and sharp, like daggers, and a wave of paranoia, something I'd never experienced before, swept over me.

"God, why did you get so high?" I asked myself.

From there it was downhill. I got down on myself for being so mean to my mother. I told myself I was a loser. I thought about school and hated that I got such piss-poor grades. I hated being fat. I hated my rotten life. I hated being high. I got abysmally depressed by what I was doing to myself.

Actually, what I was doing then was acknowledging glimmers of truth about myself. It was a rare and frightening occurrence, and the picture was as unflattering as I could imagine.

Yet—or because of it—through it all I kept taking hits off the bong, and getting higher and higher, trying to blot out all the unpleasantness.

"Do I look pale?" I asked, growing panicky.

"Not really," he said.

"Are my hands shaking as much as I think they are?"

"They're shaking a little," he nodded. "I feel strange too."

"Like you're having trouble breathing?"

We tried to count. From one to ten, and then back down to one again, trying to get a grip on our unbridled emotions. But it was too late. My chest filled with tension and my breathing got very rapid. My pulse was racing.

"This is so weird," I kept repeating. "I don't want to be this high anymore."

He was nodding.

Soon both of us were crying like babies, crying out of panic and fear, and hating what we'd done to ourselves.

God, for however long that lasted, I realized how unhappy I was and how much I hated the person I'd become.

But when we woke up the following afternoon, most of whatever I'd thought the previous evening had jelled into a single, grossly unpleasant blur. I couldn't remember anything in particular, except that I'd gotten too high, and the net result was that I vowed to lay off for a few days.

I had to cut down, too. When my mom picked me up, she knew that I'd been smoking pot. The maid had smelled it, told his mother, and she'd told my mom. When my mother confronted me, I didn't deny it.

"But it was just one little puff," I lied in a sickeningly sweet voice. "I was just experimenting. I'm really sorry."

"Okay," she said. "But stay away from that."

"I will."

The fights between Jaid and Drew became routine. Almost predictable. It was not unusual for Drew to wake up fighting mad and go to sleep after a wall-shaking blowout.

What would precipitate these imbroglios with her mother?

Nothing. They just happened, as inexplicably as spontaneous combustion.

To Jaid, the situation was a living nightmare. Drew's volatile temper recalled the uncertain behavior of Jaid's former husband and Drew's father, John Barrymore. She came home late, didn't do her schoolwork, forgot appointments, and when Jaid called Drew on it, she lashed out. There didn't seem to be any getting through to Drew, and their relationship took on an increasingly desperate timbre.

One afternoon my mom picked me up at my friend's house. It was after school and she wanted to have dinner with me. I was supposed to be at Chelsea's, though, and brushed my mom off with some rude remark. It was typical of me. But it set her off.

"You know, it's getting so I can't stand you, Drew," she started.

"Oh, just take me to Chelsea's," I snapped. "I'm already late."

"Listen to you," she shrieked. "I hate the person you've become . . ."

And that started it. I sat there, staring out the window and ignoring her while my mom raged on and on, screaming at me at the top of her voice. She called me names—loser, asshole, bitch—and I started to cry. It wasn't the names that hurt; it was that she was telling the truth. I was a loser, an asshole, and a bitch, and I didn't like hearing it one bit.

As I cried, she went on, not unlike the way I talked to her, only she was justified in her attack. But then something inside me snapped. I couldn't take one more word, not a single sound more.

I whipped around the front seat and slapped my mom in the face.

The sound of my hand against her face made a loud crack that filled the car like an explosive.

She was stunned and appalled. She pulled the car over and stared at me, fuming.

She didn't say another word till we pulled into the driveway.

"But I've got to go to Chelsea's," I whined.

She looked at me like I was the saddest case she'd ever seen.

"You're grounded," she spat out. "Two weeks."

Anything but seclusion, Drew whimpered. But Jaid was adamant about making the punishment stick, and every day for two weeks, a terribly gloomy Drew came home after school and parked her unhappy frame in her room. The company was horrible.

Depressing is more like it. I hated being by myself. I'd sit there, staring in the mirror at my fat, ugly body and shake my head.

"What happened to you?" I asked myself out loud.

The phone rang constantly. Friends checked in to see if I could get out and party. When I told them I was grounded, seriously grounded, they'd commiserate, saying, "Bummer," and then proceed to tell me what fun they were going to have.

"I'm going over to Amy's to get stoned," said Gigi. "I'll be thinking about you, babe."

"No, I'll be thinking of you," I said.

Sitting there alone, feeling isolated and having no one else but me for company, I became horribly glum. Forget changing my tune and becoming apologetic. I was too deep into my own problems, feeling too sorry for myself, to think of anyone else, like my mother. All I thought about was the fun I was being deprived of. Of course, that fun was booze and pot. Shows you how addicted I was already.

Desperate too. Even though I knew my mom would hit the roof if she caught me smoking, I lit up right there in my room. I didn't care what happened if she caught me. How much worse could it get, I thought. So I sat in front of the mirror, slipped my Marlboros out of my bag, and fired one up. What a sad picture. In baggy clothes that hid every ounce of my body, I blew a stream of smoke rings, launching them from my pursed lips, and watched them float into the air and vanish. I often wished that I could hook a ride on one of those rings and take it to wherever they disappeared to.

But there was no getting away until December when Drew was cast in the movie *See You in the Morning*, a drama about the effects of divorce on children, starring Jeff Bridges and Farrah Fawcett. It was being filmed over four months in New York, ordinarily a cause for celebration. However, Drew didn't want to go.

It was an abrupt change of face from previous films Drew had worked on. Though she'd read for the *See You in the Morning* part, then auditioned and waited anxiously to see if she'd gotten the part, when it came time to depart she balked with an extraordinary obstinacy. "Who cares about a stupid movie?"

she scoffed to her disbelieving mother. Work had always been her saving grace, a stroking of ego that she avidly pursued, and now, for no apparent reason, she wanted no part of it.

On the surface, Drew was protesting against separation from her friends. A single day away was too long, she argued. But, truth be told, underlying her complaints was a fear of being cut off from her addictions. The power of drugs and booze had seduced her into believing that being high was more appealing than making movies.

Drew fought a fierce battle to back out of the commitment. But it was to no avail. Her manager and agent decided the move was a "good career move." In January, Drew and Jaid arrived in New York for their turbulent four-month stay.

I cried all the way to the airport and continued crying throughout the plane flight. *Depressed* isn't a strong enough word to describe my condition. I imagined myself stranded in New York, 3,000 miles away from all my friends. I knew several people in Manhattan, but I had only one good friend, and he was much older than I was. There were no girlfriends for me, I groaned to my mother, no place for me to sleep over. The last thing I wanted was to be holed up for four months in a hotel suite with my mom. I envisioned us bumping into each other till one of us killed the other. And that's about what happened.

Being forced to work on the picture over my objections clinched the impression I had of my mother as the enemy. I didn't want to work, and I felt she made me. I'd forgotten that I had this career, that in the past I was always the one begging her to let me work more often, and that I actually loved working. Instead, I viewed my mom as the ruthless taskmaster, convinced that she no longer cared about being my mother. All she wanted from me, I believed, was the money I earned.

What garbage. I never once stopped and asked what my mother did with the money I earned. I didn't have to because I knew. The bulk of whatever was left over after various commissions were paid went straight into my trust fund. I've heard countless stories of parents stealing their children's earnings. Not my mom though. If anything, she has always been overly conservative about saving money. She'd give me a bit of cash, but let me earn extra spending money, which is why I worked part-time at a video rental store in Los Angeles before we left.

We set up home in our usual suite at the Mayflower Hotel, and the next day, with my mom practically forcing me out the door, I went to work. On past projects I always went to the set early and hung out as late as possible. But I'd changed in a big way. I wasn't into the work at all. I'd turned into an unhappy, mopey, downcast girl.

"I just want to go back home," I whined to my mom, "and sit in the sun."

"And I want to drink beer, get stoned, and way fucked up," I added to myself.

That was my attitude. The booze and pot had obviously made me a different person. It scared me. I mean, if I wasn't an actress, which had always been the saving anchor of my identity, then who was I?

Within the month, Jaid decided to purchase a spacious two-bedroom condo on 68th Street and Broadway. She loved being in Manhattan, and Drew was quickly changing her tune. Acquaintances she had known from previous trips turned into close friends—particularly Stacy, a beautiful seventeen-year-old model from a troubled home who shared an apartment with her older sister in SoHo. Stacy introduced Drew to New York's late-night haunts. She slept at Stacy's on weekends and the two hit the fashionable clubs from dark till dawn. There was never any trouble getting in. Stacy looked old enough, and Drew, who was a month shy of turning thirteen, was waved on by—the advantage of celebrity.

It was good business, I guess. But there was never any problem getting in, except at one particular club. I was with Appolonia, the beautiful singer who costarred with Prince in *Purple Rain*. The doorman asked me for ID. I didn't have any. "But you know who I am," I snapped, annoyed. He nodded but said I was too young to go in. Suddenly my whole life began to crumble—or so I thought. I started to cry. The clubs were my life. Everything I loved—drinks, guys, music, excitement—was inside, and it was being denied to me.

"Just let her in," Appolonia argued, taking my arm and pulling me through the door. "She's with me."

I was saved. Later that night Appolonia gave me a ring she wore in *Purple Rain*. She slipped it on the index finger of my left hand, and it's never been off since.

Getting out of clubs was an altogether different story from getting in. Ninety percent of the time I fell into a cab with Stacy and gave the driver directions. But one night I was at a club with another girlfriend and we were drinking Long Island iced teas, a highly potent mix of gin, vodka, rum, and other liquor. Not just drinking them, but racing through them as if we were gulping water on a hot day. After downing my fifth glass, I started making a fool of myself on the dance floor. I was quite drunk, but not out of control. By my seventh drink, though, I got vilely ill.

The club manager, who had said hello to me earlier, approached the table, asked me my age—even though he obviously knew I was too young to be there when they let me in—and tossed me out of the place. It was like a movie, with him behind me, pushing me out the door and scolding, "And don't ever come back!"

Somehow I found a cab, climbed in, and made it home, staggering down the hallway till I found the door. The afternoon before, I had told my mother that I would be home at one A.M. But it was nearly seven the next morning when I staggered inside the door. My mother was standing on the opposite side with a furious look on her face. She probably smelled me coming up the elevator, because I stunk like a puked-out alcoholic. I looked directly at her and said, "Hi, Mom," and keeled over.

I woke up later that afternoon with a garbage can in my face. I was so sick.

"Did you have fun last night?" she glared at me from the door to my bedroom.

"Tons," I groaned.

"Good," she said, "because that's the last fun you're going to have for a while, young lady. You're grounded for two weeks."

Sequestered in the condominium, the tension between Drew and Jaid was thick enough to cut with a knife. Instead of talking over their differences, they glowered at each other like two boxers. Drew stomped from room to room, slammed doors, and scowled like a caged animal. Her mother, she thought, was purposely tormenting her.

Their relationship was a powder keg set to ignite. As her circle of friends expanded, Drew's desire for more independence increased. That brought her into conflict with her mother. Jaid attempted to set limits to Drew's nightlife. She asked her to be home by midnight. If she slept over at Stacy's house, she wanted Drew to call every so often, and if she didn't hear from her, Jaid called there herself.

At times Jaid sounded like a broken record, constantly reminding Drew of her professional responsibilities. Drew listened—sort of. Because she admired the people with whom she worked, Jeff Bridges, Farrah Fawcett, and Alice Krige, Drew tried to maintain a line between work and partying. She confined her clubbing to weekends and tried never to go out the night before she had to answer a call on the set.

No one I worked with had a clue as to the double life I was leading. They were all nice and kind to me. If I seemed glum and depressed, which I often did, they chalked it up to adolescence and tried cheering me up. Little did anyone realize I was just trying to get through the days as best I could, thinking only of the fun I was going to have on the weekend.

But the real torture was at school. By law, I was supposed to be tutored three hours every day on the set. But my life-style made me an absolute bitch when it came to buckling down and paying attention. School was hard. I couldn't keep up with the work. Concentrating was impossible. And I didn't have the inclination to study. I made the situation even worse, too, by jerking around so much that I had to spend numerous Saturdays banking extra school hours. Which only infuriated me more. When I could've been out with my friends, I was sitting in a cold, empty room, doing schoolwork.

However, as the weeks wore on, it became increasingly difficult for Drew to differentiate between work-nights and weekends. All she talked about was being with her friends, going out, dancing and partying. Were it not for Jaid, Drew would have stepped out every night. But Jaid set up restraints in an attempt to control her daughter, and that stirred up the conflict they had hoped to leave behind in Los Angeles.

The scenes were like carbon copies of each other: I'd want to stay out later than my mom said I could, and when she wouldn't relent, I'd erupt and we'd have a huge fight. In the midst of one horrible spat, I went on a rampage, breaking vases, throwing magazines, and smashing a huge pitcher of iced tea on the floor. The pieces shattered everywhere and I yelled, "I don't really give a damn what you say!"

I ran into the kitchen, grabbed her purse, and snatched her credit card.

"I'm leaving, you bitch," I said.

My mom stood in front of the door, blocking my path. We squared off, and I thought about hitting her. I didn't want to hurt her, but I did try pushing her aside, trying to open the door. My fingers closed in the doorknob and then I backed off a little bit. But I kept yelling and stormed off into the living room.

"Why don't you just go to hell," I screamed.

My mom shuddered. Apparently I'd pushed her to the breaking

point. Unable to take any more of my abuse, she ran to the bathroom, crying. I couldn't believe it. Standing outside the bathroom door, I listened to her cry. I felt a remorseful ache in my heart. But I was too far gone to do any apologizing.

Instead, I cleaned up the broken glass and iced tea and straightened the mess. I still had her credit card in my pocket. I still wanted to split. So I plucked a wad of cash from my mom's wallet and told her I was going shopping.

"I can't stay here anymore," I called.

There was no answer. My mom let me walk. She probably didn't want me around anymore either.

Peeling the crinkled bills from her pocket, Drew bought a pair of roller skates, which became her primary means of transportation around Manhattan. Taxis were draining her of the precious cash she needed for clubs at night. With Stacy, she became a ubiquitous sight along Broadway, speeding in and out of the crowds, whipping around corners, and tiptoeing down subway steps. In peak traffic hours she could get downtown to Stacy's apartment faster than a taxi was able to.

However, the night of her thirteenth birthday, February 22, it was Stacy who skated up to Drew's house. There had been a small party for Drew on the set that day, complete with cake, ice cream, and balloons. She had even enjoyed herself. However, by nightfall, Drew's cheer had disappeared and she felt compelled to get out of the house. A premature worldliness had made her a prisoner to her age.

"Why are you so depressed?" asked Stacy.

"I don't know," I said. "But if it wasn't for you, I'd probably kill myself right now."

"Why?"

"It's my birthday. I'm not happy about turning thirteen. It's such a lame age."

"Yeah, but it's better than twelve," she said.

"That's true."

"But, hey, it's the best year for you," she smiled. "You're finally a teenager."

"Yeah, whatever. But I feel like I should be turning sixteen, not thirteen."

"I know," she sighed. "Come on, let's go out."

Nearly every weekend Drew slept over at Stacy's, which also meant that nearly every weekend she was going out to clubs without her mother's knowledge. By the end of February, the cozy duo became an even cozier trio.

I was at a club one night with Stacy and another friend of mine was also there with this guy. She introduced him. His name was Bobby. I looked into his eyes, and for some reason I immediately fell in love with him. We talked a bit that night, then went our separate ways. For days afterward, though, I couldn't get him out of my mind. I was totally infatuated with him.

For the next two Fridays I went back to that same club with Stacy, hoping to run into him. I kept thinking he'd be there. Finally, I was there one night, talking to my friend about him, when my luck changed.

"Yeah, I can't get him out of my head," I said. "He's gorgeous. But it's more than that."

"But you don't even know his name," she laughed.

"I think it's Bobby."

"Oh, my God, you're pathetic," she laughed. "Wait, hold on. I think there's a guy waving to you."

Both of us turned around, and it was him. I thought it was too good to be happening.

Bobby and I went upstairs, where he bought me a bottle of champagne. We drank it and ended up kissing at the end of the

128

night. Then he went home and I went to my house. All night I thought of him, nothing but him. The next day he called, and from then on we were inseparable.

Bobby wasn't like most of the guys Drew was usually attracted to. Like most kids his age, he experimented with drugs and drank at parties, and kept these practices secret from his folks. He was no Boy Scout, but he was a nice guy whose life seemed to be heading in the proper direction. Bobby was cleancut, a top honors student at a private New York prep school, and he had designs on college. He had already received early acceptance to New York University. He lived in an Upper West Side apartment with his parents, and his, contrary to most of Drew's friends, was a happy home.

It was no wonder she tried to spend all her free time at Bobby's. Drew's own home was anything but happy. She was more like a visitor, showing up at her apartment merely to collect a change of clothes, drop off her dirty laundry, and leave a note of her whereabouts for her mother. As for work, it was an interruption that Drew treated as a contemptible chore. She never missed a day. But she preferred to concentrate on the endless sleepovers she arranged, dates with Bobby, and club outings. If Jaid dared ask a question, Drew rebuffed her with a sharp and wicked swipe.

Drew didn't want to be bothered by her mother and went out of her way to set up smoke screens that would camouflage her clandestine life-style. Within two months of their arrival, Drew and Jaid had become virtual strangers.

I walked into our house one afternoon after having been gone for nearly two days. My mom knew that I'd been sleeping at Stacy's, but we'd barely spoken three words to each other. I'd called to check in, but that was it. She had asked me to get together for lunch or dinner.

"Something," she said. "I never get to see you anymore."

So I popped in to pick up some clean clothes at a time when I didn't expect her to be home. But there she was.

"Where're you going now?" she asked.

"Out," I said.

"You can't leave," she said. "We need to talk."

"Yeah, I can leave," I said. "I've got things to do. I'll be back later."

"I haven't seen you in two days," she said, grabbing my wrist. "I've barely known where you've been. I don't even know where you live. Now, I want some answers right this minute."

I pulled away from my mom and looked at her long and hard.

"Well, answer them yourself, because you wouldn't be happy with the answers I'd give you. You want to hear something else. But I can't say that to you."

That started the fight. We got on the subject of freedom and the shit hit the fan. My mom was trying to curtail the independence I'd carved for myself and I wasn't going to relinquish one iota of it. The more she attempted to establish some parental authority, the more vehemently I put her down. I was utterly rude and disrespectful, even calling her a "bug up my ass."

If I was going out every night, my mom was doing the exact opposite. She was a veritable hermit. As far as I knew, she never left the condo, never developed a social life of her own, and I thought she expected me to live like that as well.

"Maybe if you developed a life, you wouldn't be such a downer," I snapped. "Can't you forget business and enjoy yourself for once?"

"Yeah, maybe. But you have too much of a life," she said. "You're making a jerk of yourself."

"No, I'm not," I argued. "At least I know how to have fun."

We were screaming at the tops of our lungs. Finally, I told her what I really thought was bothering her.

"You know what?" I said with total disdain. "You need to get laid."

That was it. My mom stood up, scooped her wallet out of her purse, fished out a $100 bill and threw it at me.

"Get out!" she yelled. "You don't like it here, go find someplace on your own. See if you can do any better by yourself."

Drew didn't know how to say it any other way. "You need to get laid."

In the crudeness of such a bald statement, she unleashed years and years of resentment and hostility. Her mother had failed to supply a replacement for her father. She had failed to find a mate who could provide Drew with the paternal affection she so desperately craved. But Drew now had Bobby, a man of her own. They may not have been sleeping together, but he still provided her with the love and affirmation that filled her existence with meaning.

Drew told her mother as much, not with eloquence or tact, and not even with a modicum of respect, but she damn well let Jaid know that she had found love, and she'd found it on her own, and no one was going to rob her of it.

NINE

BUSTED!

I loved cocaine. Period.

That, I think, says it all. Part of being an addict is involvement in the continuous search for the perfect antidote to pain. It's like a doctor treating an illness with a specific antibiotic. For some addicts it's booze. For others it's pills or heroin. You go through them all, knowing that something out there is going to make you feel good.

Alcohol made me feel horrible. It caused me to forget my pain, which is what I liked about it, but I always drank to excess and I woke up sick as a dog, which I hated. Pot—that was fun for a while. Then I discovered cocaine, and it was like standing on top of a mountain and yelling, "Eureka! I found it!"

Coke was the right drug for me. Neat and quick, with no apparent after-effect, coke allowed me to soar above my depression and sadness, above all my problems. What I couldn't see is that it eventually makes you go crazy.

However, out of plain and simple fear, I didn't try coke till I was back in Los Angeles. I was scared of what effect coke might have on me. But in New York I was around it often enough to not be naive about its thrilling high. The crowd I ran with in Manhattan always had drugs. Plenty of them. Whatever anybody wanted. Marijuana, cocaine. They were as easy to get as a newspaper, and there were many times when we actually bought pot right down at the newsstand outside Stacy's apartment. It was thirty-five cents for a paper and five bucks for a tiny bag of pot.

Stacy seemed to always know someone who had pot for sale. If not, we found someone on the street who was selling loose joints for a couple of dollars. In clubs, pot and coke were even easier to come by. All you had to do was ask, order them up just like a drink. We'd either see a guy we knew, who would turn us on to a dealer, or we'd recognize someone we knew who usually sold drugs. Then a quick exchange of money in a dark corner and the deal was done.

And once we got hold of them—a roach, a joint, whatever—we went into the bathroom, closed the door on a stall, and did them. Just like that. It was something that was kept low key, but in the bathroom you could almost always smell pot or hear someone sniffing up a little cocaine.

However, I didn't have anything on me when I showed up at Bobby's.

"My mom just kicked me out of the house," I said. "What an asshole."

Bobby refused to take sides in the fighting that went on between my mother and me. He didn't really care. However, he said I could sleep over at his house. We checked with his mother, who wasn't very inquisitive about my plight, and it was okay with her. Later, though, I think she called my mom to say that I was at their house. It was pretty hard to be around me for five minutes and not know that I'd just had a major altercation with my mom.

With my lodging suddenly taken care of, I had one hundred dollars in my pocket.

"I've got some money," I said to Bobby. "Let's go out for dinner."

"And this guy I know is having a party later," he smiled. "He's getting a keg."

"Cool," I smiled. "I'm going to get so fucked up tonight."

That became the routine. Throughout March and April, Drew beat a steady path between Bobby's comfortable Upper West Side apartment and Stacy's makeshift SoHo digs, where she usually spent the night.

Half the time the three of them would go out to clubs, and half the time they'd stay home and cook elaborate meals from the pages of *Gourmet*. No matter what, though, their activities were tainted by the hue of alcohol, pot, or cocaine—one of the three or a combination. It depended on what they had at the time.

She had long since called a truce with her mother and returned home. Survival depended on it. They tolerated each other, treating home as a demilitarized zone, where they were careful not to overstep the volatile boundaries they set in order to make it through the rest of their stay in New York. Jaid didn't ask many questions and Drew maintained a minimum level of respect. Jaid worried. She spent lots of time worrying about Drew, talking to people Drew worked with on the movie, asking how she behaved, wondering just what was going on inside her daughter's pretty blond head.

But every time she tried to approach Drew, she was turned away. If she attempted to ask what was bothering her, or sought the slightest glimpse of how she was conducting her life, Drew accused her of prying or of usurping her freedom. The net result was always the same: a fight that sent them both reeling into separate corners like two combatants who refused to throw in the towel.

It was getting to be the same with Bobby too. Not because he sought to control her or set limits she thought were too harsh. No, Drew and Bobby fought because in the haze of habitual drug and alcohol use, of which both of them were guilty, relationships suffer. They have to. Inebriation is a selfish activity. It may start out with a festive whoop and holler, but the psychological effects turn it into a solo flight that eventually inhibits one's ability to cope with another person.

We were in a fight, a big one, but Bobby called me at Stacy's anyway. He said that he was coming over to see me. I asked where he was and he said that he was at a nearby restaurant. That he'd be there in five minutes, and if I wasn't dressed and ready to go out, he'd barge in, dress me himself, and pull me out the door.

"Try and make me," I said, hanging up the phone.

Five minutes later we heard rocks hitting the window. I stuck my head outside and saw Bobby on the street, three flights below.

"Come out here," he called.

Naturally, I was dressed, as he'd instructed, and I told him I'd be right out. Then I turned to Stacy and another friend. We had two joints left, and I told them if they took one hit off either of those joints or drank either of the three beers that we had in the refrigerator, I'd kill them. Then I yelled out the window to Bobby.

"Half an hour," I said. "That's as long as I'm going to stay out."

"Fine," he said.

So I went downstairs, met Bobby and his friend, Jason, and we started walking to a loft, where a friend of his was throwing a keg party. After a few blocks Bobby suddenly disappeared. Jason covered for him, cracking jokes, not telling me where Bobby went. A minute later he was back, holding a bouquet of long-stemmed red roses, which he gave to me. I smiled and took his hand as we walked.

When we got to the party, there were probably four hundred people jammed into the loft. We milled around, and then I went into the room where the keg was set up and stood in line for a beer. It was an enormous, brightly lit, overly crowded room, and I happened to stand in line next to Bobby's ex-best friend, Sam. They'd had a fistfight several weeks earlier over me when Bobby wrongly accused Sam of trying to move in on me. He'd never done that. We were close friends, but nothing more. Anyway, Bobby saw us there together and went crazy.

"There's a bedroom upstairs," he screamed, "and you guys can go fuck each other if you want."

Sam backed off, not wanting to fight.

"Don't give in to him," I screamed at Sam.

Then I turned toward Bobby, who was holding my bouquet of roses. By now people had heard us screaming and gathered around, like they do when a fight breaks out. It was better than the music, that's for damn sure. I grabbed the roses and smacked Bobby across the face with them. Everyone started laughing, but I was livid.

"You can't tell me who to be friends with," I screamed. "I'll be friends with whomever I want."

"I've just wasted my money on you, I can see that," he said.

"You can take your goddamn money and shove it up your ass," I said.

The scene made the fights my mom and I had pale. We were pushing, kicking, and slapping each other. Everyone was staring at us, and when I noticed that we'd become *the* spectacle of the party, surrounded by hundreds of gawking people, I decided that was enough.

"I never want to see you again!" I snapped, and stormed out of the room.

Holding but a single rose from the bouquet that I'd been hitting Bobby with, I stomped into the other room—the dance room—which, except for a swirling white light, was totally dark. And suddenly I heard the opening beats to mine and Bobby's song. "Blue Monday" by New Order, come over the sound system. We'd played that song thousands of times, over and over. I dropped the rose and started to cry.

Bobby was coming after me, with the whole party trailing behind him to see what was going to happen next.

"Look what you're making us do," I said, turning toward him.

"You too," he said, picking up the rose I'd dropped.

I was crying.

"I love you," I said.

"I love you too."

We started dancing, alone, in the corner of the dark room.

"Our song has saved us once again," I whispered.

He smiled and held me close.

"Bobby," I said, looking up in his eyes, "I'll always love you, till the day I die."

"So will I, Drew. So will I."

Crying, I took the rose from his hand, kissed him lightly on the cheek, and walked out of the party. He started after me, but I was gone.

I went back to Stacy's and got dizzy-eyed loaded. Stacy and I went down to the store three times that night to get more beer. Finally, we passed out.

A year and a half earlier, during the time Drew was enduring so much ridicule at school, she and Jaid had gone to the city animal shelter one afternoon and selected a fat old cat. Drew had named him Pizza, and the plump furball became the repository of all Drew's private thoughts and secrets. Pizza listened without making a judgment and purred ever so gently as Drew stroked him and poured out her heart.

"I told him everything," she says.

Everything. She'd settle Pizza on her lap in the quiet of her dark room and confess her innermost thoughts, things she rarely admitted even to herself. She told him about her smoking and drinking. She talked about the fighting with her mother. She loathed her fat body. She even cried remorsefully over what a horrible image of herself she'd turned into.

"I wish there were some way you could suddenly change everything," Drew remembers telling him.

The cat seemed to understand, rubbing his whiskered face on her T-shirt.

"I used to have another cat, little Gertie," said Drew. "I told her everything too. But she ran away. Everyone in my life has run away. Even me. I'm running away from myself."

Pizza purred as Drew petted him.

"Don't you run away too, okay, Pizza?" she said. "Okay? Don't leave me."

People always seemed to be leaving her. Or else she seemed to be saying good-bye.

Before leaving New York at the end of April, Drew spent virtually an entire day calling people to say good-bye. She must have made fifty phone calls. At least fifty. Stacy was the hardest. No, maybe Bobby was the hardest. Drew called him to say good-bye and hung up in tears. She was always getting close to people and then leaving them.

Love. It was the hardest habit to break and the craving most difficult to satisfy.

In Los Angeles, Drew's first call was to Chelsea, whom she hadn't spoken to the entire time she was in New York. For some inexplicable reason, they'd grown apart before she'd left. But Drew still wanted to check in with her and catch up on what everyone had been doing. She wanted to see who had boyfriends, and who didn't, stuff like that. Then she wanted to meet at Amy's house and get high—like they used to do.

But Drew knew by the sound of Chelsea's voice on the phone that she wasn't the same girl as before. Chelsea was glad to hear from her. However, when Drew suggested meeting at Amy's, Chelsea hesitated, and finally stammered an uneasy no. Drew was puzzled.

"I don't do that anymore," said Chelsea.

"What do you mean?" I asked.

"I'm into sobriety now," she explained. "I don't smoke or drink anymore."

"Why?"

"I went into the hospital," she said. "I had two months of treatment."

"You're kidding."

"No."

"Okay, see ya 'round."

When I hung up, I thought, "Geek city. What a jerk. I don't want her as a friend."

Then I found someone else who would get stoned with me.

Drew entered into a terminal state of high, smoking pot before school, ditching classes, and staying out late at night with her friends to get even higher.

Yeah. That was the life. One big party.

Finally, Drew got up the nerve to try cocaine. It had been a long time coming. She was at her school's prom, and everyone seemed to be snorting lines of coke.

God, I consumed so much that night. I don't even know how much I consumed, but it was very, very scary.

When it came time for me to do my first lines, I was so frightened I could barely see out of my eyes. I thought I was going to have a heart attack. A friend held my head straight so I could snort better. And I needed the help. I was so drunk and so stoned I could hardly walk.

"Do a couple lines and you'll be all right," a friend of mine coached.

It wasn't just me who was in such a bad state. All my friends were completely buzzed too. And these were the cream of the crop, the really good kids from school. If any parents had seen a picture of that crowd, they never would've believed all those kids were guzzling wine coolers, smoking pot, and laying out lines of coke like it was candy.

Then we smoked some coco-puffs—a little cocaine on a cigarette—and got even higher.

From that night on I loved cocaine. I craved it all the time. Just thinking about it caused my palms to sweat.

Television movies and talk shows have created a stereotypical image of the addict. Someone who's ragged, out-of-control, and utterly blind to the self-destructive course they've chosen. They lose their money, jobs, family. Stand them in front of a mirror and they fail to see the truth . . . until some dire accident occurs. All they want is their fix.

That was me. Gimme my coke. My mind seemed to have a huge neon sign in it that blinked nonstop: COKE. GET COKE. So I did. It was great for dieting, partying, and picking up my mood. If I did a little coke, I could drink all I wanted to without feeling it. It made me so happy, I thought coke was the ultimate in life.

But of all the times I used it, the one image that stands out is of me sitting alone on the floor in my bathroom. The door was locked, and I'd laid out a bunch of lines on a tiny mirror. Very methodically, I inhaled each one and waited for the rush. It was great. Every so often I ran out and changed the song on my stereo. I was so happy, so high. Then, I remember, I did the last line and licked up all the powder.

"More," I thought. "I've got to get more."

That's the insidious nature of the drug. You always want more. No matter what you tell yourself about rationing, conserving, or cutting down, you always want more, more, more. I remember being so incredibly high, my hands were shaking and my heart was pounding. I could hardly sit still. I imagined myself grinning from ear to ear.

But when I looked back down at the empty mirror, hoping to find a few stray pebbles, I saw that I was actually crying. Tears were streaming down my cheeks and I didn't even know it. I was miserable. I didn't know what was going on. I remember telling myself, "Get a grip, girl. Get a fucking grip." But, I guess, it was too late.

Jaid felt handcuffed. She had, she realized, finally run out of options as well as patience, and she didn't know what to do with Drew. The grades Drew brought home on her report card, though they reflected only two months of work, were dismal, setting new standards of low. When she was home, they barely communicated. They barely saw each other, for that matter. When Jaid tried talking to her, it was to no avail. When she broached the subject of counseling, Drew slammed the door on her.

That seemed to symbolize their relationship.

How could two people who loved each other sink to such a horribly low point, wondered Jaid.

Worse still was that they didn't seem to have hit bottom yet. Summer vacation promised the likelihood of additional problems, since Drew would have even more free time on her hands. She didn't have a movie schedule until mid-July, when she would be off to Nevada to shoot *Far from Home*. Till then, Jaid fretted, there was no telling what Drew was going to get herself into.

At that point Jaid was feebly resigned to the helpless position of worried parent. She sat, bit her nails, and imagined her hair turning white and wrinkles turning her face into a billboard of angst. And that's exactly how she spent the night of June 28. Sitting and worrying. Ten o'clock turned into midnight, Drew's curfew, and still there was no sign of her.

Then the phone rang.

"I want you out of the house," I told her. "When I get home I want you out. I don't think you're treating me fairly, and so I want you to sleep somewhere else tonight."

My mom was silent.

"Okay?" I asked.

"Okay, Drew," she said calmly. "I'll sleep at someone else's house tonight."

I was so out of my mind that I thought I could say something as audacious as that and get away with it.

So I hung up and thought, perfect. She'll be gone, so I can drink all I want and come home as wasted as I want and there's not going to be any mother there to yell at me.

I was out with friends. It was a warm summer night, and we were at a drive-in movie, a place where we knew it would be easy to score beers. We'd brought our own six-pack, and they sold glasses there. So we were set. And after talking to my mother, I felt free to consume as much as I wanted, which was a lot.

And I did. By the time we started to my house, I'd drunk all or part of something like twelve or thirteen beers. We were having a beer race, trying to see how many we could drink in as short a time as possible. If my mom wasn't going to be there, it didn't matter what condition I arrived in.

Needless to say, I was pretty intoxicated by the time we pulled onto my street. Drunk out of my head is a more accurate description.

The car we were cruising in was a convertible, a big old boat of a car. The guy driving was completely wasted and having a difficult time driving, but we didn't care. The radio was blasting and the hot air was rushing by. It was invigorating. We were high on alcohol, blitzed and giddy, and having the best time, laughing hysterically at everything anybody said.

And all I thought was, I have the house to myself. I can drink all the beer in the fridge. All the liquor. I can blast my stereo. I'm going to have the absolute best time.

Then we turned into the driveway and I saw it. My mom's car was there. Parked right in the middle, her usual spot. Instantly, every ounce of jubilation I'd been feeling turned into rage. I was steaming as I got out of the car and ran up the stairs and opened the front door. My mother was there waiting for me, anticipating the confrontation.

"What the hell are you doing here?" I screamed. "I told you to get out of the house!"

My mother just stood there, looking at me with a blank expression. No, an expression of disbelief and sternness. I continued to rant and rave. But she wasn't feeding into my shit, which only made the tantrum I was throwing worse. I started throwing things— glasses, vases, anything I could reach. I couldn't see straight, I was so mad. Things were shattering all over the floor, and it still didn't faze my mom. She just stood there, her hands on her hips, watching.

There was one sure way to provoke her, I thought. I'd grab a beer. That would get her. So I went into the kitchen and grabbed a can from the refrigerator.

"You can't drink in this house," she said.

I could tell she meant it too. But I didn't pay any attention.

"I'll do what I want," I replied, and then stalked into my bedroom and slammed the door.

Listening through the door, I heard my mom get on the phone.

"She's very bad," she said. "You need to come over right now and pick her up."

Panic shot through my body as if I was being scalded by hot water.

Oh, shit, I thought, the cops are coming to get me. What am I going to do now?

TEN

LEVEL ONE

Drew was shaking. Part nerves and part drunken stupor, she figured the police were on their way. She hoped they didn't blare their siren. That thought ran through her mind. She didn't want the neighbors coming out and gawking as the cops led her down the walk and to the waiting patrol car with her hands cuffed behind her back. What a disaster. In a matter of hours, she thought, she'd gone from party girl to the absolute jerk of the planet.

Fine. Then so be it. As long as the roof was going to cave in momentarily, she decided to get an ax and help the demolition. Opening the door to her bedroom, she started her wobbly body toward the kitchen with one goal in mind: to grab another beer and quickly down it before she was hauled off to juvenile hall. The walk was more of a stagger. Drew huffed and puffed her way down the hall, swearing at her mother and babbling incoherently. Still fuming, Drew believed she was spewing flames and smoke.

Then the front door started to open. She heard the handle turn and the door hinges creak. Drew stopped in her tracks. Oh, no, she thought, here it comes. When she began using drugs—marijuana and cocaine—on a regular basis, Drew vowed that she'd never find herself handcuffed and going to jail. Drew started to sob.

But it wasn't the cops. Chelsea and her mom walked through the door and I breathed a sigh of relief. But with that last breath I lost all my stamina and strength. Barely able to stand, I collapsed on the sofa. My eyes were watering and I felt incredibly sick. Chelsea picked me up. Our mothers were talking. I couldn't hear a thing they said. Nor did I care. Then they led me out to their car. Chelsea sat down next to me in the backseat. My mother got in the front next to Chelsea's mom.

"Where are we going?" I asked, though I didn't really care now that it was clear I wasn't going to jail.

"The hospital," said Chelsea. "The same place I just got out of."

"Okay," I mumbled, "no prob. I'll go to the hospital."

In whatever portion of her mind that was still trying to function, Drew envisioned herself being checked into a local hospital, like Valley Presbyterian, which was around the corner, where she'd spend the night and sober up. Sometime the following day, she imagined, her mom would arrive, deliver some grave lecture, and then they'd drive off in their BMW. No prob, indeed. She'd be wasted later that night.

However, Drew was mistaken in her perceptions. Her situation was much more severe than she believed, and, as far as Jaid was concerned, it required severe actions. More severe than either she or Drew had probably ever imagined.

But at least Jaid had been ready for it. After returning from New York, she'd spent countless hours on the phone with Chelsea's mother, commiserating, crying, and listening, and what she'd come away with was a frightening portrait of Drew that brought back all the horrid memories of the violent struggles she'd

LEVEL ONE

endured trying to get her former husband—Drew's father—treatment for his alcoholism and drug use.

Jaid had long suspected something direly wrong with Drew. The path of self-destruction she'd left behind was unmistakable. Her problems obviously ran deeper than the growing pains of adolescence. But their explosive relationship had made it impossible to penetrate the labyrinthine walls that stood between them. Confrontations led nowhere. So Jaid, following advice, had decided to wait for an incident like the one this evening and then take action.

As they drove, Drew was laughing in the back-seat.

"Would you please chew some gum," said Chelsea, disgusted. "You smell."

"Do I?" giggled Drew. "Oops."

The car pulled up in front of a long, low brick building that looked more like an office building than a hospital. It was the ASAP Family Treatment Center, a private drug and alcohol rehab facility in Van Nuys, California. Chelsea led Drew from the car. Jaid followed Chelsea's mother, who, familiar with the admitting procedures, took charge.

They took me into a small admitting room, where a blond guy, one of the night technicians, greeted us and collected the proper forms. The room was sterile, stocked with just two plastic-covered couches, a plain table, and a big ashtray. I sat there and smoked cigarettes, one after the other. Chelsea had two packs in her purse, and she had to open the second one. My mom complained that I was smoking too much, but I just ignored her and waited for something to happen.

"How many beers have you had tonight?" asked the tech.

"Oh, about fifteen," I said.

I heard my mother gasp.

"Fifteen, huh," he nodded. "And you're not drunk."

"No, not at all," I said.

The tech looked at me like I was the idiot I was being.

"Okay, I'm drunk," I laughed.

But our exchange became very businesslike and serious.

"Do you smoke pot?" he asked.

"Yeah," I said.

"Do you do coke?"

"Yeah."

"And you drink an awful lot, I suppose."

"Yeah, you can say that."

"Have you ever done heroin?"

"I don't think so," I said.

"Crack?"

"I don't know."

"You don't know?"

"No, I don't think I have."

My mom, who was crying a stream of tears, couldn't contain her shock and horror any longer.

"You've done cocaine?" she blurted out.

I turned to her and gave her a look that said, "Bug off."

There seemed no letup to the questions. The tech asked for Drew's height and weight. He ran down a checklist of illnesses and allergies, compiling a cursory medical history as best he could. He asked Drew to estimate the quantity of drugs and alcohol she'd consumed over the past week. She sat inhaling a cigarette, answering questions till it seemed she could no longer keep her eyes open. Jaid, pale and drained, sat across from them in silence, showing the same signs of exhaustion and strain. Then the tech stood and told Drew to follow him. They were, he said, keeping her overnight.

And I was thinking, Yeah, right. You're keeping me here forever.

"No," he reassured me, "not forever."

By that time it was about five A.M. and I was too tired to fight.

Three generations of Barrymore
profiles: John; John, Jr. (Drew's father);
and Drew. (UPI/BETTMANN NEWSPHOTOS)

(ABOVE) John Barrymore, Jr.,
strikes a leading man pose.
(UPI/BETTMANN NEWSPHOTOS)

(RIGHT) Jaid Barrymore,
Drew's mother. (JOHN SANCHEZ)

Before she could walk, Drew looked interested
in front of the camera.

Drew as Gertie in E.T. THE EXTRA-TERRESTRIAL. (UNIVERSAL STUDIOS)

(ABOVE LEFT) Drew with her special friend, Steven Spielberg, during the making of E.T. (UNIVERSAL STUDIOS)

(ABOVE RIGHT) The E.T. kids: Robert MacNaughton, Drew, and Henry Thomas. (PETER C. BORSARI)

On a publicity tour in Japan, a seven-year-old Drew mugs with an E.T. doll for photographers. (UNIVERSAL STUDIOS)

(LEFT) Drew and Jaid, gowned and coiffed, attended the 1983 Academy Awards. (RON GALELLA)

(RIGHT) Drew found George C. Scott "huggable" when they made FIRESTARTER. (UNIVERSAL CITY STUDIOS, INC.)

Out too late, an exhausted Drew fell asleep in the midst of a Hollywood party at Ma Maison. (PETER C. BORSARI)

Drew identified with her character in IRRECONCILABLE DIFFERENCES, a girl who tries to divorce her parents. (© 1984 ANGELES CINEMA INVESTORS)

Hollywood teens: Drew and Corey Haims.
(STEVE GRANITZ/RETNA LTD.)

At New York's Limelight club, Drew exchanged fashion tips with Dweezil Zappa. (RON GALELLA)

Drew, then a worldly eleven years old, heading inside New York's China Club. (RON GALELLA)

Actor Corey Feldman escorted Drew to the 1988 Academy Awards. (RON GALELLA)

Drew showed off dazzling Hollywood beauty at the premiere of SEE YOU IN THE MORNING. (SMEAL/GALELLA LTD.)

I followed him down a hallway that was dimly lit and extremely quiet, since everyone was asleep. Then he opened the door to a small room. I looked in. There was a bed, equipped with restraints, though they didn't use them on me. Then he gave me some blankets and told me to get as much sleep as possible.

"Wake-up's in two hours," he said, shutting the lights and closing the door.

I stood there, rooted in the dark and unable to move. It was shock or some facsimile of it, and I was so overwhelmingly scared. In the dark, the only sounds I heard were my own wheezy breaths, and that made me sick to my stomach. What a pitiful case I was, so pitiful that I couldn't even muster up the tears to feel sorry for myself. Finally, I laid my weary self down on the mattress and pulled the blankets over me.

But I couldn't go to sleep—at least right away—and so I stared at the wall for an hour, reliving the past evening and thinking about what a screwup I was, and eventually dozing off into a brief, unsettled sleep.

There were no windows in the secluded, barren holding room to indicate the arrival of morning. But at seven A.M. the fluorescent lights overhead flickered on and filled the room with their unremitting glow. A tech woke Drew, which was no easy chore, and explained that it was time to get up. She didn't argue, and allowed herself to be led to an examining room, where a nurse sat ready to take a sample of her blood.

She was still in a disheveled state, wearing the same odorous clothes from the previous evening and badly in need of a shower and change of outfit. Hung over, her head pounded unmercifully.

When Drew glimpsed the needle, she turned ghostly white and faint. Immediately the tech straightened her up, revived her somewhat, and got her to the bathroom, where she tried throwing up but couldn't. She cried and cried and cried from being sick, and they put her back to bed.

Several hours later, ASAP therapist Betty Wyman, the treatment coordinator who had been assigned Drew's case, walked into the room. Wyman, a dark-haired woman with gentle eyes and a soft, kind smile, stood over Drew's bed and looked at the sleeping girl. Her face was grimy and tear-stained, her hair snarled, and her clothes reeked as if she was a derelict off the street. "What a sad, sad kid," she remembers thinking.

She woke me up. She was basically the first person I saw with a clear head and eyes that could focus. She looked at me, and I looked at her. I didn't know who she was, her name, or her position. She could've been the janitor or the person who owned the place. For some reason, though, I got a comforting feeling from her and I wanted to reach out and hug her.

"Hi, I'm Betty," she said. "I'm your therapist. You're pretty sick, huh, kiddo?"

"You could say that," I moaned.

"You think you're going to throw up?"

"No."

"Okay. Why don't you go take a shower and come into my office when you're done."

I nodded and walked out of the room alongside Betty. Then a tech handed me some towels and a change of clothes, and took me to the shower. That was probably the best shower I've ever taken. I stayed under the hot water for half an hour, till I felt waterlogged and wrinkled, and then dressed and went into Betty's office.

Betty handed me a cup of orange juice. We started talking, then she introduced me to my roommate, and I spent the rest of the day getting acquainted with the hospital and meeting people. I heard some of the kids say, "Hey, that's the chick from *Firestarter*. What the fuck is she doing here?" But Betty intervened and told them to calm down and treat me like any other patient. That whole day it was really awkward and I was so unhappy, but I stuck close to Betty. I felt she would protect me.

Jaid spent the rest of that night and the early morning bereft of spirit, depressed, tired of crying, and too exhausted to scream. Nonetheless, she experienced a feeling akin to relief. The ASAP hospital provided her with an option that she hadn't been aware of until she started talking to Chelsea's mother. In their storm of desperation, it seemed to offer some shelter. Watching Drew being led down the hall and the door slamming shut behind her was like driving a stake through her heart. Yet, Jaid felt, she was so despondent and discouraged that anything had to be better than what they'd been going through.

Faith. That's all Jaid was going on. A faith grounded in Chelsea and Chelsea's mother telling her that the treatment worked. Not only for Chelsea, but her older sister too. Their lives had turned around. That was substantiation enough. Still, Jaid was confused.

After watching her daughter disappear behind the doors of the locked hospital ward, Jaid let loose a torrent of pent-up emotions. The techs on duty were sympathetic. Even if they'd heard parents with ravaged faces pour out their hearts hundreds of times before, they were kind and comforting and told Jaid, first and foremost, to go home and get some much-needed rest.

She was at the point where she wanted to be told what to do, she needed instruction, and she obeyed. The tech's competency, understanding, and experience gave her something positive to hold on to, the first positive sign she'd had in years. Later that afternoon she came back to finish the paperwork and learn more about the program. At last, thought Jaid on her way home, at last something positive was happening.

That feeling was only reinforced later that afternoon when she returned to the hospital to complete the admitting paperwork and receive an indoctrination to ASAP's program. The information came at her like an avalanche. Papers, terms, graphs, explanations—it was overwhelming, and she grabbed at bits and pieces, trying to assimilate the information as best she could in the condition she was in. She left with the sense that she was making the transition into a whole new world.

That afternoon, this lady, a nurse who was older and sterner and completely opposite from Betty, explained the rules to me. It was done with a matter-of-factness that made me feel imprisoned. There was no smoking, she said, until your parent signs the smoking consent.

"But your mother already signed it," she said.

"Well, there's no point in telling me that, is there?" I said.

"Listen," she snapped. "Smoking is a privilege. It has to be earned and can be taken away."

"Right."

"And there's no SAO-ing."

"Huh?"

"Sexually acting out," she said.

"What's that?"

"Kissing, making out, and all related activities."

"Oh."

And for fifteen minutes she continued telling me what I couldn't do or at what particular time something had to be done. There were appointed times for showering, for meals, there was no cutting lines for food, there was school every day and punishments for cheating, and there were particular bedtimes. That meant in bed and lights out.

"What time do I have to go to bed?" I asked.

"You're new here," she said. "Which means you start on level one. Bedtime is 10:00 P.M. on weeknights and eleven o'clock on weekends—if you earn it."

Drew was confused and frightened. Like most new patients, she didn't know the first thing about treatment. When she thought about what she was getting into, her mind conjured up the ominous scenes from *One Flew over the Cuckoo's Nest*. After all, she was at a hospital where they set down a strict code of conduct and monitored patients with hawkish attention. But the reality of ASAP was anything but threatening.

The foundation of treatment is basically a process of nurturing a sick individual to health and simpler than one might imagine. Through weeks and months of intensive therapy, the patient is made to confront and resolve the various issues that are causing their addiction. It's not enough to merely acknowledge the obvious symptoms, such as excessive consumption of alcohol or drug use. Successful recovery rests on the acknowledgment and resolution of whatever deep-seated problems cause the self-destructive behavior.

The ASAP Family Treatment Center, found in 1979 by psychiatrist Dave Lewis, is no different. At a cost of $500 per day, most of which is picked up by insurance, treatment revolves around long days of rigorous therapy including individual, group, family, and multifamily sessions. The emphasis is on family therapy, resocialization, and the daily practice of a Twelve-Step belief program like Alcoholics Anonymous.

ASAP patients, Dr. Lewis has found, span the gamut of economic, social, and family backgrounds, but share one thing in common: most usually began using drugs or alcohol around age eight, started using consistently at eleven, and were admitted to the hospital at age fifteen.

Whether or not she wanted to recognize it, Drew fit the picture perfectly.

There were usually three girls to a room, but to start with, I had just one. Her name was Tina. She was seventeen, had long brown hair, green eyes, and I thought she was beautiful. Too beautiful to be in a hospital. After introducing us, Betty left for a while, and I slumped on the empty bed.

"You scared?" Tina asked.

I nodded.

"Don't be. This ain't the greatest place, but it's not the worst either."

"How long have you been here?" I asked.

"Two months," she smiled.

Tina turned back to folding her laundry, and I sat there watching her, wondering what her story was. Later I learned that she was at ASAP for the same reason I was: drugs and alcohol. Her younger sister had recently been discharged too. They were from a nice middle-class family from Ventura. Her father was an accountant and her mother stayed home and took care of the house. On the surface they seemed like the perfect family, a family that wouldn't have a single problem, but Tina and her sister had both been messed up by drugs.

I wondered if Tina wanted to ask why I was there, but then when she didn't, I figured the answer was obvious.

I took out a cigarette and my lighter.

"Hey, no smoking in the rooms," Tina told me. "You get demerits for that, and I'm not risking any of my weekend passes. I've got my release date, and I'm not ruining it."

I put it back.

"You need to borrow some clothes for the rest of the day?" she asked.

"Yeah, that'd be great," I smiled. "That's really nice."

"Go ahead, pick something out."

Lunch was the first scheduled activity of the day that Drew actually participated in. It wasn't pleasant. The food disgusted her fragile stomach, and she just sat at the table till it was time to go to the next designated activity, which turned out to be group therapy. Betty showed her to the large room, where nearly twenty kids were already gathered, seated in chairs and on sofas.

The group was led by Dr. George Blair, the resident psychotherapist, and counselor Lori Cerasoli, a

past ASAP patient herself, who had already been designated Drew's individual counselor as well. Group,
as it was called, normally lasted one hour. That day's
session happened to be a "marathon" session, termed
such for its two-hour duration.

My first group was a marathon! Oh, God, I was thinking, please just
get me out of here. I don't want to be here. I was so miserable,
listening to people go on and on about their problems, one gripe
after another. They started out complaining mostly about the unit—
how people couldn't be trusted, they stabbed each other in the back
to get attention, people lying to each other.

Then Lori stopped the group and announced that there was a
new patient. There was a lot of audible grumbling, "Duuuh, we
know!"

I shrank in my chair and prayed she wouldn't say my name.
Don't even say my name, I thought. Don't even say part of it, please.

"Drew," she said.

I put my head down and sighed, "Fuck."

Then Lori went around the room and asked everyone to
introduce themselves to me. They'd say, "Hi, I'm so-and-so, and I'm
an addict. Or I'm an alcoholic." I nodded, "Hi." The scene struck
me as a little overly dramatic, and I was thinking, "Like I really want
to be meeting all of you in this situation. Maybe outside on the
street, but not in here."

Then Lori and Dr. Blair asked everyone how they felt about me
being there, and most everyone who said something expressed
concern that I was going to receive special treatment and too much
attention. When they made those comments, I wanted to give them
all the finger. Special attention was the last thing I wanted from any
of them. Given the chance, I would've walked at that moment.

"And how do you feel about being here, Drew?" Dr. Blair asked.

"Oh, I love it," I snapped sarcastically. But then I caught myself,
turned on the sweet little actress in me, and said, "I guess I do need
the help and I really understand."

But in my mind I was thinking, Fuck all of you. Like I really
want to be in here.

Drew was the walking embodiment of the word *alienation*. Everything about her said that. Her hunched, closed posture and tight-lipped reluctance to reveal the most basic emotions evidenced the angry thoughts that filled her mind. She told herself that she couldn't relate to anyone at the hospital. She knew that no one there would be able to understand her problems. The whole place, she thought, was "totally lame," and she spent that first night in the hospital unable to sleep.

The following evening Drew saw her mother for the first time since being admitted. Jaid was toting a suitcase of clothes, shoes, and personal articles. At first sight Drew felt as if she was going to be snapped out of a bad dream. Or that her mom was going to take her home from a slumber party. But that wasn't the case. She wasn't going home, and that rekindled the fury inside her.

Later that night Drew and Jaid attended their first multifamily group therapy session, an assembly of children and their parents, where everyone is encouraged to address the various issues discussed that session. Drew and Jaid wore all the telltale signs of first-timers. They walked in separately, not speaking. Drew, full of resentment, trailed behind, her eyes fixed to the ground. Jaid, saddled with tremendous guilt and looking as if she'd had the wind knocked out of her, was wrapped in a heavy coat and stared at the group from behind large sunglasses.

That was the first time I said, "Hi, I'm Drew. I'm an addict and alcoholic. And I have two days of sobriety."

But I was just mouthing words. Inside, I didn't believe any of that stuff. I was only obeying the rules.

Jaid says:

There wasn't really any communication between

Drew and me. Nor did we actively participate in that meeting. Instead, we sat there and began to see how the multifamily therapy functions, how people share, open their feelings and get feedback, and how they're encouraged to be straight with themselves and consequently with one another. Basically, you're taught to strip away all the facades and veneer with which you protect yourselves and, ultimately, harm yourselves and the people you love.

It wasn't so much that I felt hope after that initial meeting was over. Because I was neck-deep in confusion and trying to assimilate so much information that I didn't know what to think. But what I felt, which was very important for both Drew and me, is that we weren't freaks and we weren't alone. Instead, we were one of a great number of people who had exactly the same problems as we did. Not everyone else was functioning perfectly, as I often thought. Because there we were, among people from every walk of life, every income and social position, and we were all dealing with the same issues of drug and alcohol abuse.

Afterward, however, I felt terrible. Watching Drew leave was devastating. Without so much as a good-bye, she just walked back into the unit and the door closed behind her.

Instinctually, I felt that she needed me, that I should run after her and attend to her as a mother feels compelled to do. But they talked to me and told me to just leave her alone. They wanted to be able to work their program, to implement what they knew worked. If I was hovering, I would, as the ultimate codependent—the catalyst to Drew's bad behavior—be undoing all their effort. So I left and stayed away.

The intensive program required Drew to meet twice weekly with psychiatrist Dr. George Blair. In their first meeting Drew refused to talk about anything. She was wary, testing the doctor, and judging him. But every girl on her unit to whom she spoke about the young, handsome therapist had a secret crush on him, and on their second meeting Drew opened up.

I talked to him about being fat and ugly for the film *Far from Home,* which I had to go do in about a week. The movie, a murder mystery that involved me in almost every scene, called for me to do bikini shots, and I thought I looked too big and gross.

"Why do you feel that way?" he asked.

"Because I am," I said, starting to cry. "I mean, look at me. I hate myself."

"You hate yourself? Or the way you look?"

"Both."

"Well, why do you dislike yourself? Let's start with that."

"Nobody likes me," I sighed.

"And do you think that's really true? Nobody, absolutely nobody likes you?"

"Yes," I replied. "I mean no."

"Let's go back to you, then. You say that you don't like yourself, right?"

"Ah-huh," I nodded.

"Why?"

I took a deep breath, realized where Dr. Blair was leading me, and cried, "Oh, God, I don't want to do this."

Because film commitments allowed Drew only a brief stay at ASAP, an effort was made to pack in as much treatment as possible. So between the many group meetings each day and her twice-weekly individual sessions with Dr. Blair, Drew also took part in two hours of family therapy, which brought her into contact with her mother. To say Drew hated it is an understatement. But it was no easier on Jaid.

Family meetings were the most agonizing, the most tearful and acutely painful portion of the program. With Betty and Lori mediating, Drew and Jaid were led into a direct confrontation of the issues that had come between them, a confrontation that served as a fiery reintroduction between mother and daughter. The object was to strip away all the protective layers and lies they'd adopted over the years and to air their gripes with each other, to be raw and honest.

I was so angry I could hardly say anything. My responses varied from a terse yes or no to a venomous fuck-you. Finally, though, Lori said something that provoked a statement from my mother that caused me to scream, "Why the hell don't you be *just* my mother instead of my manager!"

"Drew, I don't think you could've said it any better," Lori applauded.

Jaid says:

We started touching on what my role was in pushing Drew to do what she did, and how my responses triggered her behavior and how her behavior triggered my responses. It was a snowball effect. Drew had tremendous resentment for the way I'd been dealing with her in life—all the yelling and screaming, which was due to my frustration.

Drew had this overwhelming feeling that I was very unsupportive and critical of her. She never heard what good I had to say about her. She heard only the bad. She felt that for many years I really tore down her self-image. That was a big issue with her.

And I was very angry because I didn't feel that way. I felt that I was trying to bolster her self-worth. We had a real difficulty in dealing with that. She saw it her way and I saw it mine.

Betty and Lori listened to us, and then pointed out that it was more important for me to not be so busy defending my perception of reality—in other words, arguing my point of view against Drew's. I wasn't listening, they said, to what was behind Drew's statements, to the need and the feeling, and to what she was *really* saying.

"Ask yourself," Betty said to me, "what Drew really means when she says, 'You're always putting me down. Or nobody likes me. Or be my mother, not my manager.' It's all the same. She's *really* saying, 'Hey, pay me a little attention. Slow down and love me. I need you.' "

The points were well made, but the breakthroughs were few. Time was too limited for that. Yet Drew gradually formed bonds with some of the other patients. Whether or not she wanted to, Drew, who sat through groups with an impassive expression and stoic demeanor, identified with a number of other kids and found herself touched by the program.

For more than a week I didn't say a word in any of the groups. I refused to utter a single syllable unless they asked something of me directly, and then I gave only the shortest answer I could think of.

But one day in group a girl began complaining about her parents and it struck a nerve. Her father constantly criticized her, she said, and her mother always made her do stuff she didn't want to. They made her life, she said, "pure hell." Well, I couldn't stand listening to that. I mean, my whole life I wanted a father, and this girl sounded so spoiled and obnoxious.

"Why don't you just be grateful that you have a mother and a father," I blurted out. "God, you disgust me. There are some people who would give their arm or leg to have two parents. You just get a little grateful, you know."

Everyone was shocked that I'd broken my silence. Someone even cracked a joke: "She can speak!" But no one was more surprised than I was. I hadn't planned to say anything. I'd been thinking that I was the worst case there. I'd convinced myself that no one could possibly understand my problems. That was one of my primary defenses. However, the more I sat in group, the more I realized there were others like me, and that was frightening. When I saw how wrong I was, it forced me to take a long, hard look at myself.

"There's a lot to think about, isn't there?" Betty asked as I was packing my suitcase.

"Yeah," I nodded. "But I'm trying."

"That's all you have to do," she smiled. "Just try."

Twelve days after checking in, Drew had to go on location. That was made clear from day one. Jaid had told them that Drew was committed to doing *Far from Home,* a murder-mystery, in Nevada and had to depart no later than July 10. Jaid promised that Drew would return to ASAP the day she landed back in Los Angeles, sometime in early September. In the interim, however, she didn't want to discard whatever benefits they'd already derived. So she asked for help.

ASAP hospital officials had never before handled a short-term emergency situation like Drew's, but they attempted to devise a makeshift plan, a rehab Band-Aid of sorts, designed to reinforce the insight and tools that Drew and Jaid had begun acquiring over the past week and a half. It was a simple plan. They assigned an ASAP tech to travel with Drew, a former patient, (as many techs were) who could function as a friend and confidante to the struggling actress.

In addition, Drew and Jaid were counseled that if there occurred a problem of any kind, whether Drew had the urge to break her sobriety or merely an argument with Jaid—anything that might tempt her into using—either one of them, or both, were to phone Betty. Immediately. Day or night, Betty emphasized, they were to call.

Believe it or not, I didn't want to leave. It surprised me. But I'd begun to form bonds with some of the kids, and with Betty, and I'd also started to feel the sense of safety and comfort that being in rehab tends to foster. Also, I guess, I feared being alone again, isolated from friends and any sort of fun.

However, I knew I had to go, and when that day arrived, I deluded myself into thinking that I was totally a brand-new person. That I was perfect. But . . . I wasn't.

ELEVEN

BUSTED: THE SEQUEL

The plane carrying Drew, Jaid, and their ASAP tech, Diane, landed in Gerlach, Nevada, early on the morning of July 11. Gerlach, a small, former mining outpost in the northern corner of the state, hadn't seen anything like the *Far from Home* movie crew since the gold rush days of the late 1800s. Overnight the local population of 350 was nearly doubled, which was good business for the town's several bars, where everyone gathered at night.

Except for me. I kept out of the bars. It wasn't difficult either. Which was surprising. If anyone had asked me one month earlier if I could've stayed sober for twelve days in a small town with just three bars and nothing else to do, I would've laughed and said, "No way."

However, not only did I survive, I had a pretty decent time being marooned in Gerlach. I hung out at the hotel and the laundromat, talked to my tech, with whom I shared a room, and got into my work for the first time since, well, since *Cat's Eye*. In that small a town it was pretty hard to get away from yourself—at least without everyone in town knowing about it—and the fact that I didn't blow my sobriety gave me a small measure of confidence that I was on the mend.

After nearly two weeks of residency in Gerlach, which crew members compared to being shipwrecked on a desert island, conditions improved markedly when the production moved to Carson City. By comparison, Carson City was a thriving metropolis, boasting hotels with room service and casinos and a round-the-clock nightlife similar to its larger Nevada cousin, Las Vegas.

There was suddenly a lot more action, and for the first time, I went to a casino. I dressed up like Scarlett O'Hara, turned on my sexy-girl act, and waltzed in with one of the crew members. Since I was doing pretty well, my mom didn't mind. Neither did the casino workers, who must've thought I was around twenty-two. Right off the bat I was offered a drink.

"No thanks," I said without a second thought.

I didn't need to drink. I was occupied. A crew member stuck a pair of dice in my hand and bellowed, "Stand back and let the lady throw. She's good luck." I was? How could I be when I didn't know what I was doing? I didn't even know the game was called craps. Even worse, everyone was watching me, waiting for the throw. Nervous, I clenched my teeth and let 'em rip. The dice flew right off the table. Fortunately, everyone laughed. "Oh, well," the croupier shrugged. "Try again."

Eventually, I got the hang of it and began having a great old time rolling the dice. Blackjack became my game. In no time I turned into an addict. I'd brought $20 with me, hoping to get into a casino. That night I played my $20 into a little over $200. Then the crew member who'd escorted me into the casino walked over, saw the pile of chips sitting in front of me, and let out a shrill, admiring whistle.

"You aren't lucky, kid, you're good," he said. "How 'bout trying the roulette table?"

"Sure," I said, scooping up my winnings and following him.

However, in less than fifteen minutes I was down to my original twenty bucks and heading back to my room. I'd lost nearly everything. I didn't mind losing the cash. It was worth it. I'd had lots of fun and I told Diane, my ASAP tech, about it. She listened, but she didn't seem happy when I let her in on my latest idea.

"If everyone down there thinks I'm older," I said, "maybe all the other clubs will fall for it too. We should try a few more of them."

"Tonight?" she asked.

"Tonight, tomorrow, the next night," I said. "It was lots of fun, and we're here for God knows how long."

"Drew," she intoned, "listen to what you're saying. You're convincing yourself that you're older. You aren't. You're thirteen years old. You're putting yourself in a dangerous position, falling back into that old line of thinking."

If my mother would've said that to me, I would've snapped at her and gone right ahead with my plan to hit the casinos and clubs. But Diane was different. That's why the hospital had sent her. For just that type of situation. We talked at length about what I was doing, and why, until I saw that I was getting back into that party-girl frame of mind.

For the first time in years I exercised some self-control. It was hard. Painful, in fact. Though I didn't break my sobriety, I still hung out with everybody on the crew in the various bars and casinos, and when one of my friends would order a drink, I'd stare at it, feeling incredibly anxious, like I wanted to grab the glass and down it. But I didn't. I really wanted to be sober. It was a constant tug-of-war in an extremely boring time.

The movie wrapped September 5 and Drew flew back to Los Angeles the next afternoon. That night a girl-friend drove her back to the ASAP hospital. She'd been away for almost two months.

It was about eleven o'clock, maybe closer to midnight when I walked back into the hospital. I was so incredibly angry that I had to be back there. I acted nice and friendly on the outside, but I was so upset that on the very day I'd flown in I had to go back in. Where's my fun, I thought. I've been missing my friends for a long time and I have to come back to this stinking prison. No way.

I didn't want to face that I was still as much an addict as when I first entered the hospital. Even though I hadn't been drinking or doing drugs, I had still been hanging around with a crowd that did.

Later I learned that's called dry time.

The morning after I checked back into the hospital I was given a school assignment to write an essay describing the difference between dry and sober time. They must've been waiting to teach me that lesson, because I didn't have a clue to what it meant.

"So ask around," my teacher said. "Look it up. That's the whole point."

The paper was due the next morning, which meant I spent the rest of the day asking people around the hospital and in my groups what the difference between dry and sober time was. I really did try to learn something. "Dry time," I wrote, "is when you continue to sit around the things you're trying to get away from, like drugs and alcohol, and your feelings are still very much involved. You don't work a program, go to meetings, or even discuss it."

"So you may not be using," the teacher said, "but you're continuing to satisfy your addiction."

On September 12, after a brief hospital stay of six days, Drew, against medical advice, flew to New York with her mother to loop dialogue for the movie *See You in the Morning* and to audition for a play. She was contractually obligated to work on the movie. The play was icing and anticipated her successful treatment and release sometime in the fall. Jaid didn't think six days in Manhattan would be detrimental to Drew's treatment. It wasn't the best situation, but she appeared to be doing well and she'd be back in the hospital in a week.

However, although Drew hadn't touched a drink or any drugs for seventy-six days, on the plane she had a bad premonition about the trip. "I was real afraid something bad was going to happen to me," she recalls.

And it did. On September 15.

Late that night Stacy and I decided to go to one of our favorite nightclubs. From the moment I returned to New York, Stacy and I fell back into our same routine of hanging out at her place, except for one big difference: We didn't drink or get high. And until that night we hadn't gone out to any clubs. But I didn't think that was a big deal, and when the subject of going there was raised, I was all for it.

We got there about eleven and sometime around twelve, I spotted one of Bobby's friends. I asked if he was going to show up, and his friend said yes, sometime, but he didn't know exactly when. I got excited. We hadn't spoken and I wanted to see him.

A bunch of us went into the ladies' room and one of the girls asked me, "Do you do blow?"

"No, no, I stopped that." I shook my head.

She already had a little packet of cocaine out of her purse and open, ready to dole out lines.

"You don't mind if we do it in front of you, do you?" she asked.

I thought it was pretty rude of her to continue, but I wanted to be cool and said, "It's okay, guys. Go ahead."

But it obviously didn't bother me that much since I didn't put up much of a fuss. Nor did I leave when they started snorting lines. Instead, I stood there and watched enviously as they inhaled, felt the burn of the coke, and then turned lively and giddy.

"Are you sure you don't want any?" the girl asked me again.

At that moment I started to cry. I felt really, really sad, overcome by sadness. I looked at my watch and blew it right there. It was 12:37 and I was supposed to be home in a few minutes. But I didn't care. I was tired and I thought, well, a little coke will wake me right up. Why bother with a cup of coffee? So I did a line. And then another.

After taking those two quick hits, I started shaking, knowing that I had just blown all my days. Even though they were dry, I was really proud of them. I got really scared and thought to myself, "Oh, God, you just had seventy-eight days sober, and now you don't even have one minute." I waited there in the bathroom, feeling really scared. When I walked out I feared everyone would know I'd blown all my sobriety. But when I looked around, everyone was smiling at me. Stacy saw something was wrong right away.

"You know what I just did?" I said.

"What?"

"I just blew my sobriety."

"No way, Drew."

"It's true," I said, half crying and half laughing. "They're going to know when they take a urinalysis at the hospital," I said. "They're going to know I did coke. Oh, God, they're going to know and I'm going to be shit."

I started freaking out, mumbling all sorts of things, crying and babbling, until Stacy grabbed my shoulders and shook me.

"Drew, get hold of yourself," she urged.

It was a crazy scene. In the midst of this crowded dance floor, with music blaring and people knocking shoulders with us, we were screaming at each other about sobriety and cocaine and boyfriends and curfews and rehab hospitals. When I think back on it, the whole thing seems surreal.

"As long as they're going to know," I told Stacy, "I might as well do some more."

She argued against it, and I asked her to do some with me. She didn't want to. She wanted to support my sobriety. But I put her in a tough position and, best friends being best friends, she caved in.

We knew a guy at the club who happened to be dealing coke, but when I approached him, he said he wouldn't sell me less than a gram. That was okay with me. I flashed a bunch of cash that I'd saved over the summer, money that had been part of my per diem on *Far from Home,* and we made the exchange in a dark corner. A few minutes later we did a line each, and then waited for Bobby to show. He never did. We hung around the club till just before dawn and then went out to breakfast.

Stacy and I were laughing hysterically when we returned to my condo about 7:30 A.M., but the minute I put my key in the door, I got real scared. Despite the drugs, it was extremely hard for me to have fun. In the back of my mind I kept seeing my mother and thinking about how much I was hurting her. Did it stop me? No. But the minute I opened the door and saw her, the laughter died and I got frightened.

I told her that I'd been at Stacy's all night. She believed me and the three of us talked for about two hours. But the conversation was all so fake. Even though my mother and I had spent several months becoming more aware of our relationship, working on our various problems, the fact that there was cocaine in my pocket suddenly put that old wall up between us. But this time, instead of blaming her, I knew that I was responsible for the hurt I was generating.

Finally, Stacy and I went into my bedroom and looked at each other.

"Do you realize what a big one we just pulled on her?" I said. "She had no idea!"

But at the same time, we both added, "God, I feel so bad."

Later that day Mom and Stacy went shopping while I rested. When they returned I took a credit card from my mom's wallet, then told her I had to return this clock that I'd bought the day before. She said fine. We were getting along really well and there was no reason to be suspicious. Then I pulled Stacy into the bathroom and flashed the credit card. "Remember the fantasy we always had?" I smiled devilishly.

We shared a fantasy, hatched over alcohol and pot, of getting on an airplane to Hawaii on the spur of the moment with nothing but our credit card and handbags.

"How could I forget?" she smiled.

"Let's do it," I said, figuring that with my sobriety blown I had nothing to lose. "I've got the credit card . . ."

". . . and we've got the drugs," she said, finishing the sentence. "Okay, let's do it."

We walked back out and I told my mother that I'd be back in an hour or so. She said good-bye. Then, without giving it a second thought, Stacy and I ran downstairs, hailed a cab, and slid inside. We looked at each other and at the same time said, "LaGuardia Airport." Forty-five minutes later we were there, and I was standing in line at the ticket counter. "Two tickets to Los Angeles, please," I smiled.

The woman behind the counter gave me a suspicious look, like "Where's your mother, little girl?" but I suddenly changed from Drew, this teenager with cocaine in her pocket who was fleeing her mother, into Drew Barrymore, the actress, complete with sweet voice and innocent eyes.

"You wouldn't believe it," I chuckled, embarrassed, "but I've got to be in L.A. at seven tomorrow for a business meeting. I can't cope with these last minute changes, the hassle . . ."

She nodded and I handed her the American Express card. A moment later she looked puzzled again.

"How come it says Ildyko Barrymore on the card?" she asked.

"Oh, that," I said, dreaming up an explanation pronto. "Well, you see, my purse was stolen a few weeks ago, and this guy tried to rob my house. Things like this are always happening to celebrities, you know. And so I thought it best to put a different name on the card."

"Sure, I understand," she nodded, and put the card through.

Five minutes later Stacy and I were walking to the boarding area, tickets in hand.

"Do you really want to live the fantasy?" I asked.

"Yeah, sure."

"Well, since the lady at the ticket counter was so gullible," I said, "let's buy two tickets to Hawaii for tomorrow."

Stacy was up for it. So we ran back to the ticket counter and purchased two tickets to Hawaii, leaving from Los Angeles the next day. It was even easier than the first time too. The guy who sold them to me hardly looked up from his computer screen. Then I telephoned my mother.

"Where are you, Drew?" she said with obvious irritation.

"Oh, I'm out to dinner with Stacy," I apologized. "I'm sorry. I know I'm screwing up, but I'll be home soon."

"In an hour."

"Fine, an hour or so," I said.

We had a brief stopover in St. Louis and I called my mom again.

"Where are you?" she asked.

"I'm around," I answered in a sickeningly sweet voice. "But it's okay. I'm fine."

"When are you going to be back?" she asked.

"Around three."

She said fine, and I began to hedge and push for a later time.

"Maybe six or nine tomorrow morning."

"If you aren't back by tomorrow morning, I'm calling the cops."

"Oh, just give me till until two in the afternoon," I pleaded, and when she gave in, I figured, "Well, if she'll settle for two, I can push for six later and go on with this forever," and we hung up on a friendly note.

About seven hours after we'd embarked on this trip, Stacy and I were walking through the front door of my condo in Los Angeles. At the end of summer my mother had sold our old house and bought a smaller, two-bedroom place that was easier to maintain. We blasted the stereo, got dressed in some of my fancy clothes, and decided to take my mom's BMW to go out to dinner. So we started downstairs in our dresses, clutching our little purses, which contained our money and credit card and drugs, and when we got to the garage, I said, "Oh, shit, my set of keys to the car are at the hospital."

"There's got to be an extra set somewhere," Stacy said. "Your mom is the type to hide a spare key."

Half an hour later I found the extra key. Stacy and I got back in the car. But the iron gate locking the parking lot wouldn't open and we couldn't find the door opener. My mom, it turned out, had inadvertently taken it to New York in her purse. So we went back inside to search for a spare opener. After nearly an hour we were about to give up when I said, "Hold on, let me get some more lipstick." It was a fortunate decision. I opened my mom's makeup drawer and there, right next to the lipstick, was the opener. "God," I said, "I guess You meant for me to do this."

I really thought He did. Everything was lining up so perfectly.

After dinner I called my mother and told her in the same sickeningly sweet tone of voice that I'd be home soon. But this time she didn't buy it.

"That's it, I'm calling the cops," she said.

All of a sudden my tone of voice turned acidy. "Do whatever the hell you want," I shouted. "See if I care."

She hung up the phone, and I knew right then that this fantasy was turning into a nightmare. A few moments later I tried calling my mom back, thinking I could convince her to forget about calling the police. By then, however, the telephone in our New York condo had been disconnected, or unplugged, and she was on her way to the airport. It turned out that she had called Stacy's sister and found out from her that we were in Los Angeles, though I had no idea.

"I know my mom," I told Stacy in a panic. "She's too smart for my shit. Let's get out of here."

We grabbed some bags out of my closet, threw a bunch of clothes inside, chucked them in the car, and took off. Even though it was around two or three in the morning, I headed for a friend's house, but took a wrong turn and ended up on Hollywood Boulevard and found myself being tailgated by a cop. Both of us started to freak because we had cocaine sitting on the dashboard, and the cop pulled up alongside the car.

"What should I do, Drew?" Stacy asked. "Inhale the whole thing or brush it on the ground?"

I don't know why I retained such presence of mind, but I said, "Very gently put your hands on the dashboard, fold up the packet, and put it in your pocket."

We finally arrived at my friend's house, but it was so late we ended up falling asleep in the car. In the morning we discovered that she was out of the country. So we went back to my house and slept a few more hours. When I got up, it was with a sick feeling that my mother knew what was going on. Talk about paranoia. I felt we had to get out of the house. We fled, first to a friend's house, where we bought some more coke—a transaction that was completed in my friend's bedroom while his parents were hosting a brunch—and then we set off for another friend's apartment.

I'm a good driver. I learned from an older friend when I was nine. But at that point I'd had too much coke. When I tried to parallel-park in front of the apartment complex, I bashed both cars, in front and back. It would've been a bad scene under any circumstance—two dented cars. But there was a garage sale right in front, and about thirty people witnessed the accident. I began beating the steering wheel, crying, "No, no, no! This is not happening!"

Only one of the other car owners was there. I gave him my address and told him I'd pay whatever it cost to fix his car. Then I left a hastily written note on the other car, and Stacy and I darted into my friend's apartment. She saw how ragged we were and asked if anything was wrong. I said, "Don't ask," and then went into her mom's bathroom and did four lines of coke. Stacy came in a minute later and did a few lines too. We looked at each other and started to laugh.

The situation struck us as funny, scary funny, and both of us, nervous and exhausted, recognized it. At that point I was so miserable that I actually entertained the idea of driving straight to the hospital. I wanted to. I realized that I was on a crash course with disaster. But I didn't know what to do with Stacy. At least, that's what I told myself. Our only realistic choice, at that time, seemed to be returning to my house, where we did some more coke.

In the euphoric daze of the coke, we decided to go to the mall. Our logic was simple: What was the point of having a credit card if you weren't going to shop? We hurried off to the stores on Ventura Boulevard, but on the way I had a feeling that my mom might've canceled the card. Or maybe she hadn't yet, but was going to. In a hurry, we grabbed clothes off the rack without even trying them on and threw them down on the counter, where the girl at the cash register recognized me. We chatted and she put the charge through without checking for authorization. But we weren't so fortunate at the next store.

"This card's been reported stolen," the woman said.

"Are you kidding?" I bluffed. "I had a mixup with my mother last week. She didn't know I had the card and called it in stolen, but I thought all that was straightened out."

"Apparently not," she said.

"Fine," I said, motioning Stacy to the door. "We're in a hurry. Thank you."

At home we cranked the stereo in my bedroom and began trying on all our new clothes. When I saw that we had about an hour and a half before our plane left for Hawaii, I started rushing around, trying to get ready. However, before we left I wanted to finish the coke. I'd passed through the airport metal detector in New York with the coke wrapped in a tiny bit of aluminum foil, and even though nothing happened, I realized that was potentially serious trouble. I didn't want to risk it.

"There're about twelve lines," I said. "Why don't you do four and I'll do the rest."

"Come on, Drew," she shook her head, "that's too much for you."

Nonetheless, we did about four lines each, catching a buzz that had our hearts racing, while still leaving just a small amount, which I stuck in my jeans pocket before taking off those pants. When I left the bathroom to change into another outfit, a strange man and woman were standing in my room.

"Who the fuck are you?" I said, thinking they were cops.

"I'm a friend," the woman replied.

"Well, friend," I screamed, "get out of here until I'm dressed."

"I'm sorry, I can't do that," she said, pulling out a pair of handcuffs from her pocket.

"Oh, shit," I thought, "here's the nightmare I've always feared, happening right before my eyes." But as they walked me outside with my hands cuffed behind my back, they revealed they were private agents hired by my mother to take me back to the hospital. When I realized I wasn't going to jail, I heaved a big sigh of relief. Stacy said she was going to wait at my house, and as I passed her at the door, she said, "I love you." I said, "I love you too," and both of us started to cry.

Driving over to the hospital, the agents started asking me about my movies, which I thought was sick. "God, you've just yanked me out of my house with cuffs on," I thought, "and now you're asking me what it was like to meet E.T. What jerks." I refused to say a word the rest of the drive. When we arrived at the admitting hall, they finally unlocked the handcuffs. Then, believe it or not, they asked me for my autograph.

TWELVE

"HI, I'M DREW AND I'M . . ."

The minutes passed like hours. Drew could almost hear the creaking of gears as the red second hand on the wall clock in the ASAP office swept around the dial. She turned her head from side to side, checking out the hospital scene. There were a bunch of new kids whom she didn't recognize, and she averted her eyes from those whom she knew. She was too exhausted to do any more than breathe, and even that was a bit taxing on her system. Strung out, sweating, and shaking, Drew imagined herself coming to the end of a long, tedious script, stopping on the final three words, "Fade to black."

"Are you okay?" a tech asked as he passed by the seated girl.

Drew mumbled something he couldn't make out.

"What?" he asked, puzzled.

"Fade to black," she muttered again. "That's what you write at the end of a movie."

I had the feeling that I'd just sat through an absolutely horrible movie, a real low-class action-adventure flick. The characters weren't likable and the ending didn't have a resolution. The entire experience was a living nightmare.

I was seated in the dining room. Everything was shaking back and forth. My eyes refused to focus clearly on anything. I tried laying low, but people who knew me from before started coming up to me and asking, "What's up?" I shrugged. A nurse came by and asked if I wanted anything to eat. Did I? For little more than three days I really hadn't eaten or slept.

"How about ordering a pizza?" she smiled. "And we'll take your vitals while the kitchen is making it."

My temperature was 102 degrees. I was dehydrated and down about five pounds from when I'd left New York. My hair was all matted and I was shivering from cold sweats, agitated, and yet too weary to even sit up straight in my chair. While the nurse continued her cursory examination, two girls I knew sat down next to me.

"What happened to you?" one of them asked.

"I fucking booked from New York," I laughed. "All I had were the clothes on my back and a credit card."

I thought I was way cool, but they looked at me and then at each other as if I were pathetic. Then my friend Edie, a girl with whom I'd grown extremely close during my previous hospitalization, pulled up a chair. She studied me up and down for the longest time without saying a word, which made me feel paranoid.

"What?" I said annoyed.

"How much sobriety do you have?" she asked.

I was going to lie. I was going to open my mouth and say, "Eighty-three days," or whatever the number was. But I knew the hospital was going to run a urine test in a few moments and then everyone would see all the coke I'd done. If I lied, Edie would find out later when it was brought up in group. I was trapped and didn't know what to say. I looked at the clock and, still reeling from all the coke I'd snorted earlier, imagined the face popping out like a figure from a Salvador Dali painting and saying, "Don't lie, bitch!"

I didn't want to answer her, but I knew I had to. They could all see right through me because they'd been working their programs and trying to get better, and I couldn't bullshit them. What should I say, I wondered. As my friends all waited expectantly for my answer, I was overwhelmed by a wave of fear.

"Twenty minutes," I whispered, and lowered my head so I wouldn't have to face their stares. "Twenty minutes of sobriety."

"Fuck, man," I heard Edie say. "She had it going so good too."

I ventured a quick glance at their faces and they were all looking at me with sadness in their eyes. It was the most severe punishment. Unable to bear their scrutiny, I bolted from the dining room, locked myself in the first empty dorm room I found, and prayed for a magic power that would allow me to disappear.

Later that night the ASAP routine was spelled out for her again in the same painfully detailed speech she'd heard months earlier. This time it was delivered with an even sterner tone that underscored the gravity of her situation. Drew wanted nothing more than to shut everything she was hearing out of her life.

Half an hour later, unbridled anger had replaced the drugs she'd ingested. Back in the dining room, Drew had gone off the deep end. Taking offense at the way another patient had been treated by several techs, she threw a temper tantrum so great that four techs were needed to wrestle her to the ground.

Restraints, not commonly used at ASAP, had just been placed on Drew when her therapist, Betty Wyman, and counselor, Lori Cerasoli, arrived after being called in from their day off. Drew saw them, sighed, "Oh, shit," and calmed down. "I felt really manipulated," Wyman recalls. "Therapeutically, I believe she felt so guilty and so shamed over breaking her sobriety that she had to let us know. Basically, it was just a display by a little girl who wanted the moms in her life, Lori and I, to come in and tell her, 'Hey, it's okay. We love you.' "

The remainder of the evening passed uneventfully, and Drew was awakened by a cautious tech at 7:30 the following morning. She cleaned her room, ate breakfast, and was in school by five minutes to nine. She picked a seat in the back corner, which became her permanent place, and rested her head on the desk. At noon, instead of eating lunch in the dining room, she carried her tray into the ASAP office, where she sat by herself in a corner.

Isolation was my big problem. I didn't want to be where anybody else was. I felt so unsafe. The only two places where I felt comfortable, which is a stretch of the word, were my room and the back corner of the ASAP office. It took me a long time to adjust to being around people.

Indeed, for several days Drew was a withdrawn shell of the individual who had begun participating in groups and among the patients on her ward the previous July. She resembled that person only in appearance. In group she sat with her knees drawn tight to her chest, her arms clenched and her head lowered.

In this one group, where everyone was talking about their problems, Lori suddenly interrupted the flow and said, "Okay, now we're going to do something else." Then she turned toward me, though I wouldn't make eye contact with her, and said, "Drew, now that you've been on your escapade and broken your sobriety and set yourself back as far as possible . . ."

As I listened, I called her every swear word in the book. I knew Lori was about to drag me through the embarrassment, the shame, and everything else you go through when you're made to own up in front of everyone. It's a real do-or-die moment where you're backed into a corner. You can no longer pretend you're not there, you can't hide, and, worst of all, you can't pitch a bunch of bullshit in front of a group that's expert at bullshitting. You have only one choice: to tell the truth.

"So Drew," Lori said, "let's be honest here—something that you don't know that much about—but let's try it."

"What?" I scoffed.

"I just want you to answer this one simple question," she said. "Have you hit your bottom?"

I understood what hitting bottom meant. It's a phrase that's used throughout treatment and especially in AA. Countless times I'd heard people explain that you couldn't begin the process of recovery until you had hit bottom. If you hadn't, you were just paying lip service to all the groups and programs you participated in. But once you knew, people said, it was suddenly like opening a window on a gloomy day and letting in a ray of bright light.

I looked at her. My impulse was to run out of the group and hide in the closet in my bedroom. But I didn't. I think that moment will be crystallized in my mind forever. At that moment, I realized that I knew what hitting bottom felt like.

"Yes," I said in a voice that was barely audible. "Yes, I've hit my bottom."

She wasn't alone. Jaid felt as if she, too, had hit bottom. When she arrived back in Los Angeles, she immediately telephoned Betty Wyman, who filled her in on Drew's condition. Jaid wondered when she could visit Drew. Betty didn't know. If treatment was going to work, she said, unlike the past time Drew was at ASAP, Jaid was going to have to abide by some strict limits. Drew couldn't leave for movies or interviews. Her recovery had to be the number-one priority.

Betty also established herself as Drew's in-house manager, taking over what had previously been Jaid's responsibility. "Drew was going out the first time she was in," Betty says. "She and Jaid were treating this almost as if it were hotel ASAP. But this time her stay wasn't going to be like a guest-spot appearance."

Jaid agreed. "I just wanted Drew to get better. I needed to get better myself. I'd hit my own personal bottom as well. Both of our lives had to focus entirely on recovery and nothing else. That I saw clearly."

For Drew, it was nothing short of a revelation. She sat in her room that night and in her mind replayed the scene from group. "Have you hit your bottom?" she heard Lori ask over and over.

After that I became aware of what my situation really was. I saw the amount of work I had to do. I knew that I'd hit my bottom. That's how people get into the program. Knowing that made me recognize how similar I was to everyone else in the hospital. We'd all hit our bottom.

My thinking was radically altered by that realization. Before, my attitude had been that no one could understand me. No one could relate to me. I was totally different and I couldn't relate to them. But once I saw that we all shared a similar experience, I thought, "Well, maybe I can relate to them. Maybe I am just like them."

In subsequent groups, even though I still didn't talk that much, I began to listen. From that, I became aware of people's problems— my own included. Once I started to listen, I couldn't help but reflect on my own problems. And slowly, I began to try. I wouldn't show anything outwardly. After a while, though, I saw myself progressing and it was feeling really good. "Maybe you should try being really open," I thought to myself. "Take a risk. Be honest."

"Write down your issues," Dr. Blair told Drew during one of their early sessions. It was Drew's first written assignment since being back. Identify ten issues that need exploration, he said, thus beginning the initial process of recovery, which, basically, consists of confronting and then resolving the issues that caused her addiction in the first place.

In no particular order of importance, this is what I wrote:

1. working out problems with my mom
2. working out problems with my dad
3. getting to know myself
4. overcoming my little and big fears
5. learning to deal with rules
6. accepting things I can't change
7. facing the real world
8. respecting people, places, and things
9. sex
10. boyfriends versus father figures

I wrote that all on my own, without any help or suggestions from Dr. Blair, and when I looked back over the list, two things shocked me. One, my honesty. That I was owning up to myself marked a big change. And two, I was amazed that when I looked deep within my bruised and battered self, I saw these things so clearly, as if they had already been written out and were waiting for me to come stumbling upon them.

"Looking at that list," Dr. Blair asked, "what can you tell me about yourself?"

"Uh, that I have trouble relating to people?" I answered hesitantly.

"Okay," he smiled. "Why do you think that is?"

Braced to tell the truth, I said, "Because I don't like myself all that much. Because I think of myself as this lowly, unworthy creature."

He shut his notepad, signaling the end of our session.

"If you don't like yourself, or respect yourself," he said, "then it becomes difficult to like and respect other people."

Drew was wondering where her mother was. At some point each day, Drew expected to be summoned to the reception desk, where she'd find Jaid standing with a supply of new clothes. After all, Drew hadn't seen Jaid since she'd walked out of their condo in New York. Nor had she spoken to her since their last conversation—whenever that was—which had been no

more than a cocaine-flavored singsong that ended with
a rancorous hangup on both sides.

"I feel empty," I wrote in another paper Dr. Blair assigned me,
"because I feel that I've now lost everything. I mean, I lost my dad a
long time ago, but now the one person, the only person I have, is
my mom, and now I have lost her too. I finally pushed her too far,
and now she's gone. I hope that I will have her back in my life. I
feel like I have nobody. I don't know where my friends are. I don't
even know who they are. I feel as if I've lost the only true friend in
my life, my mom. I've never gone this long without seeing her. Or
at least talked to her on the phone. I used to want to get away from
her all the time, but now that she's away, I feel horrible."

Finally, after some determined pestering, Lori told
Drew that her mother hadn't abandoned her. Actually,
Lori said, Jaid was in New York, where she was carrying on with her life. The news nearly caused Drew to
turn blue in the face with anger. If she had to suffer
through the constant demands of the hospital, then
she wanted her mother to suffer too. Drew didn't want
her mom to enjoy herself in her old stomping grounds
while she was a virtual prisoner.
    Two weeks passed without a word. Then . . .
    "You've got multifamily tonight," Betty unexpect-
edly announced to Drew one afternoon.
    "What?" Drew replied surprised. "Don't I have to
go with my mom?"
    "She'll be there," she said.

Even though I had missed her, I was pissed. For the first time I felt
as if I were doing good, like I was stretching and really attempting
to express myself honestly. Then my mom reappeared and all the
negative feelings I had been harboring toward her came back also.
    "Hi," I said to her with obvious disdain in my voice.

"Hello, Drew," she smiled.

My mom was still quite angry with me too. I sensed that much, but I was more concerned with punishing her for all the pain and hurt I felt she was inflicting on me, not to mention those recent feelings of abandonment. However, nothing I did—dirty looks, snide, sharp, sarcastic remarks—nothing got a rise out of her. No matter what I tried, she wasn't allowing me to manipulate her, or, as they say in the hospital, "feeding into my bullshit."

Seated beside each other, we might as well have been strangers. The unspoken tension between us was palpable to everyone in the room. We didn't say a word—to each other or the group—and that hour-and-a-half session was one of the longest, most tedious ninety-minute periods of my life.

"So I guess I'll see you later," I said at the end, trying to sound unaffected by our strained relations.

My mom looked at me with such sorrow in her eyes that I really wanted to reach out and hug her. And I bet that's what she felt like doing too. But we were too angry with each other to show such emotion. We had to relearn how to express ourselves before we could hug and truly feel it.

"Good-bye, Drew," my mom said in a restrained tone of voice that echoed her injury.

I turned and walked back into the ward. That was how our relationship continued over the course of the next few months. Unless it was in family session or multifamily, she never called. She never even came to visit me. I couldn't believe it. If I asked her to bring me some things, she replied, "When I have time." Which meant no.

The estrangement was unnerving. I'd never gone more than a day or two without seeing my mother. And before this, I don't think an entire day had ever passed without us at least speaking on the telephone. It reinforced all my feelings of abandonment and of being unloved. God, was I ever pissed.

Jaid was being kept away from Drew for a reason. The staff wanted to spend a concentrated amount of time working on Drew herself. They'd ease into the family therapy. Betty and Dr. Blair believed Drew had to confront herself first. She had to be dragged, kicking and screaming if need be, into the harsh glare of reality.

ASAP's daily schedule was unremitting in its intensity. After school and lunch, Drew, along with the others, sat through Therapy Group, primarily a discussion of what everyone was feeling. Then everyone was shuffled into Doctor's Group, moderated by the staff psychiatrist, which was essentially a continuation of therapy group. Following that was Step Study, which focused on one of Alcoholic Anonymous's Twelve Steps.

This long afternoon was followed by a series of less taxing activities, including stress management, anger reduction, biofeedback, and physical conditioning. "These are all things," therapist Betty Wyman explains, "to gear the young addict or alcoholic into means of dealing with problems other than self-medicating. They're taught that when they have problems, they can share in groups, exercise, listen to relaxation tapes, and work on AA steps. They don't need to get high to feel better."

But the day wasn't over yet. Recovery group, a problem-solving session that wrapped up the day, followed dinner, and after that patients were siphoned off to substance abuse programs, like Cocaine Anonymous and AA, depending on their particular problems. Additionally, once a week Drew and Jaid met to participate in Multiple Family Group, an innovation unique to ASAP but since copycatted by other treatment centers, where patients and parents collectively discuss their issues as a single community.

Multifamily is often likened to an emotional roller coaster that replaces inhibition with insight. Discussions ricochet from anger to sadness to uncontrollable laughter, all exposing the unpredictable nature of family life. "It's absolutely the most powerful dynamic I've witnessed in terms of recovery," Betty Wyman says. "Most people enter into treatment believing they're the only ones in the world who have these problems. But multifamily takes them out of that isolation, which is one of the most debilitating factors of addiction, and into scenarios similar to theirs."

The basic issues Drew needed to confront—low self-esteem, depression, relationships with her mother and family, her difficulties with the opposite sex— were obvious, even to her. She became adept at identifying those various issues that had led her down the path to drug and alcohol abuse. Articulating and working through the next step required a far more dramatic leap than Drew had ever taken.

Drew's counselor, Lori Cerasoli, needed only a single word to explain how Drew could accomplish that. "Honesty," she said. "Honesty is the biggest part of working your program."

"Working a program," a phrase Drew heard often, meant different things to each patient, but the crux of it boiled down to the same primary element: staying sober. To Lori, a recovering addict herself, working a program meant "the difference between life an death." To others, it was defined by the original Twelve Steps of Alcoholics Anonymous.

"But with a kid like Drew," Lori says, "I don't even try to explain what working a program means. With Drew, when something came up, I threw a step in her direction and we worked to understand that. Otherwise, working a program was understood to mean honesty and communication. Basically, it was— and is—talking about all those things she'd never been allowed to talk about."

Everything I did was designed to get me in touch with my feelings, to confront myself. It was something I'd avoided for years. "Write a list," they constantly told me, and I swear, I made lists till they were coming out of my ears. One day, for instance, Lori asked me to make a list of things I was willing to do in the hospital. "And be honest," she intoned. This is what I wrote:

My Priorities in the Hospital

1. work a program
2. stay sober
3. deal with my dad
4. deal with my mom
5. find out who I am
6. deal with my fears
7. live up to my own expectations, not others
8. abide by rules
9. deal with my age and not growing up too fast

When I compared this list to the list of issues I'd made three or four weeks earlier, I saw that they virtually overlapped except for two monumentally important additions: working a program and staying sober. "What do you think that means?" Lori asked.

"That I'm being honest with myself," I replied.

"Yeah," she nodded. "And what else?"

I didn't know.

"That you want to live," she smiled. "That you've got a vested interest in your own life."

In reality, the picture wasn't as rosy as it appeared on paper. Changes occurred subtlely, almost imperceptibly, in the textures of Drew's mind. As Betty Wyman says: "Progress was inconsistent." There were good days when Drew tuned into what was going on. But for weeks on end the bad days outnumbered the good. She didn't want to get out of bed. She balked at attending school. Worse still, Drew received "goodbye" letters from several close friends, a ritual connected with discharge from ASAP, which sent her into a depression.

All my friends were leaving—maybe not all—but that's what I imagined. What really bothered me about their departures was that there was still no end in sight to my hospitalization. For a brief time I felt as if I didn't have any close friends in whom I could confide. Then this guy came in and for some reason I liked him. I don't know why. His name was Rick. He had blond hair, blue eyes, and was real tough, a gangster type with a lengthy criminal record. Not a good person, basically, but that was the kind of guy I was attracted to. It was part of my self-destructive tendencies.

Rick was always kind of rude to me. But one night I confronted him in the hallway and we sat and talked for about an hour and a half. A few days later, we exchanged notes, which eventually led to us secretly becoming boyfriend and girlfriend. We couldn't ever do anything, though, or we weren't supposed to, since it was against the rules to SAO—sexually act out.

Unfortunately, once I started to like him, the little progress I'd been making disappeared as all my issues with males came back. I saw guys as the answer to my problems with low self-esteem. I obsessed on winning their affection. I had to prove I was worthy of their love. Of course, in the process, I ended up hurt more often than not.

Rick proved no different. With my mind fixated on his dreamy eyes and long blond hair, I lost control of myself. Even though I knew he wasn't a great guy, I ceased to care about anything except his attention and finding the satisfying love my father never gave me. The consequence of that was disastrous: Everything I'd been working on, everything that had made sense to me, suddenly went down the tubes and I became a hellion again. I quit sharing in groups, working in school. I got put on something the hospital called a "male communication freeze," which meant that I couldn't talk to any males in the hospital, and that lasted for a few weeks. It was supposedly to help me explore my problems with boyfriends and relationships.

The freeze ended the day before a weekend dance, where we planned to see each other. Through friends, Rick and I arranged to meet in a storage room, where we planned to finally kiss. After weeks, we still hadn't gone past exchanging notes or stealing glances. When none of the techs were looking, both of us slipped into the pitch-dark room, but instead of kissing, we just talked in excited, breathy whispers. Still, a tech caught us, which cost us any future privileges we might've been expecting on upcoming weekends. Ticked off in a major way, I ran into an adjoining room, locked the door, and started to climb out the window. I was going to bolt from the hospital. AWOL as it's called. Unfortunately, the tech nabbed me again, and this time they gave me three days of ITP, which was a huge drag.

Intensive treatment program. Three behavior violations earned the dreaded ITP, which confined a patient to their room in place of free periods between scheduled activities. It was nothing more than being grounded, part of the hospital's effort to enforce definite limits to the patient's behavior, something that was often lacking at home. The worst part of ITP, Drew thought, was having to write out the assignments she was given as part of her punishment. Her first topic: Is Rick just another number on your long list?

"Well, to be completely honest," I wrote, "he really isn't. I feel like I'm completely in love with him. I'm probably not really in love, but I care about him so much. In a way, I regret what I did last night. But to me, Rick is worth it. Sometimes when I see him, or think about him, I get scared that he's screwing around with my head. He tells me that he loves me and I believe him. But I'm scared of getting hurt."

In her first month and a half, Drew was slapped with ITP more than fifteen times. It was a hospital record as well as irrefutable evidence of her lack of self-control and the wanton way in which she exercised restraint over her various impulses. Her infractions varied from general tardiness to an unkempt room to smoking cigarettes in her bedroom, which wasn't allowed.

Among the worst of her violations was being caught making out in Rick's bedroom.

I was sneaking down the long hall, feeling so sly and smart as I sprinted back to my own side of the ward. When I heard over the loudspeaker—and I do mean *loud*speaker—"DREW! Get to the ASAP office NOW!" I changed directions, then opened the office door, where I was greeted by one very unhappy, unsympathetic tech. "What were you doing in Rick's room?" he asked.

"I wasn't in there," I said in a bitchy tone. "So get off my case."

"You were caught," he snapped. "You've got ITP . . . again."

"Shit!"

"Go to your room," he said, "and no passing Room Four"— which was Rick's room—"on your way there."

"Don't worry," I said. "I've already had enough of that tonight."

A week or so later, my heart sank when I spied another girl's bracelet dangling from Rick's wrist. I was angry and Rick wouldn't look at me. He wouldn't give me the time of day. I couldn't confront him since I was on a male freeze again. Then I found out that he didn't like me anymore. "Why?" I wondered. "What had I done?"

Instead of letting these disparaging feelings gnaw at me un-checked, Lori had me meet them head-on by writing down how I felt. The words poured out of me. "I feel used, abandoned, lied to, fucked over, angry, sad, mad, hurt, and like I don't even exist," I hastily scribbled. "To be honest, I feel like a piece of shit!"

"What do you think is the problem with you and guys?" Lori asked.

"I just feel that if I get into a relationship," I said, "I'm definitely going to get fucked over."

"Why?"

"Because that's what happens all the time," I replied.

"Why do you think that?" she asked. "Whose fault is that? Yours? Or the guy's?"

"They're all scum," I said testily.

"You're attracted to scummy guys, right? Why? Why not aim higher?"

"Because I'm not worth any better?" I asked, hoping it was a correct answer.

Lori smiled. "Think about that yourself."

Like other patients, Drew's highs and lows vacillated as regularly as a swinging pendulum. After her breakup with Rick, though, it was apparent that Drew had slipped back into a rut. She slunk down the halls, isolated, withdrew in groups, and kept her eyes low to the ground. She was licking her wounds, wallowing in the pain rather than treating the injury.

I reverted. I rolled up inside myself and disappeared into a black hole of self-pity and remorse. But there was a subtle difference this time. I sensed it inside. My eyes were slowly being pried open and what I saw was an ugly sight. I wasn't able to articulate it, but looking back, I'd describe that rough period as the reemergence of my conscience. There was right and there was wrong, and I saw which side of the line I was standing on.

It was painful for Betty and Lori to watch. Yet they continued to exert the pressure. Experience had taught them that almost anything could reverse a tailspin. You could prod with exercises and questions, but no matter how well you knew someone, it was impossible to predict what might set them off. You just had to keep trying. Occasionally, though, an unexpected occurrence proved remarkably serendipitous.

There had been some speakers at our group that afternoon, a bunch of people who came and spoke about their drug and alcohol problems and their ongoing recoveries. I remember paying attention. I don't know why. For some reason I identified with the story this one girl told about her growing up in a broken home, always feeling lonely and unwanted.

Anyway, afterward I was summoned over the loudspeaker to the ASAP office, where Lori was waiting for me. Normally, she would've been kidding around with me or asking me a question about the group that had just finished. But her face was too serious for the moment.

"Call your mom," she said.

"Why? What's up?"

"Just call your mom," she said. "She's got some bad news."

When Lori refused to give me any more information, I gave up and telephoned my mom.

"Hi, Mom," I said.

"Hi," she said in a soft voice, a near whisper really.

"What's wrong?" I asked.

"I have something to tell you."

"What?"

"Well, your grandfather died," she said.

Not even listening to the rest of what she had to say, I burst into tears. A few minutes later I said good-bye and dropped into a chair. Lori asked if I was okay, but I couldn't stop crying. I'd been so involved in my own dark, selfish world, I didn't think anything could affect me. But I was wrong. The news of my grandpa's death touched me in the one place I'd deemed off limits to everyone: my heart.

It ached in a way that, in months past, would've had me running out the door for a drink or drugs. Anything to numb the pain rather than face it. But that was out of the question. I was made to confront the situation head on. "Deal with it, Drew," Betty urged. I was given no other choice. Friends talked to me about it. They smothered me with advice and sympathy. Others, it turned out, had lost parents and grandparents. "You aren't alone," I was told repeatedly. In group the next day we talked about it too. "You've got to let him go," a girlfriend told me. "There's nothing you can do about it, Drew. It's not your fault that he died. The only thing you can do is pray for him, and in your prayers tell him that you loved him."

So I prayed. And I told him that I loved him. And in group the next day I took a big risk. I told everyone that, although Grandpa Mako was one of the people I loved most in the world, I worried that the chance to tell him that had passed by because I was into my teenage bullshit and rotten drug use. I wasn't being myself. The last time I'd talked to him, I said, I'd told him that I loved him, but I feared that wasn't enough.

"Then write it out," Betty urged. "Say good-bye to him."

Dear Granddad,

I don't know how to start his letter, because I'm speechless. I can't picture you not in my life anymore. I'll always remember the wonderful times we had together. Like when we'd go feed the animals in your backyard. And that incredible treehouse you built me. And how we'd go sit inside it and talk about adult matters. Just being with you always made me feel happy.

I don't know if you'll understand, but for the past several years I've been wrapped up in the teenage scene. Maybe you thought that I treated grandparents as if they were convenient and cool only when bringing me presents. I never thought about you that way. I truly loved you. I'm sorry if I didn't show it.

I just want you to know that you mean a lot to me. I love you. No matter what you will always be with me. Your soul, our shared memories, and your love will always be in my heart. I love you . . . and good-bye!

Love,
Drew

In the quiet of her dimly lit bedroom Drew read and reread the letter, scanning the paragraphs over and over again and finally stuffing it into her tattered composition book. She dabbed her eyes with a tissue that came back dry. She'd cried until there were no more tears. But the weeping was not just for her grandfather. Drew was also crying for herself. His passing, she realized, had turned out to be one of the first life experiences in many years that she'd actually allowed herself to feel. She was vulnerable. She felt it all. But rather than run, Drew had wrestled it to a draw. She'd survived. That alone made her feel better, stronger.

The meaning of that didn't escape her. In her grandpa's death, Drew saw, she had discovered her own miraculous rebirth.

It's funny how you hear things repeated endlessly and yet never really hear them. They don't make a lasting impression. And then, for what reason I don't know, it all suddenly clicks.

That's the way it was for me whenever people talked about the Twelve Steps and working a program. I always thought, "Yeah, sure, I'm working a program. All I have to do is be honest." But I never really thought deeply about what honesty to oneself really meant until my grandfather died. Then, I couldn't help but be honest to the very core of my soul, because that was the only way I could purge myself of the sorrow, pain, and guilt that I felt.

Honesty. When you arrive at ASAP, they hand you a stack of books. There's your composition book, which is full of the blank pages you write on. There's the "Big Book," the bible of Alcoholics Anonymous, in which the Twelve Steps are listed. And then there's a pretty light-blue book of daily meditations called *Day by Day*. It provides a different thought for every day of the year.

Several days after my grandpa died, I had some free time before an AA meeting and picked up that book for lack of anything better to read. Naturally, I turned to my birthday, February 22, and read:

Taking the Steps

We used drugs for many reasons. Often it was to take the edge off life. In the beginning drugs made the world more beautiful, more satisfying to us. Toward the end we used chemicals to turn off our guilt, our fear and our loneliness. It was hard to see when we passed over the line where using began to be more the cause of conditions than the cure. Finally, our using met none of our needs at all.

However, by taking the steps, we can relearn how to meet our needs in constructive rather than destructive ways. Am I taking all the steps necessary to meet my needs without chemicals?

"Well, are you?" I imagined my grandpa saying to me. I heard his voice loud and clear and I didn't know what answer to give.

"No," I said softly out loud. "But I'm going to start."

Later that night in the AA meeting, I had to identify myself to a new member. I always hated that. As I stood up, my sentiments were still unchanged. I still hated hearing myself say, "Hi, I'm Drew and I'm an addict and I have so many days sobriety." But if I was going to be honest with myself, I had to fess up to the hard, cold fact. In a clear voice, with my eyes directed toward the new member of the meeting, I said, "Hi, I'm Drew and I'm an addict and I have fifty-one days sober."

THIRTEEN

LITTLE GIRL FOUND

Four-thirty in the afternoon. Penalized for a series of minor indiscretions, Drew, on ITP, again was stuck in her room, pondering her second essay of the day. The topic: What I am willing to do in this hospital.

It was a good question, one she hadn't thus far given much consideration.

Toward the end of October, Drew had come to terms with exactly why she was at ASAP. "I'm here because I'm a drug addict and alcoholic," she had written several weeks earlier in a different essay. "I started using to run away from my problems." Even the problems were getting less fuzzy than before. "I have very bad family problems," she wrote. "My dad is an abusive, bad-tempered alcoholic-addict, and my mom and I don't get along."

Up to this time the primary focus of treatment had been Drew's self-image. Betty, Lori, and Dr. Blair had forced her to stare at herself. She admitted feeling ugly, fat, and always inferior to her peers, and then she was made to explore how all that related to her substance abuse. "She felt she had to get more loaded than the next guy to prove she was older, bigger, and badder," Betty Wyman says.

Without drugs, however, Drew had to confront these issues and, ultimately, herself. She listed the things that she wanted for herself. She made lists of her priorities in life. "Finally," Betty explains, "we essentially stopped her in her tracks and said, 'Hey, this is who you are. This is what you say you want. Now, what are you willing to do about it?' "

What I Am Willing to Do in This Hospital
by Drew Barrymore

I am willing to get to know myself. Not Drew Barrymore the actress, but just plain Drew. I want to know and be at peace with the person who no one knows.

I am willing to try to accept the things in life that I cannot change, and to change the things that I can by working on them. I want to find a balance that allows me serenity.

I am willing to come to terms with myself. To do that, I have to be willing to face my problems, which I am. I can't run from them any longer. I have to break them down, understand them, and then try to prevent them from happening again.

I am willing to do everything it takes to stay sober and to be healthy and happy. I can no longer abuse myself or other people. And I am willing to become someone who helps myself and others.

Despite the insights and resolutions Drew enumerated on paper, treatment proceeded on its own painstaking schedule. Improvement was slow and vague. Drew's problems with self-image marked only the tip of much larger troubles.

Drew still had to face and resolve the source issues that had made her life so unbearable: her combustible relationship with her mother and her estrangement from her father. By early November these were subjects that had only been hedged at in the handful of family sessions that had brought Drew and Jaid together.

Jaid says:

Seeing Drew at those initial family sessions was like facing a stone wall. She was very resentful and angry. If there was any communication, it was very accusatory, sarcastic, and hostile. I wasn't equipped to deal with it. I didn't know how. Either I'd yell out of frustration. Or I'd withdraw. Or I'd become as resentful as Drew. Both of us cried a lot.

My mom would share some of her feelings about me. She told me how she felt about my escapades in New York, the lies I constantly told, and the way I'd methodically shut her out of my life.

"We've practically become enemies," she said in one of those early sessions. "Strangers at the very least. I don't like that. I don't want that."

"I don't really give a flying fuck what your opinion is," I said in a kind of disinterested singsong.

"Drew!" Betty snapped. "Now, instead of being rude, why don't you try explaining what that very eloquent statement really meant?"

I hated being called on my bullshit, but Betty and Lori never gave me an inch.

"I mean what I said," I replied.

"Well, we didn't quite understand," Betty said. "Try restating it."

"I don't care how she feels," I snapped. "Everything she says is negative. I hate her."

My mom, looking like she was going to scream at me, suddenly changed expressions and started to cry. I started crying too. That's how it went for a long time. Afterward, I'd walk back into the ward with my head lowered, not even saying good-bye, and feeling so incredibly empty in my soul.

"How come you can't speak to your mother?" Dr. Blair asked Drew the next time she saw him.

Every session of therapy, individual or family, was gone over, or "processed" as it's called in the hospital. If an issue was raised, it was processed from beginning till end, from ambiguity to complete understanding. Over time, the skills required to handle that issue were taught.

"Because I can't," Drew said.

"Do you actually hate her, as you said?"

"Sometimes."

"And sometimes not?"

"Yeah."

"Why not talk to her about those things you don't hate?"

"Because I'm scared."

"Dear Mom," I scrawled in a letter Dr. Blair had me write in my composition book. "I really don't know what to say because I'm really scared of how it might come out. I feel like I hurt you so bad. I really am sorry about all that's happened. I don't know if we will ever be the same, but I hope that you can forgive me for what I have done. I can accept that it won't be easy. I'm sorry. I love you. I'm really going to try the next time I see you. I really want to set myself straight."

Meanwhile, events transpired that shook up the comfortable routines Drew had created for herself in the hospital. First, Edie, a statuesque teenage model with long brown hair, received her discharge date and sent Drew a good-bye letter. Drew read the emotional two-

page missive, which was written in red ink and deco-
rated with hearts, and cried.

Dear Drew, my best friend,

I'm really going to miss you. We've been through so
much together. When I first saw you and asked why you
were in here, Lori said, "The same reason you were put in
here." We have so much in common. Despite our ups and
downs, you are a true friend. I want you to know I'll
always be there for you.

When you left the hospital to go shoot the movie in
Nevada, I really closed up. I hope that doesn't happen to
you, because I lost a lot from it. Learn from my mistakes.
When I think about leaving here, I get really paranoid. I
never thought I would be anything but overjoyed to leave,
but I am sad, sad, sad and very scared. I hope life does go
good for me.

I hope you keep going forward. When you lost your
sobriety, I was very angry, but more sad. I care about you.
Please! Don't be so self-destructive. Write about your
problems, talk them out. I wish I could explain my
feelings better, but they are all jumbled inside.

The very best I can say is 1) I love you, and 2) the
program really does work.

> Love always
> (and we'll rage when you get out),
> Edie

Then, within days of Edie's departure, another friend
transferred to another hospital. Minus her two closest
friends, she backstepped her way into a morose frame
of mind. It wasn't long before she was acting up, a
reaction to the isolation and alienation she suffered.
Then a letter from Edie arrived. A tiny card, actually,
festooned with hearts and arrows and happy faces.

Drew Bear,

Hey babe! I looked for you Wednesday to say bye, but you disappeared. A word of advice: You have to stop torturing yourself. Don't fret on being in there. Don't obsess. All that does is make you 1,000 times worse. You'll miss that crazy farm when you leave, I guarantee you. Drink up all the love and support you're getting. I'm happy I was there. It really helped my life. One hundred twenty-two days sober now! That's a *long* time!

Keep your eyes as open as your heart . . .

Edie

I was so sad. Without my friends I felt very lonely. For several days I went through the motions, going to group, going to my therapy, all that, without participating. But I did listen. And I did, as Edie advised, keep my eyes open.

What I saw jarred me. In group one day, I noticed a guy—his name was Ned—looking at me with such a sad expression on his face. He was staring with an intensity that unnerved me. We hadn't really spoken to each other before. I knew his name, but that was about it. He seemed nice. I pegged him as a quiet type, kind of out of it, and soft in the way that Rick had been tough and hard. His hair wasn't exactly right. He wore glasses. I didn't know about him.

A girl named Alice, a fifteen-year-old with a big-time alcohol and Valium habit, was talking about being jealous of her older sister, who, she claimed, was always stealing her friends. She found it difficult to trust anyone, and felt as if she lived in a dark cave, alone and miserable. Suddenly Ned began to cry. He was looking at me and crying. I don't even know if he was listening to Alice. Lori asked him what was up, if he wanted to share what he was feeling. "I've never told anyone," he sniffed, wiping his nose.

"It's okay," Lori said. "We'll listen to you. We'll support you in whatever you say."

"Well, I used to . . ." He lost it and continued to cry.

"Try to get it out," someone said. "It'll help if you just say it."

He rubbed his eyes, looked out the window, and then turned back toward me.

"I used to have trouble with my father," he stammered. "He . . . he . . . when I was littler, he molested me. There was arguing between him and my mom. I'd hear the yelling. He'd be drunk and angry. And later in the night, when it was finally all quiet, he'd come into my room and do things to me."

Ned broke down and started sobbing. So did I. So did everyone else in the room. It was like that in group, not often but enough so that if you'd been through it several times, those stories affected you. How could they not?

The next day Ned was again talking about his father. Lori led him into a discussion of the emotional distress his abuse caused. It turned into another teary session. When Ned started talking about how awful his father made him feel about himself, how empty and devoid of love he felt, I couldn't help but recognize how closely his story seemed to mine.

"It's not your fucking fault," I piped up without even thinking about contributing to the group. "He's the one with the goddamn problem."

"Drew?" Lori said. "Can you relate?"

I gulped. I suddenly regretted my intrusion into the group and wanted to shrink back into whatever dark hole I'd come from. But I didn't. To me, the moment was like going off the high dive for the first time. You're petrified of the jump, but you know that you'll feel stronger for doing it. I felt the pull of that strange connection between Ned and me and looked directly at him, perhaps gathering strength from his ability to have shared something incredibly painful and secret as he did the day before.

"Yeah, I can," I said in a muffled voice. "I've never shared this with anyone before either. But my father hit me and abused me, not sexually but physically and emotionally . . ."

Then I started to weep. Like Ned, though, I wasn't alone. When I looked up, wondering whether or not to continue, I saw that everyone else in the room was crying with me, for me. They shared in my suffering and cared about me. Had that ever happened before? No, I didn't think so, and that gave me the courage to go on talking about my dad.

In braving one of my deepest secrets, something I'd never even told my mom, something that had made me feel unloved, unworthy, and so alone, I found the shared sympathy and comfort of a group and saw that I was none of those things. If it sounds quick, it was. I felt it immediately.

I'd crossed a line I'd never dared cross before, and from then on, it became easier to share. Not long afterward, in another group, a girl began talking about how her grandfather was dying from Alzheimer's disease. When Melissa had last seen him, he hadn't even recognized her.

I told Melissa how crummy I had felt over not being able to say good-bye to my grandfather before he died. We talked a lot in that group about losing people we loved and about loving the people we had, things that I was only beginning to be aware of. After, we hugged and decided that we could help each other. "If you can't make yourself feel any better," I said, "find me and we'll talk about it."

I knew I was changing. I recognized that I was able to help Melissa. Equally important, though, I was being helped too. Both felt good.

Something was stirring inside Drew's head. Betty Wyman had seen it happen countless times before to kids just like Drew. For whatever reason, they suddenly "got it." "Many times with kids around Drew's age, it begins with a challenge of some sort," she explains. "They take on the program and their sobriety as if it were a challenge. That's fine. Anything to get the momentum going."

That's the way it was with Drew too. For two months she had been one of the most unstable, bedeviled patients in the hospital. She had been content in that role, which suited her self-image. It had almost become expected of her by friends. That's how she imagined herself and that's how other people came to view her. However, once Drew's closest friends were out of the picture, Drew's antics no longer got the same reaction. The rewards of acting up vanished. She had to find something new.

I wanted Growth Group, which is where you are allowed to leave on weekend passes with people with whom the hospital sets you up. All of a sudden I wanted it really badly. You get it by working and showing improvement, and so I started working really hard, sharing in every group and getting out my feelings. But what happened next was totally unexpected.

Throughout treatment, no one ever really talks about why the process works. You don't really think about it either. It's like you've been flailing in the water, struggling to stay afloat. And suddenly, in the seconds just prior to drowning, someone you've never laid eyes on tosses you a life preserver. Instead of asking questions, you grab on and let them pull you ashore. When you regain a bit of strength, you kick some, and after a while you find that you're trying to swim again.

I recall some of the speakers we had visit our groups mentioning a moment of spiritual awakening or a sudden sense of clarity, where they opened their eyes and surrendered or accepted their addiction. In working a program, "acceptance" is an important concept, one that's drummed into you over and over again. "Until I could accept my alcoholism," the Big Book states, "I could not stay sober; unless I accept life completely on life's terms, I cannot be happy.

"I need to concentrate not so much on what needs to be changed in the world as on what needs to be changed in me and in my attitudes."

I wasn't a good addict. I'd had that discussion several times with Betty, and I understood. Drugs had caused me to be handcuffed and led into a psycho ward. I'd bought plane tickets to Hawaii with a stolen credit card. I'd destroyed my relationship with my mother, the one person who'd been with me through my entire life. I didn't want to be that person. I saw that drugs and alcohol weren't solving my problems, only making them worse.

I had my moment of clarity.

As I shared, I found, "Wow, this feels really good. I'm really opening myself up. People are learning to accept me and I'm learning to accept myself. I talked my head off. I became close to people. I interacted in games, activities, and started coming out in the open.

The roll call for Growth Group was every Tuesday and Thursday after Doctor's Group, and despite my efforts, I didn't hear my name called. Finally, after about three weeks of concentrated effort, Lori read off the names of everyone who was getting Growth Group. Mine wasn't one of them. I slapped my desk out of frustration and said, "Damn!"

"Wait a minute," she smiled. "There is one more name."
Everyone started drumming their desks and Lori looked at me.
"Hey babe," she smiled, "you got it."

It was a milestone whose importance can't be under-estimated. Growth Group eased patients into the out-side world again. Chaperoned by former patients on Saturdays and recovering adults on Sunday, they at-tended movies and concerts, visited parks, played softball, went bowling and miniature golfing, or bar-becued hot dogs and hamburgers at the beach. The lesson was simple: They could have fun without get-ting high. For most, it was the first time they had ever done any of these things without drugs or alcohol. For Drew, it was the first time she had done many of these things, period.

Growth Group kept me hungry. I didn't want to give it up. It made me try hard in groups and in my family sessions, and the harder I tried, the better I felt. The more I dumped, the less pressure I felt. It didn't get any easier to express myself. I had to force myself at times. But I actually felt the weight I'd been shouldering lighten.

Drew was responding to ASAP's nurturing atmosphere. She reacted positively to the community, which was built on shared feelings, understanding, healing, and love. As Betty Wyman saw it, among the most important things she and Lori provided Drew at the hospital was a stable healthy relationship. "We were constant and consistent in our rewards or punishments," she says. "We loved her, but we also told her no. We were firm. And later on, we taught Jaid how to do that. You build a trust, but ultimately you want everything the patient shares with you to be shared with their family." That meant tackling the issues of Mom and Dad.

The two were separate problems and yet they were inextricably intertwined. They had to be dealt with individually and simultaneously. It was a bit like taking two movies with similar themes, splicing them together, and trying to ferret out a single story line. In the early going, Drew would simply erupt, "I am so fucking confused!"

On the one hand, Drew had to relinquish her longtime fantasy that her father would waltz into her life, clean and sober. She had to, as they told her, recognize him for what he really was and let him go. At the same time, Drew had to come to terms with Jaid. It was as if the mother and daughter had to be reintroduced.

Our family sessions didn't turn around until I'd acknowledged the benefit of taking a risk. For a long time my mother had been willing to communicate, to air her gripes and to listen to whatever I had to say. But I'd been so negative that our sessions served only as evidence of the incredible hurt and anger that had driven us apart. She spoke, I swore, and both of us cried endlessly.

But shortly after I earned Growth Group, we had our first good family session. It began, as usual, with my mother talking about how emotionally bruised she was. The difference this time is that I was listening to her. God, I hated hearing her tell and retell the lies I'd told her over the years, how she felt mistreated and taken advantage of. It all sounded so one-sided, and in my mind I thought, "Did I do all that? Am I that much of an asshole?"

"How does listening to that make you feel?" Betty asked.

She'd often posed that question, and normally I answered with a flippant, "I don't give a shit. I don't care one way or the other." Truthfully, though, I did care.

"If I could only climb inside your head and see what you're feeling, Drew," my mom sighed, shaking her head. "I'm so frustrated. I know it's not all you. But I can't learn if you don't share with me."

All of a sudden I just started to cry and cry and cry. I saw the frustration on her face, and in my heart I wanted to reach out to her. I wanted her to be my mother, like the other kids had, but I didn't know how to go about it.

"Okay, okay," I sniffed.

"Take a deep breath," Betty advised. "Dry your eyes."

"What do you want me to say?" I asked, not knowing how or where to begin.

"How about telling your mom how you feel about her?" Betty said. "We've made lists of likes and dislikes. Try remembering what you wrote."

I saw my mother stiffen in her chair.

"Well, the things I like about my mom," I said to Betty, "are, well, one, she cares about me. She truly does love me. I know that. She must, considering what a total jerk I've been. And she's always there when I need her. She's easy to manipulate. I mean, I've gotten away with murder. And she gives me freedom, kinda, and lets me be my own person."

"Good," Betty smiled. "And the dislikes?"

"When I was younger she was never there for me," I continued, though it was harder this time. "That's the way I felt, at least. And these days she takes everything out on me. I mean, she is always so negative. She compares me to my friends. She's greedy with all our money, hardly giving me any. She's all business and no pleasure. And, I think, she gives me too much in some ways and not enough in other ways."

Jaid bit her lip. She wanted to defend herself. Her impulse was to offer a terse rebuttal to Drew's complaints. The picture was clear. As a child, Drew felt abandoned by Jaid's absences. That was an all too common issue in single-parent families. "But someone had to go out and earn the money to pay the bills," she wanted to say. And as for the negativity, she wanted to scream, "Hold up a mirror, honey. Do you honestly believe you've been an angel?"

But she didn't. She held herself back and listened to her daughter, which was something new on her part, trying to understand and gain insight.

Jaid says:

I was learning and changing too.

When a response to a given situation is the same over and over again, regardless of whether it's effective or not, it strengthens the conditioning from which that response came. It's as if you were on automatic pilot. When you act like that, you aren't even consciously aware of what that response elicits. It's like doing the same script over and over. Given that circumstance, it's impossible for the situation to change. It feeds on itself and perpetuates itself. That's a pretty good definition of a codependent relationship as well as a description of the way Drew and I had been speaking to each other. I screamed without listening.

Early on I was giving those kind of knee-jerk responses. Betty or Lori would point out that they were not only ineffective, but they created the exact reaction on Drew's part with which I couldn't deal. Things just got more out of control. I needed to pull away, they instructed, from being a totally subjective participant and find a perspective from the outside looking in. I had to think, "What does that response elicit? What's the result of that response? Is it positive? Or does it only perpetuate the misery and the problem?"

In effect, Drew was correct in her comments of my negativity. I couldn't see it. As far as our arguments went, I was constantly backpedaling, trying to show what I was doing that was productive and positive in the relationship, essentially defending myself, and constantly being frustrated by not getting the reaction I wanted because of my behavior. I had to change my behavior.

I learned to pull back and stop buying into her manipulative behavior. I learned to stop being codependent. If Drew, for instance, accused me of feeling a particular way that had no validity, instead of arguing with her and justifying my own position, I'd just stop and say, "Fine. You're entitled to feel that way. But I've heard that excuse before and if you can't come up with something new, then it's time for me to back out and leave." When I did something like that, she'd look at me in shock and say, "What do you mean, you're leaving? You don't care about me." And I'd say, "No, it's not that I don't care. I do care, and that's why I'm not going to feed into your bullshit. I'm not going to be a stupid, naive jerk anymore."

As far as discipline went, whatever threats I imposed, they told me, I had to come through on. But the threats couldn't be an emotional response. They had to be something that was logical, objective, and very clear. I had to pull back from my ridiculously overblown emotional investment in every move that she made. When she said that I didn't care, I had to tell her that wasn't it. I was just no longer being manipulated.

And when I changed my response, Drew had to change her response as well. The concept was so logical that I felt like an idiot when it was explained to me. We were like two people who fight year after year, learning their moves and punching on automatic. But when one person finally slips in a new move, it changes everything. That's what I did.

Change didn't come overnight, no matter how aware Jaid became. In fact, there were slips. Visiting hours at the hospital were from six to seven at night. One evening Jaid arrived five minutes past seven and persuaded the nurse on duty to allow her back to Drew's room for a few minutes. Toting a script under her arm, she handed it to Drew, who burst into a raging temper tantrum.

"Can't you just be my mom for a goddamn minute!" she yelled. "Don't you listen to a thing I say? I don't want you to be my manager. I want a mother. Other kids' parents bring them McDonalds. Why do I have to get scripts?"

Jaid shrank out of the hospital, distraught, realizing she'd made a huge mistake. In the following family session, Drew's fury was still in the danger zone. "Sometimes I don't want to work," she said. "I just want to be a little girl. I just want to be ordinary Drew. Not Drew Barrymore."

Jaid got the point immediately. "First and foremost," she recalls, "Drew was my baby, my child, and she made me realize that I needed to reconsider my actions. My priorities weren't wrong, I don't think, but the manner in which I showed them needed revamping. I wasn't listening to what she was saying to me."

Later that night Drew was summoned to the ASAP office, where a package overflowing with ribbons and balloons was waiting for her. Hurrying back to her room, she ripped open the gift-wrapped box and pulled out a pair of fluffy, cow-shaped slippers. The card read, "I am *very proud* of the way you dealt with everything today. Things have been so hard for us, but I feel that you were really honest. I know you really want things to be better. So do I. I thought these little cows might make you feel a little cozy when you put them on. Love, Mom."

She sobbed and fell asleep that night wearing her slippers.

It meant so much to me. That night someone asked where I got my slippers and I smiled. "My mom brought them to me." Kids were always getting little gifts or presents. Everyone, it seemed, except me. What did my mother bring me? A script. She wanted me to work, which I knew I wasn't ready for. I told her that in the session after I blew up at her, and though she said she understood, I wondered. But when I finally got that special little something that told me she cared and that she loved me for being me, well it sounds stupid, but it made a difference.

Jaid says:

When you make a new resolution, you have to keep strengthening and nurturing and reinforcing it. When you've had years of practicing a pattern that you're asserting over and over again, in order to change, you have to build a new foundation. If it's not a tremendously conscious effort at every moment, it's easy to slide back to where you were. It's like putting on this old, comfortable pair of shoes. You have to break the new ones in, and that takes time. And it's uncomfortable at first.

You feel so ashamed for backtracking. Your self-esteem is at stake. When you realize what a jerk you're being, you vow to get tough.

I had to work through tremendous guilt, which I saw every other parent suffer. Eventually, I began to see that the guilt is an inadequacy to deal clearly with a situation. Guilt is an easy copout, an easy way to rationalize. If you buy into it, you don't have to look any further. You don't have to get more complex and search your soul and your child's soul. You have to dig deeper and look at things you don't want to look at in yourself, your child, and your relationship. You have to dredge up things about yourself that you never had to resolve and never had to own up to. You have to be really honest with yourself. If not, nothing works.

One day in an individual session concerning my relationship—or lack of one—with my father, Dr. Blair asked me how Mom and he met. I tried my hardest to remember, but ended up giving him the typically vacant look I always gave whenever he asked a question about my family. "I don't know," I said.

Suddenly, my family sessions struck me as extremely one-sided. There I was, spilling my guts to my mom every week, telling her all my feelings about her and dad, my inadequacies, my obsession with guys. All that stuff. But when I thought about it, I realized that I didn't know all that much about who she was as a person—besides, of course, that she was my mother.

When I thought about it, she'd never really told me about her life. Of course, I'd never asked. But she'd never made herself available in that way.

At Betty's suggestion, my mother showed up at our next family session carrying a large, beat-up scrapbook that I'd never seen before. It was stuffed with pictures of her as a young actress and model and yellowed and torn newspaper clippings that showed my father as a younger man.

"That's Dad?" I shrieked incredulously, turning the pages quickly. I'd never seen him without the long white hair and scraggly beard that made him look like a freaked-out hippie Frankenstein from some punked-out horror movie. "What a hunk!"

I turned a few more pages and saw a black and white photo of my mother. She was beautiful. "God, Mom," I gushed. "You look wonderful."

"Well, I had a life before I had you," she laughed.

"I've never known about it," I said, turning serious. "How about you and Dad? How'd you guys meet?"

"I never told you?" she asked. "Oh, God, it seems like another lifetime, maybe two or three lifetimes ago." She sighed. "Okay, though. We met at the Troubadour, you know, the music club on Santa Monica Boulevard . . ."

"Yeah, the metal club," I added eager to identify.

"Right. But it wasn't heavy metal then. It was very cool then, the center of the L.A. music scene. Jackson Browne played there, James Taylor, Elton John, The Doors. All those people played there in the early days. I was a waitress there, oh, gosh, for a long time, and that's where I met your father. He came in with friends and, well, you saw, he was extremely handsome . . ."

"A hunk," I quickly interjected.

"Ah-ha," she smiled. "Very movie-starish. He had a certain way about him that I found attractive, and, I suppose, I had a certain way about me that he also liked."

"And so, like, when did you get together?"

"We went out several times, liked each other, and really, we just dated for two years before . . ."

"You had sex?"

"Before we did anything, yes," she said. "We were caught up in the bohemian life, very artsy-fartsy and actorish. We didn't have any money. For a while we lived together at a friend's house. Then we finally got our own place in West Hollywood, not far from where our first little apartment was when I brought you home from the hospital."

"And Dad," I asked, "what was he like? I mean, was he a total schmuck then, like he is now?"

"No, not at first," my mom answered. "No, not that I saw. He was quite charming, actually, very suave, almost as if he were playing a role. We were poor, but on the few occasions we did have any money, he bought me little presents or took me out to dinner. That was nice. And when we didn't have any money, we sometimes just laid on the bed and talked and cuddled all night. It was romantic. But he changed. As soon as he knew he had me, your father turned into a different man. It was as if he were possessed and . . ."

"He turned into the shit that he is," I said.

"Yeah, I guess that's one way of putting it," she answered.

"I wish it had been different," I said. "But you must've felt the same way as me when Grandpa divorced your mother, right?"

"Drew, that's so long ago," she sighed. "I don't know."

"I think that's a good question," Betty prodded.

"God, I haven't thought about this for centuries," my mom huffed. "But yeah, when I think back, I suppose I was mad and angry and hateful at my parents for splitting. I didn't have a close relationship with my mother though. Now that I'm remembering all this, I realize that I was rebellious, something of a renegade. I mean, there I was, stuck in Pennsylvania, and all I wanted was to go to

Hollywood, be an actress, and hang out with rock stars. I fought with my parents all the time for more freedom and understanding. . . ."

"Listen to what you just said," Betty interrupted. "You fought with your parents for more freedom and understanding. Does that sound familiar to anyone in this room?"

"Oh, my God," my mother realized. "It's me. I mean, it's you."

"That what I used to say all the time when we fought." I nodded.

"We were so much alike in some ways," she said, daubing her tear-filled eyes.

At that point I got up from my chair, walked over to my mom, and hugged her. It was very emotional. All of a sudden I felt so close to her. It was the first time we'd hugged, really hugged, in, well, longer than I could remember. She hugged me as hard as I was squeezing her and said, "I love you, Budgie."

"I love you, too, Mom."

Despite the strides with Jaid, there was less apparent progress where Drew's father was concerned. Drew was reluctant to give up her fantasies about him. Then Betty got an idea, a long shot that required time to set up.

With Drew working hard to maintain her weekend pass privileges, Betty arranged for her to go out on Growth Group with a friend of hers, Jan Dance, the wife of rock star David Crosby. Both Jan and David were recovering addicts whose problems with substance abuse had been well chronicled in the media. But the pairing was arranged "because," Betty explains, "Drew responded so much better to adult companionship. She enjoyed being with kids her own age, but she delighted in the nurturing of a stable adult relationship."

Drew's relationship with Jan and David also looked forward to the day when she would be out of the hospital and need a network of sponsors, surrogates for Betty and Lori, whom she could call in times of crisis. They hit it off perfectly. Drew attended AA meetings with Jan, went out to dinner, ordered in pizza, and watched movies. "I found I could talk with Jan about anything," Drew says. "Guys, the hospital, my mom. I also listened to her. She'd been through what I was going through, and that counted for a lot."

Jan, it seemed, knew just what to say when Drew turned up feeling anxious about the work she was doing with her mother. "It's so hard," I told her. "Sometimes we'll get along, but then she comes down on me and I hate her for it."

"You know, you have to accept your mom for the way she is," Jan offered. "You can't change her. The only person you should worry about changing is yourself. When you turn eighteen, you don't ever have to see your mother if you don't want to. But you can't get away from yourself until you're dead."

"Why's it have to be so hard and confusing?" Drew said. "I just want to get out of the hospital."

"Don't rush it," Jan responded. "You'll know when it's time."

Through an informal discussion outside of group, Lori discovered that Drew had never seen any of her father's movies. Nor had she watched any of her grandfather's films. Lori and Betty were amazed. Determined to change that, the following Saturday, Lori and Drew went to the video rental store, selected the classic *Grand Hotel*, starring John, Lionel, and Ethel Barrymore, and the B-movie *High School Confidential*, featuring an appearance by John Barrymore, Jr., Drew's father.

"It was cool seeing everyone's names in the first movie," Drew recalls. "But I was mesmerized when I saw my dad. At first I was shocked just being able to look at him. Once that wore off, though, it became painful. My dad played a drug dealer in the film and that was too close to the guy I already knew."

The following weekend she told Jan and David about watching the movies and was flabbergasted to learn that David had actually known her father. Years ago they'd run in the same social circles, hung out and gotten high together. Drew ate up every word David said. "What was he like?" she asked, panting for any morsel of information that would make him seem palatable. "Wild," David recalled. "Not really a nice guy, basically. But it's so hard to remember."

Drew, who hadn't seen her father in seven years, hungered for more. Coincidentally, Betty's husband, Dallas Taylor, a respected drummer who was one of Crosby's close pals as well as a recovering addict himself, had known Drew's father in the same way that David did. That's when the idea struck Betty.

Over the years she had concluded that role-playing as a therapeutic device had very limited value. Most kids, she found, weren't able to suspend their ties to reality. But Drew's ability as an actress made Betty think it might accomplish something in the way Drew perceived her father. Finding someone to convincingly act out the part of John had been the problem—until she realized David and Dallas knew him.

Her first thought was David, who had a background in film, but he tended to be too nurturing where Drew was concerned. Then she asked Dallas, and he agreed to try.

As we sat down in front of the group, I remember wondering if I'd be able to get into the role. I mean, Dallas was Dallas, not my dad, and when I looked at him, I saw this guy who was always so incredibly nice and supportive of me. But surprisingly almost from the word go, I started crying.

"Drew," Dallas nodded, "you've grown. It's been what now, seven years since I've seen you?"

'Yeah."

"Doing anything lately?" he said.

"Not much, really."

"Got any money?"

"What's it to you?" I said, getting into the part. "You're just going to use it to buy drugs and get loaded."

"So what. That's my business, isn't it?"

"I wish you wouldn't. I wish you'd pay some attention to me. I mean, I am your daughter. I haven't even talked to you in seven years."

"Right," he grumbled. "But I'll let you in on a bit of reality, something you should've picked up by now, daughter. I need my drugs a lot more than I need you. If it came down to choosing, I'd turn my back on you in an instant."

By then I was sobbing. I couldn't even look at Dallas, and he kept up the attack.

"So do you have any money?" he goaded.

"Is that all you care about? Money?"

"Right now, hon," he said. "But hey, don't get riled. Maybe I have something you want in exchange. What do you want?"

"What I want is a dad, you asshole!" I screamed, by then oblivious to the fact that twenty people were watching us and Dallas was only pretending to be my father.

"You got that already," he said. "You're looking at him."

"Oh, right," I spat out. "Like I need that. Every single hurt you ever inflicted has stayed with me. I can still hear you telling me, 'Daughter, I wish that you'd never been born. It was a mistake.' And I, like a jerk, believed you. And those times when you hit me, I'm still in pain and bruised. Those injuries don't just go away. They've been incredibly damaging."

"Well, what do you want me to do about them?"

"Uggggh!" I screamed out of frustration. "Why did Mom have to marry someone like you? I don't know what to do!"

That's when Betty and Lori jumped in. "What you do is let him go, Drew," they advised. "Love him if you want, but recognize that he's never going to be there for you, at least in the way you imagine."

It was a heavy session, one that required lots of processing, and the next afternoon Dr. Blair asked Drew to write a letter to her father, explaining how she felt about him.

Dear Dad,

This is how I feel:

I feel like you were never there for me, and when you were there, it was only to hurt me. I really wish you would tell what you feel about me and tell me why. I never did anything but love you and keep forgiving you. And you never did anything but hurt me and cause me pain. Well, I'm all out of love and forgiveness for you. Love is a two-way street, and your street turned out to be a dead end.

If I had one wish, it would be for you to straighten up and get your goddamn act together. So many people have tried to help you, but all you've done is fuck them over. I was like that too. Are you happy? Is that your wish? For your kids to be as messed up as you are.

I'll tell you one thing though. I'm going to get out of this and live a happy life, and unless you do a lot, you won't be a part of that. I hope I'm wrong. I hope you will be a part of it. Somehow. I really would like to hear you say, "I love you, Drew." I really would.

But I guess I never will.

Something unexpected occurred several days later. Out on Growth Group with friends, Drew went to a park on a picnic. She was having "a really good pass," playing Frisbee, enjoying herself and not thinking about the hospital. However, in the park she spotted a tall, rail-thin man with a wild shock of white hair and a long beard. Drew studied his movements carefully as he searched through trash cans, read a newspaper on the bench, and drank from a bottle of cheap wine. She thought it was her father.

When she returned to the hospital later that night, Drew was quite anxious and animated and telephoned

Betty right away at home. Rambling on and on about what she believed was a chance sighting of her dad, Drew took several hours to calm down. Betty suggested she write another letter to her father, telling him what she might've said to him if that had indeed been him at the park and they had talked.

Dear Dad,

Well, I guess I could start with the present, since our past really isn't worth talking about. I am now in the hospital for drug abuse and psychiatric problems. I'm living here. I wonder what you think of that. Probably a waste of time, huh?

Anyway, in my family sessions—more like mother-daughter sessions, since I really wouldn't dare call us a family—you've been the main topic lately. I'm so angry at you. To tell you the truth, something I've never had the chance to do, I resent the hell out of you.

Even so, I really want to see you, just once, and tell you everything you have done to me that's messed me up. I also need to tell you that I love you—while I still have the chance. I'm really frightened that you're going to die from drugs and I won't get a chance to say it.

Love,
Drew

The next day I had a family session and I shared all my feelings about seeing him. Surprisingly, my mom didn't seem that affected. I tried convincing her that it was him, but she adamantly refused to believe it.

"How do you know?" I asked.

"Because he's in Taos, New Mexico," she said.

I got really angry at that point, thinking that she had known where he was this whole time and was keeping it a secret from me.

"No," she said. "I just found out a few days ago. He called your agent, asking for you."

"Really?" I perked up.

"I think he wants money," she said.

I knew my mom was probably right, but she didn't end the conversation there, as she would've done in the past. Instead, she told me that she had thought long and hard and decided it was unfair to completely shut him out of my life without at least asking me. "He is, after all, your father," she said. My mom was willing, she explained, to send him one lump sum of money. He could use it to clean himself up or flee the country and start over, which he expressed some desire to try. Whatever he wanted. But, she added, it was the last time she was going to give in to his demands.

"So what do I do?" I asked, curious.

"Well, I got his telephone number and if you want, you can call him up."

We scheduled the call for 4:30 the next day. That entire morning and afternoon, all I could think about was that telephone number. I went over the digits in my head till they were ingrained in my memory. Despite my negative feelings about him, I couldn't help but be drawn to speaking to him. Maybe he wouldn't be as bad as I remembered or as everyone said. Maybe he would've gotten himself together and he'd be really nice, you know, the dad I'd always wanted.

So I went into Betty's office, dialed, and asked the hotel operator for the room number. It rang twice.

"What?" snapped this mean-sounding voice on the other end.

He knew I was going to call and, hearing his voice, my heart sank like an anchor in a swimming pool. You could hear it crashing on the bottom.

"Daddy?" I said, my voice trembling. "This is your daughter, Drew."

For about fifteen minutes, the conversation went nice and slow. My dad asked what I'd been doing, how life was treating me, that kind of stuff. I asked if he was okay, if he felt healthy. It was more than I ever expected and everything I wanted, really. I felt a swell of emotion in my throat.

"I love you, Daddy," I said on the spur of the moment.

I nearly froze out of fear once the words came out. I didn't know how he'd reply. And there was a long pause afterward, a silence that filled me with dread.

"I love you, too, daughter," he whispered emotionally.

I started to sob and nearly dropped the phone. Betty, who was half monitoring the conversation, pulled up a chair for me to sit in. I didn't know what to say next. But my dad did, and he didn't waste any time in saying it either.

"Drew, I could really use a little bread," he said, beginning the old manipulative song and dance that I'd heard so many times.

"No," I said, gaining strength with my anger. "Mom just gave you a thousand dollars, and we're constantly giving you money, and I don't want to give you another cent."

"Listen, call me right back," he said. "I've got to go to the bathroom."

In the ten-minute interval that followed, I dried my tears and sipped on a cup of tea and lemon, gathering support from Betty and Lori. Then I dialed again, and when my dad answered, it was obvious from the sound of his voice that he'd gotten high. I was so angry. I wanted to say, "You sick jerk," but I held back and listened to him babble on for a few minutes. Finally, I just didn't want to listen anymore. "Listen," I said, interrupting, "I've got to go now. But do me a favor and call my agent once a month and let me know you're okay?"

"Sure thing," he laughed, and hung up without even saying good-bye.

Drew spent hours over the following weeks in groups and in family and individual sessions grappling with the topsy-turvy emotions elicited by the phone conversation. She had been, she felt, understanding what it meant to let him go, and then, suddenly and unexpectedly, he came waltzing back into her life on the telephone and that screwed up everything.

Eventually I recognized the truth. It was still hard for me to accept, and it's still something I find confusing. I replayed our conversation over and over in my mind and thought about all my past experiences with him, trying to get one clear picture of the man my dad really was. It took time and courage, but I tried to be honest with myself. He wasn't a good guy to me.

I was in my room one night, exhausted from hashing out the issue in group, wanting nothing more than to smoke a cigarette in a calm moment where I could be by myself. There was a knock on the door and a girlfriend of mine walked right in. In the hospital, people tend to get excited and emotional when they have something worthwhile to share, something they think will help a situation. And she was worked up.

"Drew," she said with a degree of urgency, "I lost my dad. He died. There wasn't anything I could do to bring him back, no matter how much I wanted to. I loved him so much. I cried for weeks. And I finally had to let him go. For myself. But your dad is a fucking creep. Can't you see that? He's treated you like shit all your life. Don't stop loving him, if you want, but just don't obsess on the guy anymore. He's already ruined enough of your life."

Then she turned and walked out. Just like that. It was like a sudden thunderstorm. Thunder, lightning, and then quiet. But I sat there thinking about what she said, and it made sense to me. I could love him, but I didn't have to have him in my life. It made sense.

FOURTEEN

DAY BY DAY

Throughout the first part of December, Drew talked about nothing but her discharge date. Not a word about her release had been mentioned by either Betty or Lori, but that didn't matter. She sensed the time was getting near. A number of her friends had already left, and watching some of the other kids leave before the Christmas holiday only made her more eager to hear her discharge date.

I made it a bigger issue than it was supposed to be. I constantly asked, "When am I going home? What about me?" I was pretty resentful watching everyone else leave. I'd been there, it seemed, longer than anyone.

Then my roommate got her d.c. date and I was so jealous. That night we got into a big fight, and the following day in group I talked about how envious I was of her. "I'm always nagging and being told, 'Not now. We'll tell you,' and that just makes me furious."

Afterward Betty came up to me and asked, "Well, do you want your d.c. date?"

All of a sudden I got sick to my stomach. I thought, Well, I should say no, because I figured she was just putting me to some kind of test. If I answered yes, I thought, she'd just say, "Well, how does it feel to want something?" That's one of the biggest jokes in the hospital. However, in a voice that was nervous and scared, I said, "Yeah, I'd like to know," and Betty smiled. "In seven days," she said. "Next Wednesday."

I was already crying before she finished. Lori laughed and told me to pull myself together, but I couldn't. I got so excited and scared. I thought, "Great, I'm finally getting out. But what if I don't do something right, like brush my teeth, and they tell me I have to stay longer and work on that?" God, I was such a mess I joked to myself, "Girl, you need to check into a hospital."

The day after receiving her discharge date, the *National Enquirer* fiasco occurred. Immediately, there was lots of scrambling to protect Drew from the commotion the disclosure engendered. Reporters, materializing out of nowhere, sniffed around outside the hospital grounds. The switchboard lit up with hundreds of telephone calls from reporters throughout the world, all wanting to know if the reports were true. Was the little girl from *E.T.* really battling a cocaine and alcohol addiction?

Betty worried about Drew's reaction. Her condition was fragile enough without the attention. Her reemergence into the outside world posed enough temptations. She didn't need the burden of public shame and humiliation piled on top of all that. Ironically, a week prior to the incident, Drew had spoken to Jan and David about the pressures of getting out. After all, her discharge was something she had thought about every day for three months.

"It's hard," David had said to Drew. "You worry about how people will react. But you can't buy into the shame, because it's not shameful to have gotten treatment. You just tell yourself, 'A really great thing came out of all this—me.' Work your program and you'll be strong."

Edie sent Drew a tiny clipping about her addiction

from the *Los Angeles Times*. One sentence described Drew as living "a charmed life." Edie underlined that and wrote in the margin, "Ha-ha! If they only knew!"

Miraculously, though, through the frenzy, Drew remained relatively stable and centered. Compared to her mother, she was the Rock of Gibraltar. She even hatched the plan to tell her story, in her own words, to *People* magazine. If her drug and alcohol tribulations were going to be public, she determined that, at the very least, the story should be factual and honest, and if possible, it should act as either a deterrent or an inspiration to people her own age who might also be struggling with similar problems.

In the midst of the tumult, Betty asked Drew if she wanted to discharge prematurely and handle the pressure of exposure at home, where she could lay low until the fuss died down.

For three months and one day I'd thought or talked about nothing but getting out of the hospital. I'd even tried AWOLing. Then, of course, I received my discharge date and that was great. But what happens next? Betty asks if I want to leave even earlier than that.

If anyone had told me that I'd turn her down, I would've laughed in their face. But it was true. I gave it very serious consideration and finally said, "No, that's okay. I'll wait till next week."

Would a few days really make a difference? Yeah, I thought so. When I asked myself if I was ready to go, I answered, "Almost." The reason was simple. I felt that I hadn't shared enough about leaving, which is an important part of completing the whole experience of treatment. Even if I didn't have any real close friends left in the hospital, I still needed to say my last good-byes.

Drew was busy in those final days, participating in the regular hospital routine, packing her belongings, contacting friends on the outside, and making arrangements for follow-up treatment after her departure. In addition, she spent seven hours over two days presenting a highly emotional account of her plight to *People* magazine, an experience that reinforced her decision to go public. When that task was completed, it was time for Drew to compose her three good-bye letters and then read them, as was tradition, before the entire group.

My letters were quite short, since there wasn't anyone left with whom I felt especially close. But as I read them, I still couldn't help myself from crying. "I'm so especially grateful to everyone for helping me," I read. "I can see that I made a lot of progress and that I was very lucky to have come into the hospital, even though I can honestly say that I hated almost every minute of it. But it probably saved my life. I'm sure of that much.

"However, if I'm going to be truly honest, then I have to say that I'm *really* scared of leaving. I always thought I'd skip outside, climb into my mom's car, and take off back into my old life. But what I realize is that my old life's not there anymore. Or at least I can't let it be. That's what scares me too. I don't want to go back to my old ways. I don't want to fight with my mother. I don't want to start using again. I like how I am now. But I'm really frightened that it won't last.

"That's not the way I want to say good-bye though. I'm happy to be leaving. Very happy! And I don't want to ever have to come back."

I sat down and Betty walked over and put her hand on my shoulder. "It's okay to be scared, Drew." She smiled. "The real world is scary. That's part of life. You just have to be prepared for that and you have to be strong."

"You'll do okay, Drew," my friend Amy added. "It'll be a lot different for you this time. Now you have lots of people who love you and who you can call anytime for support."

"Thanks," I said, wiping a tear from my eye.

Drew left the ASAP hospital on December 21. It was three months and one week after she'd been brought in by two private detectives with her hands cuffed behind her back after a delirious, forty-eight-hour cocaine-powered cross-country romp. She walked out twenty-five pounds lighter than when she'd arrived, with her hair brushed and gathered in a pink ribbon, holding her head up high and waving a tearful farewell to those patients who watched with their noses pressed to windows. She looked beautiful and felt even better. She kissed her mother hello and climbed into the car beside her.

She had ninety-six days sober.

However, a week that should have been full of celebration was in fact tainted by conflicting emotions. On the one hand, Jaid and Drew spent a quiet, pleasant Christmas together in their Sherman Oaks condominium, exchanging several small presents and sipping iced tea. Drew, who complained of not having any time to shop, gave her mother several novels. Jaid gifted her daughter with two large amethyst crystals. But what they actually savored was being in the company of each other. That was the real gift. On the other hand, the National Enquirer's story was out that week and the telephone rang off the hook. Friends, people Drew had worked with, acquaintances from years back, all wanted to know if it was true and, if it was, how Drew was doing. Reporters stalked the front of their house. They had to sneak outside through back doors and neighbor's cars. It wasn't a pleasant scene.

But I didn't let it get to me. I was so delighted to be outside again and able to enjoy my freedom. I packed in as much activity as I could, because the following week, I started filming an ABC Afterschool Special titled *Getting Straight*, a pretty accurate drama about teenage drug use starring me, Tatum O'Neal, and Corey Feldman. Ironically, it was shot at the ASAP hospital I'd just left.

During the second week of filming, the *People* magazine story came out, and I was so relieved to have my version available to the public. Doing it, I recognized, was a risk, not unlike sharing in group for the first time, but it seemed stupid to me to hide all that I'd been through as if it were something to be embarrassed about. Not getting help would've been something to be ashamed of. In addition, I planned to have a long acting career that over time would require me to give lots of interviews, and I didn't always want to have to talk about my ordeal. If I told the story from beginning to end, once and for all, then, I thought, when the topic arose I could simply tell interviewers, "I've already dealt with that extensively. I'd like to move on." Still, I couldn't help but wonder how people would react.

Drew didn't have long to wait. For the next several weeks, the letters poured in. In just the first week *People* magazine was out on the stands, one hundred seventy emotionally charged responses streamed in, far above the average for an issue. Nearly ninety percent applauded Drew's courageous battle, including thirteen readers who were themselves recovering from drug or alcohol misuse. The ten percent who wrote in negative comments expressed astonishment and disgust at the way Jaid parented her child. "That was to be expected," Jaid says. "If people wanted to use me as a scapegoat, fine. It was Drew's decision to tell her story, and I was determined that it be *her* story, not mine.

"I blamed myself plenty and got over that. The real story is told in those multifamily groups we attended. You walk in thinking you're the worst parent on the planet, but then you see that kids and families from every possible situation are represented and you think, 'My God, we've all ended up at the same point. It couldn't be just me.' "

The negative letters bristled with disdain for Drew and Jaid, evidencing little understanding or compassion for the underlying complexities of addiction. "Feel sorry for Drew Barrymore?" a reader from Brooklyn, New York, wrote. "No way! Instead of putting her on a national magazine cover, someone who has an interest in her well-being should give her a good spanking."

"I am disgusted by Drew Barrymore and angry with you for giving her a forum," a reader from La Mesa, California, commented. "If she were an ordinary child she would now be in foster care, her mother would be charged with child endangerment, and the adults who furnished her with addictive substances would have faced appropriate legal action."

However, there was no question that Drew, as she intended, made the biggest impression on those of her own generation who faced the same problems and temptations she did. "I have just finished reading your article on Drew Barrymore, which I must say has made a large impact on myself," a girl from Connecticut wrote. "At first I thought a thirteen-year-old addicted to drugs and alcohol was ridiculous. But after reading the article, I could really relate to many of her emotions. I myself, only fifteen, grew up without a father— he was addicted to drugs—and found it difficult. All my friends are considerably older. I have used many drugs and alcohol and have been since the age of twelve. I am also very harsh and irate toward my mother. Drew's story had really made me think about myself. I believe her story was great and I give her credit for sharing it."

"Thank you, *People*, and Drew Barrymore, for sharing her story about teen alcoholism with us," an anonymous reader responded. "After reading the story, my fourteen-year-old sister came forward to let the family know that she, too, had a problem with drinking. Like many others, I'm sure we always had the attitude of, 'It would never happen in our family.'

By sharing her story, Drew allowed us to catch the problem before it got completely out of hand."

We got tons of mail at home too. I read it and tried to answer most every letter.

Without question the response made me feel as if I'd done the right thing by going public. There's absolutely no shame in helping other people.

But Drew wasn't allowed to sail off smoothly into her life. Just when it seemed as if the furor had subsided, a bombshell was unexpectedly dropped in an issue of *The Star* dated February 14. "E.T.'s Drew Barrymore Falls Off the Wagon," the headlines screamed. "Back in late-night clubs just four weeks after leaving drink clinic . . ." Then the story announced that Drew was "drinking again" at a Hollywood party.

According to an anonymous "insider," "After the party, our worst fears were confirmed when we went to the trendy 20-Twenty Club for some dancing. Drew couldn't order a drink herself, but she managed to get blitzed by sneaking sips of everyone else's drinks when they got up to dance.

"Everyone was horrified when they realized poor little Drew was drinking again and that nothing had changed."

It wasn't true. Not a single stinking word of it was true. But what was I going to do?

According to what my mother told me, one afternoon two men buzzed our condo, identified themselves as reporters, and asked for an interview. My mother told them to go away. When they persisted, she went out to ask them nicely to please leave, that I wasn't giving any interviews. With that they got all huffy and indignant and said something like "If that's the way you want it, then we're going to get even with her. We'll show you what you get when you don't cooperate."

A few weeks later the story came out. I saw it on the racks in a 7 Eleven, got angry for a little bit, then flipped the thing off and tried to forget about it. As far as my mom and I were concerned, the best way to deal with stuff like that was to not deal with it at all. Just let the lies pass and go on with life.

Life. That was enough to handle. Drew was healthier than ever before and better able to handle her problems. But she still wasn't out of danger. She wasn't even close. She was still very much an addict-alcoholic. And she was still an adolescent who alternated between good and bad days with the predictability of the weather. Blowups with her mother were unavoidable. Wrestling with the destructive components of her personality was an ever-present reality she had to confront. She still suffered the frightening lows of depression. Her therapists, aware of the high relapse percentage, worried about slip-ups. Issues popped up all the time.

That's what they told me would happen. I didn't walk out of the hospital cured. It's not like I got a shot of penicillin and everything was fixed in three days. Every day is a struggle. The difference is that I'm aware of it, and, hopefully, I have the tools to help me get through my various crises without having to lose myself in alcohol and drugs.

How do I handle my lows now? Well, I call people who I trust and talk out my feelings. Or I write about them. Basically, when something happens, I first isolate for a little while, gathering the energy and strength to deal with whatever it is, and then I get myself out into the open and confront the issue. I don't let problems simmer anymore. I work through them right away.

It's not always easy. Not too long ago I was looking through a photo album, and most of the pictures were taken before I went into rehab. In most of them I was really loaded. You could see my eyes dilated. Or I was falling over, about to pass out. Or I'd passed out already. In others I was just getting out of bed, holding a glass of water in one hand, a bottle of aspirin in the other, with a little sign taped to my shirt that read HANGOVER—OUCH!

I was laughing as I leafed through the pages, remembering all the fun times, and all of a sudden I had a really bad anxiety attack. I started crying hysterically. I thought I looked so happy in those pictures. I wanted to be like that again. I started breathing heavily, and then I stopped altogether and fainted. When I woke up, I sat there, contemplating everything I was feeling, really debating whether or not I wanted to use again. As I was catching my breath, I was tempted to just run into the kitchen and scream, "Fuck sobriety," grab a beer or whatever I could find, and get so loaded—just like it used to be.

It was the closest I'd ever come to using again. I was ready to say, "Screw everything!"

Instead, I waited there, not moving except to light cigarette after cigarette, until my mom came home and I could talk to her. Then I called Jan. They talked to me, soothed my anxiety, told me that I was a better person sober than loaded, and reiterated that they loved me. Afterward I calmed down and decided that I was glad that I didn't use. The way I was thinking, that I needed to drink or use till I was obliterated, is just a one-way ticket to death. I'm an addict and there's no middle ground.

Needless to say, one of my biggest fears centered on my social life. There was no going back to my old friends, that was for sure. But I wasn't going to be a hermit. I wanted to go to parties, to spend Saturday nights with friends, and to date, normal things that teenagers do. I just worried about what other kids would think of me now that I was straight. Except for the people I knew at ASAP, I figured from experience most teenagers dabbled in drugs and alcohol.

In the middle of March a totally cute guy from Beverly High asked me out. His name was Sam and he was sixteen. I'd seen him around a few times and really liked him. Dark hair, nice face, good body. But I didn't know anything about him personally. When he asked me out, I immediately said yes, but then I panicked. It was one of my first dates since being out and I was really nervous about what, if anything, he knew about me.

Anyway, he picked me up at seven in his parents' BMW. We had a sushi dinner that we rushed through out of nerves, but I was having a good time. We were hitting it off, it seemed. Then he suggested going down to the marina, where we could sit on his parents' boat and talk. "Talk?" I questioned him.

"Yeah," he smiled. "I don't really know you that well. But I'd like to."

That sounded nice. Twenty minutes later we pulled up beside the dock and I was thinking that Sam was pretty darn cool. We'd chatted nonstop, laughed, and were obviously liking each other. He bolted out of the car to open my door. "How gallant," I laughed. "I thought chivalry was dead."

"Not yet," he smiled.

Then he ran around to the back of the car and opened the trunk. "Don't look," he called. But it was too late. Out of the corner of my eye I caught a glimpse of an ice bucket and a bottle. My heart sank. Sam told me to walk on up to the boat, which I did, and he followed behind, holding the ice bucket behind his back. I wanted to cry. We'd been having such a good time, and I was jazzed that this was the first date I could recall where I wasn't getting loaded. Then this.

"Sit down," he motioned, "over on the sofa."

I did, all the time wondering how I was going to explain my problem and all I'd been through. Obviously, he didn't know. He'd somehow avoided all the stories about me. But I didn't want to explain everything. What a drag.

"Okay, close your eyes," Sam said, which I reluctantly did, and then he said, "Okay, now open them."

I was prepared to handle myself calmly. I was going to say simply that I didn't drink and that if he wanted the date to continue, he shouldn't drink either. And that would be it. When I opened my eyes, though, I broke out in a huge smile. Sam was standing across from me, holding two crystal goblets, and in the ice bucket was a big bottle of Evian water.

"Would the lady care for a drink?" he smiled.

In the months after that, Drew continued to fight her battle on a daily basis. She went to therapy, she participated in sober dances with Chelsea and Edie, and she attended weekly AA meetings. With a great sense of accomplishment, she accepted her six-month chip for sobriety and looked forward to celebrating a full year of sobriety.

And like everyone else, I got up at those meetings and said, "Thank you, and I am very grateful for my sobriety."

I thought about that every day.

All addicts do. You are never without the fear of returning to your old ways and losing everything that you've gained. When you're sober, you don't forget what it was like to use. It's hard, really hard, and you take it day by day, hour by hour, minute by minute. That's the way it's going to be for as long as I'm alive.

But at least I'm alive.

FIFTEEN

RELAPSE

And she lived happily ever after.

That's the way Drew wanted her story to end. That's the way she hoped it would end, the way she dreamed it would end. However, the reality of her life, like that of many recovering alcoholics and drug addicts, was much different. It was different in a way that those close to her could not imagine and Drew could not admit.

Little more than twelve weeks out of rehab, Drew suffered a gross error of judgment and responsibility as well as an abdication of willpower.

I blew it.

And I was too frightened to tell anybody about it.

On the night before what would've been my sixth month of sobriety, I went out with my friend Andie, a bubbly party girl a few years older than me. She had her own car, and we went driving around Hollywood. Andie was wild, one of the things that made her so fun, and that night she had a couple joints of marijuana on her. So we decided to get high. For no good reason other than that.

We had the pot and decided to get high.

Only every place we thought of lighting up made me paranoid.

This street, that street. We drove around forever, or so it seemed, and every place made me uncomfortable. Finally, we turned up a dark street that wound up a hill and dead-ended in total seclusion above the twinkling lights of the city. No houses around, nothing. Just a big red brick wall that we slowly approached.

Andie lit the joint and inhaled. I smelled the all-too-familiar sweet smoke, an aroma that momentarily made me nauseous with fear. Then she exhaled and handed me the joint.

I'd like to say that I trembled as I held the tiny stub between my fingers, but I didn't. My eyes fixed on the burning orange tip and followed the thin trail of smoke up into the dark sky.

"Well, Andie," I said, "this is happy six months."

She laughed and then I laughed. Nervously.

"I can't believe I'm going to do this," I said.

"I can't believe I'm going to *let* you do this," she said.

But I gave Andie a shrug as if to say "Don't worry," and explained, "Oh, well, I would've done it with someone else, anyway. It's not to blow my sobriety. I'm just looking to have fun."

That's really what I believed. After all I'd been through, my twisted mind convinced itself without much difficulty that smoking dope was still nothing more than a brief amusement. But the bottom line was that I just wanted to get high. Nothing more, nothing less. I guess I missed it. My life at the time wasn't so rough that I couldn't get along without it. I simply wanted to get high. No other reason.

A couple of puffs, that was it, and I was really, really stoned. I started rolling down the hill, laughing and babbling and having the best time.

For the hour we were up there I suffered no remorse. No guilt. No repentance. My feelings were so numbed. I felt nothing but the phony joy of being high and carefree and above the city.

Then we got in Andie's car and drove around, cruising without a destination while letting a blasting radio serve as our company. The pot began to wear off as we sped down the hill on our return to the Valley and I started to think about what I'd done by getting high. "Fuck it," I thought, "I got high. What's the big deal?"

Well, I knew what the big deal was. I wasted a lot of time and effort and emotion. "But," I asked myself, "what had all that hard work been for?" Not for me, it seemed. I guess among the primary motivations of my sobriety was proving to the magazines, the gossip columns, and everyone else who seemed to be holding my every move under a microscope that I could stay sober. That I wasn't a drug addict.

However, I had truly enjoyed it. I liked feeling healthy and natural and in control. I liked knowing myself, being comfortable with myself, knowing how to deal with problems rather than hiding from them. It wasn't easy, not by any means. In fact, it's hard to describe the effort sobriety took, but I imagine that at times it was no different from running two or three marathons in a single day. Suddenly, I felt horrible for turning a cold shoulder on all that positive work.

"Shit, Andie," I said, turning down the music. "Do you believe what I just did?"

She turned to me and said something. I don't remember what. Because at that very moment a car traveling in the opposite direction crossed over the center line and slammed into us at thirty miles per hour. My head slammed into the windshield and I was knocked out. Andie pulled me out of the car and laid me on the sidewalk, by which time I was awake though woozy, and then pulled the car over and took care of things with the other driver.

Several hours later we got to her house. I was shaken and upset, a package of frayed nerves, but I was all right. I phoned my mom, who wasn't home, and left a calm message. "I'm at Andie's, and everything's cool."

The next morning I called my mom again and told her about the car wreck. She was great. She smothered me with concern and motherhood, saying all those soothing things mothers say in times of crisis. When I finally got back home late that morning, it was as if she'd done nothing other than wait for me. I opened the door and, almost immediately, she hugged me.

"You have six months today!" she screamed joyfully. "I'm so proud of you."

"Yeah," I agreed somberly. "Six months and one day."

I disappeared into my room, slammed the door, and telephoned Andie.

"What are you going to do?" she asked.

"What can I do?" I said. "I just gotta keep on lying. I'll never tell her. And I'll never do it again. If I told, it would just screw everything up. So keep it a secret, promise?"

"I promise."

Two months passed, during which Drew pushed her secret to the farthest, darkest corner of her mind and continued with her life as if nothing happened. She studied hard in school, earning three A's and two B's, her best grades ever. She went on auditions. She dated on and off a twenty-two-year-old actor named Peter. She attended ASAP's outpatient day care and her regular therapy sessions. And she went to her weekly AA meetings. Before long she had erased all memory of the night she got high with Andie.

Everything was okay. Once in a while I thought about what I'd done, like when I was with Jan Dance, my friend David Crosby's wife. But honestly, I blocked it out so much that I stopped remembering about it. I was still going regularly to meetings, to day care at the hospital, to therapy sessions. I guess I lied so much about it that, actually, I almost convinced myself that I'd never broken my sobriety . . . even though, inside, when I looked at myself in a frank light, I knew the truth.

Then, sometime during the week of what everybody thought was my eighth month of sobriety, I did it again. I got high with Andie. We got stoned in the afternoon at her house, went to lunch, and then picked up tickets for a concert later that night by the Bangles. However, when we returned to Andie's house, we got stoned again, fell asleep, and missed the concert.

I felt like a jerk. The lamest jerk in the world. I think the only thing running through my mind was how purposeless getting stoned was. I'd promised myself I wasn't going to do it anymore. And here I was, breaking that promise. I felt like the total jerk.

So what'd I do?

I made the same promise to myself.

I looked in the mirror in my bathroom at home and said,

"Drew, you're never going to get high again. Do you hear what I'm saying? Never!"

This time, unlike the previous incident, I found it more difficult to forget my lapse. Not that it constantly weighed me down. I didn't allow that. Or, rather, I couldn't allow that and pretend to be getting along like I was.

One time, though, the reality of my increasingly cumbersome lie hit me, and hit me hard. Not surprisingly, that was all it took to begin the slow and painful dismantling of the delicate facade onto which I'd been so desperately clinging. I was sitting in an AA meeting and this girl got up and shared how she'd gotten loaded and lied about it for a long, long time. I found it eerie and unsettling as she described how she kept her lie going right up until a cake celebrating a full year of sobriety was wheeled out. As she began pulling out the candles, she broke down and cried. "I can't do this. I'm not sober."

I sat there and listened intently, but I did so without the slightest expression on my face. To look at me was to see an impassive girl with blank eyes. Inside, though, I wanted to jump out of my chair and scream, "That's me!" It took monumental strength to restrain myself, but it was more than supplied by the incredible fear I felt about coming forth. I wanted to admit everything. I wanted to get real with myself. But I was just too damn scared.

I looked over at an acquaintance from ASAP with what I imagined was a sad and mournful expression. She returned my look with a supportive "Cheer up, Drew" smile.

But that was out of the question. I was miserable when I got home that night. The lie was hanging over me like a ticking time bomb. I couldn't imagine it getting any worse. I cried and cried, and when I believed my tear ducts were thoroughly drained, I cried some more. I heard my mother on her way out with Peter, my on-again off-again boyfriend who, at that point, was more on than off.

As she pulled the car out, I bolted out the back door and virtually dove under the car. My mom jammed on the brakes and shot out of the car. I made her sit there with me while I cried my eyes dry. She stroked my head softly and asked what was making me so upset. But I wouldn't—couldn't—tell her. I just cried instead. And inside, the whole time, I was thinking, "Mom, I wish I could tell you this. I got loaded twice and have been lying to you and everyone else."

Mothering is what I wanted. Mothering and being smothered with love and care. I knew if I told her the truth, she could make me feel better. But I couldn't. I didn't have the courage. The more I thought about how tangled I'd become in the complicated cover-up, the harder I cried. My mom didn't know what more to do and, understandably, got frustrated.

"What's wrong with you?" she shrieked. "If you're not going to tell me, I'm going to leave."

So I made up another lie.

"Oh, I'm so lonely," I whimpered. "I just feel so all alone and isolated."

I wasn't that, though. It was that I felt so horrible about myself that I had gone on lying. Now I was running out of steam. The strength required to maintain such a complicated lie was ebbing. I could accept just fine that I'd gotten stoned and broken my sobriety, but I found it too hard, almost impossible, to handle that I couldn't be honest about it and accept the consequences for my actions.

And what were those consequences, after all? Just taking responsibility for my actions. As plain and simple as that. Just owning up to what I'd done. But that also meant starting all over again and going through the immense humiliation of admitting I'd messed up. I knew, realistically, that those people closest to me were only going to be sympathetic and loving. But that wasn't convincing enough.

Instead, I feared the onslaught of public scrutiny and imagined my mom, irreparably disappointed, hating me, and all my friends in the program feeling ashamed of me, mad that I let them all down. I was so scared of letting everyone else down that I embraced the lie more closely than ever. I had to, I convinced myself, for my own good.

In reality, though, the lie wasn't for any of that. I lied to avoid letting down the one person who mattered most.

Me.

It was all about me.

And I knew it, which made the experience all the more painful. Emotionally, I thought of myself as an hourglass, a beautiful, fragile hourglass full of sand, that had been turned over with a single puff off a joint the night I broke my sobriety. From that night on, for three and a half months, the sand had slowly been trickling out, slowly, ever so slowly, through the tiny hole. Until now, finally, the last few grains were gone, leaving me empty and hollow.

From then on, hers was a fast slide downhill. The more Drew chastized herself for spinning this tangled web of a lie, the more the rest of her life became unglued. Fights with her mother grew in frequency and ferocity, and the old tendencies of codependency they had worked so hard at ASAP to understand surfaced out of self-preservation. Drew also battled incessantly with Peter. There was no way for her to maintain those relationships when she could not deal with herself.

And that heaped on top of all her other troubles proved too much for Drew to shoulder.

I couldn't get on with either my mother or Peter. However, they became friendly with each other, and that annoyed me no end. I understand the situation now. The less they got from me, the more they found in each other. It was as if they were waiting for me to get over whatever I was going through. However, then I wanted so much to be part of them, individually and as a group, but I'd made myself too much of an outsider. It drove me nuts.

So one morning before school I ran away. It wasn't school I was running from as much as it was my home and my life. My mother and I got in a huge fight, I slammed the door and tore down the driveway, running as fast as my legs would take me. I heard my mother's pleas to return fade into the background until all I could hear was my own breathing. I stopped at a pay phone and called my friend Edie.

"I can't come pick you up," she told me. "I'm not going to feed into this."

I slammed down the receiver just as my mom screeched her

car into the parking lot. I took off running, turning down side streets, and then hiding behind someone's garage until I thought I'd lost her. Then I went walking, on one street and then another, not consciously following any pattern. And then, somehow, I found myself standing in front of the old condo we had lived in until several months earlier.

It was eight A.M., I guess, and I recognized some of the people who were leaving for work. It was weird, like I was standing in the midst of a movie I'd seen before, in it but not of it. I watched for a moment, desperately wanting someplace safe to go. It seemed I should have someplace where I could take shelter. So I sat down on the steps in front of my old building. I wanted to go in but didn't have a key. I was so sad, and tears began falling from my eyes.

"You know," I thought out loud, crying, "things were going good when I was living here. Ever since I moved to the new place, my life has gotten so shitty. I wish I could move time backward."

Eventually I got up and wandered down to a main street, where I found another pay phone and called David Crosby. David and his wife, Jan, both of whom were close friends of my therapist, Betty, acted as an invaluable support team to me, like surrogate parents. They were always there for me.

"David, I'm scared," I said. "I just ran away."

"I'll be right there," he said. "All I have to do is put on some pajamas."

He pulled up a few minutes later—yes, in his pajamas—and took me back to his house, where we sat in his car and talked for almost two hours. The topic: my mother and Peter. My inability to relate to them translated itself into a jealous hatred of their healthy friendship. I cried my heart out to David, and he told me, in a lot more words, that I needed to let go of both of them to a certain extent and deal with myself.

I took in his advice and tried to understand as we went inside and cooked breakfast. But the talk and the good food was nothing so much as a Band-Aid.

Around two I called my mom and, of course, we got into a screaming fight.

"Look," she said, "if you want to come home, then you're going to have to start acting a certain way."

I wanted so badly to scream "Look, you've got to compromise too. It's not all me." But I didn't. The fight went out of me and I just listened to what my mom said, no argument. I was so confused, disoriented. I didn't understand anything that was going on in my life. I didn't understand what I was doing so glaringly wrong that both my mother and my boyfriend should abandon me.

By the time school let out for the summer, Drew's home life had become the ultimate codependent nightmare. She and Jaid bickered constantly. There was no middle ground, no island of calm, no refuge from the way they seemed to set each other off. Despite months of working on their relationship, they had become full-time combatants.

Finally, I simply said, "Mom, I'm moving out."

She looked at me totally shocked, but she couldn't have been too surprised. I'd been working up to that for a while, explaining that I couldn't handle life the way it was going, that I didn't think she could either, and something had to give. I was the logical one to go. It was total manipulation on my part and sheer acquiesence on her part.

That I'd gotten the best grades of my life also helped persuade her, I thought. Later, my mother told me she gave in only because she knew Edie and I could never live together without coming to blows. We were too competitive with each other. My mom only let me go because she expected I'd be coming back home. She wanted me to learn a lesson.

So we made a deal. If I got a job, I could move out. Several days later I got work through well-connected friends as a door person at three different clubs, working three nights a week for sixty dollars an evening.

That opened the door for me and my friend Edie to go apartment shopping, a frustrating two-day experience that did a lot to convince me that independence isn't as great as I imagined. We budgeted ourselves six hundred dollars a month in rent, and in Los Angeles it's ridiculously hard to find a place two girls can share in a safe neighborhood for that amount of money.

But we did it, finally, taking a tiny apartment in West Hollywood with two dinky half bedrooms, a kitchen, and a living room.

We cleaned like crazy and got all our stuff moved in one long, tiresome day.

I was excited to be living on my own, but I wasn't fooling myself completely. I knew I was also doing it in part to give my mother the major burn. Only as Edie and I drove away, I grew extremely sad because I realized that by moving out, I was giving the house to my mom and Peter.

The month of June passed quickly and without incident. Drew enjoyed her freedom. She worked her various jobs. She went out with friends. She stayed in touch with her mother, checking in on a regular schedule. She attended meetings and worked her programs as diligently as possible. Seemingly stable, she also got involved with an upstart actor in his late teens, a relationship that began slowly and then intensified as quickly as it burned out.

Our relationship was nice while it lasted and it made me feel less lonely. But after we broke up—actually, he lost interest—I got down on myself, angry and depressed. I hated that my mother and Peter were such good friends and that I couldn't get along with either of them. And then, of course, I began to think about my busted sobriety. The dam was beginning to burst. My lies suddenly consumed me in a way I'd been able to prevent. They haunted me day and night. Where it was once so easy to ignore what I'd done, now the fact was impossible to escape.

Edie and I were fighting, the result of my mental state and some natural competition between us, but God, suddenly, the apartment was way too small for both of us. Unfortunately I didn't have anywhere else to go. Though I wasn't even considering using alcohol or drugs to blot out my troubles, I saw myself quickly sinking into a dark abyss.

I had few options, I felt, except to plod forward, absorb the pain that was due me, and just try to survive. After all, how much worse could things get?

A lot worse.

On the afternoon of July first I walked into the apartment and played back the messages on the phone machine. There were several from friends, but the last one on the tape was a strange, gravelly voice of an older man.

"Drew, this is your father," he said. "Please call me back. It's an emergency."

An emergency, huh. Right. I'm sure. Still, of course I would call him back. Even though he's never been there for me, not one single time, he's still my dad and I still crave the love I've never had from him. Rationally I know it's crazy, destructive, nothing but a dead end. Nevertheless, I called the number and he answered.

"What's the emergency?" I asked.

"I need money," he said. No hellos, how are yous, or anything like that. "I want some money, Drew. I need some money in a big way."

"That's it?"

"Yeah, right way, daughter."

Well, that fired me up.

"Personally, I wouldn't give you money for the bus," I snapped angrily. "If you need money, I saw a Help Wanted sign down the street. Go apply."

"You won't even give me a dime?" he pleaded, trying to tug on my heart. "You're my daughter, for Christ sakes."

"Dad, there're dimes on the street. Go find some. And besides, I don't have any money. What do you think I am, a money tree?"

"What about all you make on those movies?"

"Almost all of it goes into a trust," I said. "The rest I spend to make me happy. It's not to give to you. Sorry."

"Okay, then," he said, and I could tell he was done with me. " 'Bye."

I hung up and felt good about myself for a while. I'd been strong. However, later that night it hit me. I felt bad, guilty, because I refused him money. I didn't please him. I'm his daughter and I didn't help. Though I know what the situation is, there's a remote part of my brain that still desperately wants his love and will do anything to get it.

The rest of the night and the following morning turned into

one extended bummer. I didn't like work. I had no money. I fought with Edie. I didn't get along with my mother. Peter was out of the picture. And I couldn't get another guy. I hated myself. I felt ugly, fat, and useless. I started going crazy. I felt as if I was hexed.

I felt desperate, hopeless, backed into a corner.

That afternoon I went shopping with Andie and we bought some pot right on Melrose Avenue. We smoked it in her car. Right there, smack in the center of L.A.'s busiest street, in plain view of anyone who wanted to see, I was getting high. It was as if I were hoping to be seen by someone, to get caught and turned in, and then the lie I'd been living would be lifted from my back.

Indeed, I wanted to be discovered, shamed right out of my self-inflicted misery. But no such luck.

Edie was out when I got back to the apartment, which gave me time to ruminate about everything I'd been going through. That was the worst thing that could happen to me. My mind was reeling. I called my mom and complained about guys and feeling lonely. She told me to remember that she was always there for me and that made me feel better. For the moment I felt safe, safe but very low and sad.

That night I lit a candle and put my favorite song, Peter Gabriel's "In Your Eyes," on the stereo and set it to play repeatedly. Then I crawled into bed and cried and rocked myself to sleep just as the candle was flickering out.

In the morning I called my mom. She detected something in my voice and asked if anything was wrong.

"Oh, no, everything's fine," I said. "I'm doing great."

"Oh, listen, I have something to tell you," she added, almost as an afterthought. "Peter and I are going to New York for a few days."

"What!" I said, incredulous, shocked, dumbfounded, and pissed off.

"Since we're selling our apartment there, I thought I'd go and pick up some things. It'll just be a few days."

"And Peter? Why's he going too?"

"I need help moving and lifting. I can't do those things by myself."

"Fine, you two have fun," I snapped.

"Listen, Drew, I don't like your attitude. I don't like the way you sound."

"Sorry, I can't be happy about this," I said, and hung up.

I stayed out practically all night, clubbing, dancing, eating, and visiting friends. I didn't get high. I was on the run, more like a pinball caroming from bumper to bumper. In the morning I called my mother in New York.

"You know what, it really pisses me off that you didn't even invite me to go along," I said.

"It's because of the way you used to act in New York," she explained.

"But I have ten months sober," I argued, feeling the sharp pain of my secret like a pin pricking my insides. "You couldn't even invite me. That's so sick. I just want to tell you that makes me really angry."

"Drew, I'll see you in two days and we can work it out."

That was it. We hung up and I stormed out of my apartment, heading for . . . nowhere, really.

SIXTEEN

COMING CLEAN

E.T. STAR, 14, ATTEMPTS SUICIDE BY SLASHING WRIST.

That was the headline of the *National Enquirer* dated July 25, 1989. The page-long story, illustrated by a photograph of a tender, sweet-faced six-year-old Drew and E.T., went on to describe how on the afternoon of July 4 the pained young actress, wallowing in depression, tried to end her life by slashing her wrist with a knife. Discovered by friends, she was rushed to a nearby hospital and treated in the emergency room.

Was it a cry for help? asked the tabloid. Or was the fourteen-year-old really attempting to take her life?

More important: Was the story true? Only one person could provide the answers.

I spent the night at Andie's—we didn't get high—and I went back to my apartment late the next morning. I was going to do something later that night with her, but Edie had left a note asking me to go out with her instead. Fine. So I canceled Andie and waited for Edie to show up. She called a while later, though, angry about something or other I'd said to her a few days earlier, which made me feel like a failure.

I hung up the phone and crumpled on my bed like a deflated balloon. All of a sudden everything in my life seemed to be piling up. Peter and my mom were in New York together. I was on my own, working to support myself, but barely able to make it. Edie was mad at me. I hated my apartment. I had no life, no friends who I considered good friends. I thought I was fat and ugly. It was Fourth of July. I was unhappy, depressed, and sinking even lower fast. And on top of all that, I had broken my sobriety and lied about it.

I cried and cried until I was curled up and soiled like a spent tissue. I don't know how much time passed. Then the phone rang. It was Edie calling back. I cried some more to her. Sensing my distress, she told me not to go anywhere, that she'd be right over.

I was still in the grips of my hysterical crying fit when Edie and her boyfriend came charging into the apartment. Obviously I was depressed, abysmally so. And Edie tried talking me out of it. But I wasn't having any of it, and the talk soon escalated into yelling and screaming. She said one thing, I said another. I was like a runaway train, speeding dangerously downhill and out of control, and no matter how hard Edie applied the brakes, I kept picking up speed.

The next few minutes unfolded like a surreal picture, with me watching from afar as if it were all happening to someone else. I wanted simply to collapse on the floor and tell Edie that I needed help, that she should quickly call someone who would take care of me. I'd gone out of control. But I couldn't bring myself to mouth the words, to tell her, and she didn't seem to pick up on the direness of my actions. When I wailed I was a bad person, she argued I wasn't. And on and on like that.

Finally, out of a desperate need to convince her of what I couldn't articulate, I picked up a knife from the kitchen counter. I didn't want to kill myself. I didn't ever once intend to take my life. I repeat: the thought never, not for one second, crossed my mind. I know too well the consequences of such dire actions, having heard the gruesome stories from kids who had actually come close to killing themselves.

I did, however, think of the knife as a giant exclamation point, something that as I brought the blade to my wrist would allow Edie to hear my cry for help and convince her beyond a doubt that I needed professional attention, and needed it fast. I made one very small scratch on my left wrist, then another, and in the heat of our back-and-forth argument, I made yet another. And that was the mistake. That third scratch. The knife slipped, I pressed too hard, and the blade sliced into my flesh.

Eckh! The rest is a blur. I caught one glimpse of the blood and passed out cold.

Edie and her boyfriend whisked me to the emergency room at Cedars Sinai Medical Center, located only several minutes from our apartment, where my wrist was treated with stitches. A nurse called my mom in New York and got permission to do whatever was required. Then I got on the phone, woozy and tired and resigned to the truth.

"Mom, you know what?" I said softly from my hospital bed. "I have something to tell you and it's so scary."

"What is it?" she asked.

"I don't know how to say it," I said, and started to weep in great big sobs.

"I think I know," she said. "Did you have something to drink, honey?"

"No, not really." I gulped down some tears. "I smoked some pot."

There was a long moment of silence and then my mother said, "It's okay."

With that one comment, those two little comforting words, a blanket of calm descended over the situation.

Cedars had already telephoned ASAP and arranged for my return. On my own, in a moment of clearheadedness, I had told the doctor that I wanted to return, that I knew I needed to go back to ASAP. But telling my mother that I'd smoked pot and then hearing her say "It's okay," that only underscored my feeling that it really was okay to reenter the rehab hospital.

I was going to be all right. I wasn't a failure. I was in need of help. I knew that. I just hadn't been able to articulate it any earlier.

Finally, though, I'd reached the end of the line—or the end of the lie—and it was a welcome relief.

Because it was a holiday weekend, ASAP's wards were practically deserted when Drew was brought into the admitting area. Most of the kids had left on passes. She sat by the nurses' station while a nurse took her vitals: pulse, temperature, and blood pressure. She blinked her eyes and looked around the familiar surroundings, inhaling the smells and sounds as if she were experiencing a déjà vu. She didn't see Ted, a friend from her previous stay, wander past.

He stopped dead in his tracks and exclaimed, "Oh, my God! Are you visiting? Or are you really here?"

"I'm really here, Teddy," I said.

A few days later everyone was back, and it seemed as if they were all coming around to get a glimpse of me. It wasn't as if I were a stranger. I was at the hospital every week for day care and visits, so I knew almost everyone. They all asked if I was visiting, and when I said no, they were shocked.

But the transition to hospital life wasn't as distressing as in previous times. The reason: This time I wanted to be at ASAP. It was my own, my first, choice. ASAP represented safety to me. I felt comfortable, secure, like I had come home—not to be coddled, but to be healed.

I immediately fell into the old routine of groups and therapies and tried to work really hard, but it didn't feel good. I knew why though. I'd admitted to Betty and Lori that I'd gotten loaded, but not that I'd smoked pot at six months and eight months. I was just too frightened to tell them everything, and that was holding me back.

To my mother I told the truth, the whole truth, and she accepted it with a measure of sadness and sympathy that was comforting if not anticlimactic.

Jaid says:

These many months later I really think that Drew had to go through that and feel the pain. It's not what I ever would've wanted for her. But I think she had to discover for herself how impossible it is to live a lie. No matter how much someone might've lectured her about the price she would have to pay for breaking her sobriety, it might not have mattered. She had to experience it for herself. That's part of growing up. Everybody that age does something bad, makes a poor choice, or lies. Unfortunately some have to pay a higher price for their mistakes than others do.

Drew learned her lesson. Without a doubt, she learned her lesson. Now, I think, her foundation is stronger because of it.

However, it took me a while to come clean with Betty and Lori, probably because I was so frightened of disappointing them and losing their love and respect, which I cherished.

Then I was surprised one day in big group. Shocked out of my socks is more like it. In the midst of a discussion concerning honesty, Lori turned sharply toward me and, in front of the twenty or so people in the room, said, "So, Drew, you're the one who got high at six months and eight months. Tell us about the value of being honest with yourself."

My mother had obviously filled in the blanks to Lori and Betty. The entire room woke up, bristled with electricity, and all eyes centered on me. "Great, my covers have finally been pulled," I thought as my face turned red and I contemplated how I might crawl under the carpet and disappear without anyone noticing me. Talk about finding yourself in the hot seat. I felt bad, so incredibly bad for being caught in the lie. But I knew that sooner or later I would have to accept the consequences, and that's what happened. With my cover blown, I knew it was time to admit everything.

"Yeah, you're right," I muttered. "I'm sorry I didn't become honest earlier, but I was too scared of what people would say."

"That's bullshit," someone spoke up. "You weren't scared of

letting everyone down. You were scared of being honest with yourself."

And it went on and on like that, as if I had been sent back to square one of rehab. It was a lot like starting over. Not exactly, since my previous work wasn't all for naught and I knew what was coming. As expected, I was whipped and flogged with the truth, totally humiliated by the group, as I knew lying would eventually make me feel. But that's exactly what I needed to set me on the right course. I had to look myself straight in the eye without flinching, which I did in big group that day.

I went to bed that night exhausted, weak in the knees but strong in the heart. From that point on I resolved to tell the truth. No more lies. "This time do it for you, Drew," I chanted over and over to myself while falling asleep. "Be true. Be strong. Do this for yourself."

When I was in the hospital previously, I'd worked only on myself, concentrating on issues concerning my sobriety. I'd gotten into other things, of course. But not the issues I had to explore this time, issues I never thought I could bring out into the open with anybody. In the past I'd hate myself for withholding them, because I knew they were there. But they were my deepest, darkest secrets, things that if revealed I thought would send me plummeting into a dark, inescapable void.

I'd gotten honest the last time, but only to a certain point. This time I decided to wring the towel out, to get every last drop of moisture.

About the end of July, I walked into the office and told Betty that I couldn't take it anymore.

"We have to do something about my mother," I said.

This was the test, the big risk. But, hey, I'd admitted I'd gotten high and survived. Probably I'd even come out a stronger person for it. So why not go the distance and talk about my mother?

Sure, I had to face up to many of the problems I'd confronted previously. My self-esteem, for instance. And how I tried to find happiness in material things; how I got upset if I didn't look absolutely perfect; and how I used guys to try to find the love I never got from my father. But the biggest issue of all, by far, concerned my mother.

We got along, we didn't get along. Our relationship was a vicious tug-of-war that had no winner. We were each other's family, and if we wanted a sense of family, we had to learn how to keep company with each other. She was mother, yes, but she was also my best friend. And vice versa. I was her daughter, but I was also my mom's best friend. It was a relationship worth fighting for, but that didn't make it any easier.

Looking back on it, in the past my mother and I perhaps didn't push far enough in our search for a better relationship. Maybe we didn't examine how we dealt with each other as carefully and honestly as we should have. Maybe we left some things untouched, unconsciously off limits, for no reason other than when it came to family, we were all each other had. In retrospect, though, that's the number-one reason that we should've pushed to an extreme.

We had to try to work things out. And it couldn't be just me making the effort.

Betty and Lori agreed, and they recommended my mother go to The Meadows, a rehab place in Wickenberg, Arizona, where she could immerse herself in therapy for codependency.

Fine. Everybody agreed. So my mother went to The Meadows, checked in, and then checked out six hours later, and went to sleep that night at home. I was irate when I found out, and told her so when we talked.

"You know what?" I told her. "I'm going to tell you something, and it's going to be short and simple. I'm fourteen years old. I've spent seven months of my life in this hospital, working damn hard to get better. You've spent six hours in a hospital. How dare you do that when you say I'm important to you.

"This is important to us. Stop being so goddamn selfish. This is not about you. This is about *us!* This is to get you better so we can have a relationship. What do you think I'm doing in this hospital? I'm not working completely for you. I'm trying to make myself better so we can go home and live in a healthy, natural environment.

"And if you don't go back . . . I mean, if you can check out and I can't, well, that's just game-playing. My life is not a little game. So if you don't go back, please don't be surprised when I don't return home."

That did it. My mom turned around and checked back into rehab.

Jaid says:

At first I was resentful about going there. Damn resentful, honestly. I felt incarcerated at The Meadows. The program is intense. Six days a week, starting at 6:30 A.M. and lasting till 8:30 P.M. And then you do homework. You are allowed no visitors. No passes. Only one five-minute phone call a week. There's no way you can help but learn.

I realized that I was at The Meadows for a reason. When Drew went back into the hospital, we had a meeting—Betty, Lori, Drew, and me. It was decided that whatever my contributions to the relationship, they were not working. If I wanted to be involved with Drew and have a healthy relationship, I had to make some incredible changes. It wasn't enough for her to work on herself.

For Drew and I to have a healthy relationship, for her to eventually come back and live at home, we all felt I needed to learn how to deal with my codependency. Leaving that first night was simply my reaction to the incredible fear that one has when forced to face yourself.

However, when I returned for the six-week stay, I knew what I had to do. There was no hiding from myself. They make you be scathingly honest. You deal, for example, with the issues of your past, what brought you to where you are, what tools you lack and why you lack them.

Basically, for six days a week, fourteen hours a day, you hold yourself under microscopic scrutiny and perform a sort of unrelenting emotional and mental probing. It's difficult, intense, grueling, and completely beneficial.

At the end of August I went to Wickenberg for The Meadows' family week. I hadn't seen my mother for more than a month, which made our reunion really scary. I didn't know how to react. While she was in Arizona, I'd been working hard on really sorting out who my mom was and what she meant to me. My conclusion: she has never been a mother to me in the normal sense and it was silly to try to create that relationship. We've always been more like best friends, I decided, and truth be told, I really did miss her friendship.

Needless to say, when my mom saw me, she started to cry. I hugged her. The feelings were genuine. However, I couldn't help myself from wondering if the tears weren't her attempt to manipulate me so I wouldn't be angry with her. That's natural, I think. Rather than say anything, though, I saved it for discussion group.

This week was full of heavy-duty confrontations and confessions. The first day I opened up completely, telling my mother with total honesty everything I felt. But I protected myself as well. I spoke without exhibiting any emotion. It was as if I wanted a wall between us. I was too frightened to let my guard down right away. But that reserve bothered everybody else. The group confronted me on my icy demeanor, and that was discouraging. After revealing a lot of deep feelings, they accused me of being insincere, and that wasn't true. I was just frightened.

Frustrated, I skipped the next day's lectures and workshops, which ticked everyone off, but then I resolved to dig in my heels and the next few days I poured out my heart with honest, uninhibited emotion. I was going to do it, and break through. I was determined about that. It felt good, my mother responded, and I thought we made some worthwhile progress.

One exercise, in particular, had us sitting beside a stack of tissue boxes. Each box represented a different issue, and as we talked about the issue, we removed a box. Our boxes represented topics such as my weight, my father, my career, and my mother's lack of a career, and so on—a lot of the same issues we'd worked on before. But this time we attended to them in depth and also delved into my mother's involvement.

The work got to my mom early. She was mean and crude and nasty. I started to cry. I couldn't believe she was acting like that. I was pouring my heart out and she was being sarcastic. However, my mother's means of self-protection is verbal, and eventually things got better and better. By the end of the week we could talk about anything with openness and encouragement.

I returned to ASAP expecting to dive into therapy and do lots of good work. But it wasn't at all like that. I didn't say a word in group, not a single word. I was numb, tired, and though I didn't realize it, I was also sick of talking about all my problems. That and I just didn't want to. But I couldn't see that. I only saw myself working hard and not being well received. Finally, one afternoon, I was out on the patio, crying to a tech, telling him how I couldn't handle not being understood by anyone.

"What do you mean?" he said. "People understand you. You just aren't saying anything."

"What?" I asked.

"You haven't done or said anything since you got back," he told me. "Open up, relax, and get real with yourself. Don't worry, people will respond."

Well, that shocked me out of my sleep, and ever since I've been working extremely hard to raise myself to a stable place of health and happiness. And people have responded, especially that one person I really needed to respond—my mom.

Jaid says:

By the end of family week I had changed. I have no doubt of that. I realized that I had to let go of my hold on the relationship. I wanted our relationship to work, and that meant more to me than the control I exercised over Drew. I saw that I no longer had to have her feel like I did, see the world the way I wanted her to, experience life the way I wanted her to. She had to be allowed her own life.

When she saw that breakthrough in me, that change, she also responded. In that week there was a lot of conflict, a lot of emotional investment, and pain, lots of pain. But from that we came to a better understanding of each other. Drew saw that. She couldn't help but see it, feel it, and ultimately respond to it.

I made so many mistakes, I discovered, because I never actually learned how to be a parent. I never had a family that was functional on any level. It was violent, under duress, miserable. I never had a situation where I could have possibly picked up the tools that would enable me to have a healthy relationship with my own child. I had to learn about them, work on acquiring them, which I have finally done.

When I came back to Los Angeles, Drew was nervous. We'd made so much progress, progress that was plainly obvious to both of us from the end of family week on, and she was afraid—rightly so—that we'd return to our old patterns of behavior. I understood and said to her, "I can't promise you anything. But what I can say is that I'm a different person than I was when I went to The Meadows. I know myself and my role as mother better, and I can now care for you on a level of mutual respect and care and love. Let's just let it evolve." And that's what we've been doing.

Now I feel I can deal with Drew in a healthy and productive manner. Before, honestly, I didn't have a clue. But I am more knowledgeable now. I can come up with a logical answer to a problem. I still have to set the rules and regulations. However, now I understand it's the way I communicate them that's going to make the difference in how she responds.

The mistakes I made in the past were harmful, I know. A relationship, though, is two people making contributions, positive and negative. We're taking it slowly, but it's positive these days. We listen, we laugh, we communicate and confide, we even argue. But we like each other as people. We love each other as mother and daughter. And I think, as time passes, we're going to make it.

As I work on this last passage, I'm in the final weeks of rehab, awaiting discharge in thirteen days. A lucky number, thirteen. I'm looking ahead to the start of school—maybe even getting straight A's this year—making movies, and just being honest with myself. I'm getting along great with my mother, seeing her almost every weekend and having fun when we're together. And I'm just feeling stronger personally.

And that's me, Drew Barrymore, age fourteen, today.

I have to accept this person, frailties and all, for who she is, and not try to be someone else. I can't obsess about my weight. I can't compete with my mother. I can't find love where there isn't any love to be found. I can't go on beating myself up, emotionally and physically, or else I'll have the miserable life I've been trying so desperately to escape.

Basically I have to love myself unconditionally, exercise responsibility, and work the program.

Am I going to get high again? I hope not. I don't want to. But it's a question with no certain answer. Last time I was sober I thought about getting high a lot. I put myself in situations filled with temptation. This time I won't. This time I've had emotional urges to get high, but not the difficult physical urges. When I got an emotional urge recently, I pulled a friend into the corner and told him that I needed to talk about it before it got overwhelming. Afterward I felt so much better.

However, this time around I realize that I can't have too many expectations for myself. I can't let other people have too many expectations for me either.

What I can do is enjoy what it means to be alive. What I have to do is live, not one day at a time, not one hour at a time, but one minute at a time. I have to work my program. If I don't, I won't last. I'll be dragged down. I have to work it whether I need to or not.

Unfortunately there isn't a nice and neat ending to this tale like in the movies. But that's what it means to be a recovering addict or alcoholic. Recovery is an ongoing, life-long process. Still, mine is a happy ending.

I'm not a miracle worker. I'm not someone special. Whatever I've accomplished has been through hard work, tears, pain, love, and more hard work.

My goals are simple: to stay sober and to live a good life.

All I can do is the best I can.